Supervision of Drama

Supervision of Dramatherapy brings together experts from the field to provide a thorough overview of dramatherapy supervision and the issues that can arise during the supervisory task. This book examines the supervision of dramatherapy in a range of contexts with a variety of client groups, including forensic work, intercultural practice, and dramatherapy with children. It draws on research into the contemporary form, content and practice of supervision.

Contributors present original research, theory-based debates, analysed accounts of practice and illustrative examples to demonstrate supervision in dramatherapy. Topics covered include:

- processes at work within supervision
- the roles of the supervisor and supervisee
- how supervision benefits the client
- the major forms of dramatherapy
- issues and developments in dramatherapy supervision.

Supervision of Dramatherapy offers practical guidance and theoretical grounding that will appeal to the supervisor and supervisee alike. It will also be useful for psychotherapists who use dramatic methods in the supervisory setting and to those interested in research into professional practice.

Phil Jones is a Reader in Childhood, Carnegie Faculty, Leeds Metropolitan University. He has lectured widely in the art therapies and has provided clinical supervision in his postgraduate teaching of Dramatherapy.

Ditty Dokter is head of the Arts Psychotherapy department at the Hertfordshire Partnership Trust and senior lecturer in Dramatherapy at Roehampton University. She has supervised both individuals and groups of art therapists since 1988.

Supervision in the Arts Therapies
Series Editor: Joy Schaverien

'This splendid series breaks new ground in its depth, breadth and scope, guided by Joy Schaverien's recognition that the time is right for a comprehensive, multi-faceted study of supervision in the arts psychotherapies. With each volume, the reader is invited to imagine, explore, and reflect on the expressive qualities of a particular art form in clinical supervision, turning special attention to art, music, dance, drama, and sandplay through contributions by leading experts from different parts of the world. These five volumes will make a lasting contribution as essential reading for supervisors and supervisees across the psychotherapies. The series also contributes towards a deeper understanding of the mentor–student relationship and the healing power of the arts.'

Joan Chodorow, Jungian Analyst and former President of the American Dance Therapy Association

'This new series of *Supervision in the Arts Therapies* is both timely and necessary. Now that all the arts therapies are established as state registered professions in their own right, there is a lack of resources that can support both the more advanced practitioner and the student. The writers of these individual titles are leaders in their respective fields both as researchers and practitioners. These publications make very important and innovative steps, and should be read by everyone in related fields of work.'

Dr Sue Jennings, Consultant Dramatherapist and Supervisor

'Each volume will not only communicate across the arts therapies but also to colleagues in other psychotherapies and health professions, to our mutual benefit.'

Diane Waller, Professor of Art Psychotherapy, Goldsmiths College University of London, President of the British Association of Art Therapists

This innovative series comprises five edited volumes, each focusing on one of the arts therapies – art, music, drama, dance or sandplay – and reflects on the dynamic nature of the presentation of that art form in supervision. The series reveals similarities and differences encountered in the theory and practice of supervision in each modality and within a range of contexts, and with diverse client groups.

Supervision in the Arts Therapies makes a timely contribution to the literature and will be essential reading for experienced practitioners and students of the arts therapies, as well as psychotherapists and other professionals engaged in supervision.

Titles in the series

Supervision of Dance Movement Therapy
Helen Payne

Supervision of Art Psychotherapy
Joy Schaverien and Caroline Case

Supervision of Sandplay Therapy
Harriet Friedman and Rie Rogers Mitchell

Supervision of Music Therapy
Helen Odell-Miller and Eleanor Richards

Supervision of Dramatherapy
Phil Jones and Ditty Dokter

Supervision of Dramatherapy

Edited by Phil Jones and Ditty Dokter

Routledge
Taylor & Francis Group

LONDON AND NEW YORK

First published 2008 by Routledge
27 Church Road, Hove, East Sussex BN3 2FA

Simultaneously published in the USA and Canada
by Routledge
270 Madison Avenue, New York, NY 10016

Routledge is an imprint of the Taylor & Francis Group, an Informa business

Copyright © 2009 Selection and editorial material, Phil Jones and Ditty
Dokter; individual chapters, the contributors.

Typeset in Times by Garfield Morgan, Swansea, West Glamorgan
Printed and bound in Great Britain by TJ International Ltd, Padstow,
Cornwall
Paperback cover design by Sandra Heath

British Library Cataloguing in Publication Data
A catalogue record for this book is available from the British Library

Library of Congress Cataloging-in-Publication Data
Supervision of dramatherapy / edited by Phil Jones and Ditty Dokter.
     p. ; cm.
   Includes bibliographical references and index.
   ISBN 978-0-415-44702-7 (hbk) – ISBN 978-0-415-44703-4 (pbk.) 1.
Drama–Therapeutic use. 2. Psychotherapists–Supervision of. I. Jones, Phil,
1958- II. Dokter, Ditty.
   [DNLM: 1. Psychodrama–organization & administration. 2. Administrative
Personnel. 3. Organization and Administration. 4. Psychodrama–education.
WM 430.5.P8 S9593 2008]
   RC489.P7.S873 2008
   616.89'1523–dc22
                                                        2008012659

ISBN: 978-0-415-44702-7 (hbk)
ISBN: 978-0-415-44703-4 (pbk)

Contents

List of illustrations

Boxes

Notes on contributors

Madeline Andersen-Warren is a dramatherapist, supervisor and trainer. For 15 years she was employed as a dramatherapist in the NHS. Her background in theatre enabled her to be an innovator in the performance aspects of dramatherapy; she has facilitated a therapeutic theatre group whose work gained national recognition. Publications include: 'Therapeutic theatre' in *Dramatherapy, Clinical Studies*, edited by Steve Mitchell (Jessica Kingsley Publishers 1995); *Creative Groupwork with Elderly People: Drama* (Winslow Press 1996) and *Practical Approaches to Dramatherapy* (with Roger Grainger) (Jessica Kingsley Publishers 2000). She has also contributed to several research-based publications and is completing doctoral research into dramatherapy and text.

Noelle Blackman is a dramatherapist and assistant director of Respond. In 1997 she founded the Roc Loss and Bereavement Service, an NHS therapy service for people with learning disabilities and within Respond she recently set up the Elder's Project. Noelle is also deputy co-ordinator and co-founder of the National Network for the Palliative Care of People with Learning Disabilities. She has presented papers nationally and internationally. Her published work includes *Living with Loss* (Pavilion), *Loss and Learning Disability* (Worth Publishing), *When Somebody Dies* (Books Beyond Words), *Caring for People with Learning Disabilities who are Dying* (Worth Publishing) and a chapter in *Intellectual Disability, Trauma and Psychotherapy* (Routledge).

Adam Blatner, MD is board certified in adult and child/adolescent psychiatry, a trainer of psychodrama, and the author of several of the most widely used textbooks on psychodrama, as well as numerous articles and chapters in other books. Though now retired after over 40 years of clinical practice, he teaches about practical applications of psychology to various groups and continues to write. He resides in central Texas.

Mandy Carr is a dramatherapist, supervisor of arts therapists and teacher. She has set up dramatherapy in a wide variety of educational contexts. An

elected member of the executive of the British Association of Drama-
therapists for four years, she currently convenes its Equal Opportunities
Sub-Committee. Her chapter on the use of story in dramatherapy appears
in *The Power of Words: Social and Personal Transformation through the
Spoken, Written and Sung Word*, eds Mirriam-Goldberg and Tallman
(TLA Press 2007). Mandy is a graduate of the BADth approved Creative
Arts Supervision Training (CAST).

Ditty Dokter, PhD is a registered dramatherapist, dance movement therapist
and group analytic psychotherapist. She is Head and Professional Lead of
Arts Psychotherapies at the Hertfordshire Partnership NHS Foundation
Trust. She has held posts as principal lecturer and course leader in masters
courses in the arts therapies, and currently teaches at Roehampton University, London and Codarts, Rotterdam. Her research is in intercultural
arts therapies practice and she has lectured and published in this area
internationally. Her publications include: *Arts Therapies and Clients with
Eating Disorders* (Jessica Kingsley Publishers 1994), *Arts Therapists,
Refugees and Migrants* (Jessica Kingsley Publishers 1996) and *EXILE,
Arts Therapies and Refugees* (University of Hertfordshire 2000). She is
currently coordinating a systematic review of dramatherapy evidence on
behalf of the British Association of Dramatherapists.

Judith Glass Collins, PhD is a licensed clinical psychologist in the states of
Washington and California. She is also a certified trainer, educator,
practitioner in psychodrama, sociometry, and group psychotherapy, and
a registered drama therapist. Dr Glass Collins published the chapter
'Working Toward Aesthetic Distance: Drama Therapy for Adult Victims
of Trauma' in *Expressive and Creative Arts Methods for Trauma Survivors*, edited by Lois Carey (Jessica Kingsley Publishers 2006). Judith's
one-act play, *Veterans' Day*, recently won the twelfth Annual Playwright's Festival at the Key City Public Theatre in Port Townsend,
Washington, and was produced at the beginning of the theatre's 2008
season.

Clare Hubbard works full time with adults with severe and enduring mental
health problems as a part of a dramatherapy team in an NHS mental
health trust. Since qualifying in 1998 she has also worked with adults with
learning disabilities and in older adult mental health. She completed her
Masters in 2003 at the University of Hertfordshire. Her dissertation was
on 'The Dramatherapy Group on the Acute Psychiatric Ward'. Clare is a
registered supervisor with the British Association of Dramatherapists.
Currently Clare is Vice Chair of the British Association of Dramatherapists and convener of its NHS sub committee. Before qualifying as a
dramatherapist, Clare worked for some years as a residential support
worker with adults with learning disabilities. Her first degree was in

Theatre and Media Drama. Publications include 'The Expressive Body: Finding Another Language', *Journal of The British Association of Dramatherapists*, Spring 2008, and co-author of 'Therapeutic Interventions' in *Caring for Adults with Mental Health Problems*, eds I. Peate and S. Chelvanayagam (Wiley Series in Nursing 2006).

Marina Jenkyns, MA (Cantab) is a state-registered dramatherapist, trainer and organisational consultant. Under her chairpersonship of the British Association of Dramatherapists, mandatory supervision of newly qualified dramatherapists was implemented. She created and was director of the first two-year supervision training for dramatherapists in Britain. She is the author of *The Play's the Thing; Exploring Text in Drama and Therapy* (Routledge 1996), which unites her understanding of dramatherapy and psychoanalysis with her previous careers in education, academia and theatre. Other writings include 'Gender Issues Supervision' in *Dramatherapy, Theory and Practice 3*, ed. S. Jennings (Routledge 1997), 'Training the Supervisor Dramatherapist: A Psychodynamic Approach' in *Supervision and Dramatherapy*, ed. E. Tselikas-Portmann (Jessica Kingsley Publishers 1999) and 'Dramatherapy and Psychoanalysis: Some Links Explored' in *Where Analysis Meets the Arts*, eds Y. Searle and I. Streng (Karnac 2001).

Phil Jones (PhD) is Reader in Childhood, Carnegie Faculty of Sport and Education, Leeds Metropolitan University, and has held the posts of principal lecturer and course leader on masters courses in the arts therapies. He has published and lectured widely on the arts therapies and on childhood. His books have been translated and published in Chinese, Korean and Greek, and include: *The Arts Therapies* (Routledge 2005), *Drama as Therapy* (Routledge 2007), *Childhood: Services and Provision for Children* (with Moss, Tomlinson and Welch) (Pearson 2008) and *Rethinking Childhood* (Continuum 2008). He is series editor for 'New Childhoods' (Continuum).

Roshmi Khasnavis is a UKCP registered integrative arts psychotherapist with an MA from the Institute for Arts in Therapy and Education. She has worked within statutory, health and corporate settings, specialising in work with people from diverse ethnic and cultural backgrounds. She piloted an intercultural arts therapy project with Maple Access Practice in Northampton, a general practice which provides healthcare services to refugees, asylum seekers, the homeless and travellers. Roshmi has run training workshops for health and social care professionals in the therapeutic application of the creative arts. Her current work is with an independent fostering agency where she provides therapy and consultation in the context of families in transition.

Emma Ramsden, dramatherapist, supervisor and behaviour consultant, is a freelance practitioner and a doctoral research candidate with Leeds Metropolitan University. Emma's history has been working with homeless adults, in forensic psychiatry with adults with addictive and violent behaviour and in education both as a therapist and consultant, supporting teachers, learning support mentors and consulting on behaviour management with children and families in deprived settings. Her publications include contributions to *Touch Papers*, edited by Graeme Galton (Karnac Books 2006), *Supervision of Dramatherapy*, edited by Phil Jones and Ditty Dokter (Routledge 2009), and *Drama As Therapy, Theory, Practice and Research* by Phil Jones (Routledge 2007).

Professor Joy Schaverien, PhD is the series editor of *Supervision in the Arts Therapies*, a Jungian analyst in private practice, a member of the International Association of Analytical Psychology and Visiting Professor in Art Psychotherapy, Northern Programme for Art Psychotherapy, Sheffield, UK.

Anna Seymour, PhD, CertEd, BA(Hons) DipDrth, DipSup, is a state registered dramatherapist, supervisor, trainer and academic. She has worked in the UK and internationally with individuals and groups of all ages. As a professional actor and director she was involved with more than 30 shows specialising in radical theatre for particular communities. She is a director of the training organisation the Northern Trust for Dramatherapy, and visiting lecturer in drama at the University of Sheffield. She was editor of the British Association of Dramatherapists Journal for five years and has published numerous articles on theatre and dramatherapy, most recently contributing to *Dramatherapy and Social Theatre*, ed. Sue Jennings (Routledge 2008).

Sally Stamp is a dramatherapist, supervisor and group analyst and has worked in a range of forensic settings since 1989. She is Head of Arts Therapies for the Adolescent Directorate and one of the Men's Directorates in West London Forensic Services. She has presented papers at national and 7international psychotherapy conferences and has been published in *Prison Theatre* edited by James Thompson.

Preface to the series and this book

Supervision of Dramatherapy is a title in the five-volume series *Supervision in the Arts Therapies*. The series was conceived as a result of collaboration with colleagues from the fields of art and music therapy, drama and dance movement therapy, as well as the related discipline of sandplay therapy. This led to creative discourse regarding the roles of the various arts media in therapy and supervision. The common element in the practices explored in this series is that in each of the arts therapies an object, sound or action (or series of objects, sounds or actions) mediates psychological processes within the context of a therapeutic relationship. The evidence is that there is a developing body of theory specific to the fields of supervision in the arts therapies but there is relatively little literature on the subject. Thus the idea of a series of books on *Supervision in the Arts Therapies* was envisaged and, with the encouragement of Joanne Forshaw at Routledge, the series came into being.

It is a great pleasure to introduce this book on the *Supervision of Dramatherapy*. Dr Phil Jones and Dr Ditty Dokter are leading practitioners, educators and theorists in the field of dramatherapy. They have assembled a group of contributors who are all highly experienced therapists working with dramatherapy and psychodrama, from diverse backgrounds. The result is a book that is an exciting and lively contribution to the literature.

Drama offers the opportunity for a specific experience that is qualitatively different from other forms of psychotherapy, and this is reflected in supervision of the practice. It is anticipated that, along with its companion volumes in the series, *Supervision of Dramatherapy* will interest a wide readership: supervisors and supervisees, whether experienced practitioners or students of dramatherapy. However, the anticipated readership is not limited to this group; it includes practitioners of the other arts therapies, as well as analytical psychology, child and adult psychotherapy, education, counselling and integrative arts therapy. All who supervise dramatherapists, and all who are interested in understanding the role of drama in professional practice, will find this book an inspiring read and an essential companion to supervision.

Joy Schaverien, May 2008

Introduction

Phil Jones and Ditty Dokter

The process whereby the novice or trainee enters a craft or profession through apprenticeship to a skilled practitioner, or overseer, is common to many areas of experience in many cultures, from juggling to healing. Lave and Wenger (1991) have traced it as a form of entry into particular 'communities of practice' from tailoring to midwifery. Early forms of variations on this process within charitable and social agencies have been identified and studied by Peters (1967) and Kadushin (1992). The nineteenth and twentieth centuries saw further developments in a variety of health professions, and the notion of 'supervision' has emerged from such apprenticeships and trainings. Contemporary supervision has been defined in many ways and takes many forms. The original connection to training and professional identity remains, but it has expanded beyond the remit of the development of expertise into the life of ongoing professional practice. Chapter 1, for example, points out that 'in essence, supervision can be seen as one worker meeting with another to enable them to reflect on their practice' (p. 13), but that the nature and use of this 'meeting' is varied and complex. Supervision in health professions such as dramatherapy is enmeshed with processes as diverse as management, professionalisation, clinical governance, support, education and the ensuring of safety and quality. This diversity can be seen as a response to the central concern of the act of supervision and of this book. This concern is: how best to deliver therapy for the clients with whom the therapist is working. The following basic questions are reflected in various ways within this book, and act as an agenda to help enquire how this concern is worked with.

- What are the processes at work within supervision?
- What are the roles of supervisor and supervisee?
- Does supervision benefit the client in dramatherapy?
- How is the relationship between supervision and the idea of 'good practice' seen?
- What are the ways in which dramatherapy supervision is currently conducted? What are its major forms and ideas?

- What issues are alive in the developing field of dramatherapy supervision?

This book contains a range of different voices involved in these questions about the supervisory space and act, from the intimate thoughts of a diary kept about supervision:

> I wrote in my diary: 'she said she had big concerns about this, particularly as it is not what therapists in the Trust do.' But then she suggested we take it into the next supervision and think further about my role at the unit and why I was feeling the need to blur it. I wrote in my diary: 'I felt upset after supervision, as if I had been told off by a teacher, but once this immediate response had gone I felt I could bring it back to the next session. I wonder what else I am reluctant to share with my supervisor, what I hide and whether this is because she is my manager.'
>
> (Hubbard, Chapter 9: 150–51)

to interior monologues from the process of a supervisor:

> She finds herself getting uncomfortable and wanting to intervene. She decides to hold on and see what she begins to feel. She also waits to see what happens to the therapist in the role-play. She knows the therapist will come out of the enactment if she feels she needs to. This is an agreement between them when using enactment in supervision. So she waits. The silence grows, the supervisor begins to feel it's unbearable, but still she hangs on.
>
> (Jenkyns, Chapter 6: 107)

to research which asks dramatherapists questions such as what would life would be like without supervision,

> Without supervision I would become less flexible in my ways of thinking, would see a narrow understanding rather than a broader one (someone else's eyes) have less creativity and be less emotionally aware.
>
> (Jones, Chapter 3: 63)

The opening chapters of this book draw on original research conducted by the editors into dramatherapy supervision within the UK. Chapter 2 describes and analyses the process and results of this research and notes its origins in a way that relates to the basic questions above:

> The first was a response to the lack of structured investigation into the general experience of supervision within dramatherapy. The second was

connected to the needs of the British Association of Dramatherapists. The Association wanted to obtain data concerning the ways in which supervision was being used by its members.

(Jones and Dokter, Chapter 2: 33)

The processes at work within dramatherapy supervision are complex and varied. An aspect of this research explored the ways in which drama-therapists understand and use the supervisory process, and this book offers the findings of this research in Chapters 1, 2 and 3. It looks at the ways in which supervision contributes to the experience of the client in drama-therapy and the maintenance of effective work. The book looks at these issues concerning supervision and its relation to effective and good practice in a range of ways. Chapter 4, for example, explores its role within training and professionalisation, tracing how the 'development of supervision started in 1983 and went hand in hand with the development of profes-sional recognition and registration' (p. 68).

Jenkyns, in Chapter 6, examines the power of enactment and counter-transference within dramatherapy supervision, and illustrates through example how 'the art-form of drama itself, the theory and practice on which the therapy rests, has become a projective object for all the participants in the supervisory triad. Our own experiences and attitudes, our self-image as practitioners of the art-form, our internalized objects which form that image must be attended to' (p. 109).

Such concerns about the role of the arts in dramatherapy supervision echo through the book. In Chapter 9 Hubbard, for example, talks about the role of creativity and enactment in dramatherapy supervision. From the point of herself as supervisor she observes:

As a dramatherapist it seems natural to use the art form in the super-vision when this can add something helpful. I think that our drama-therapy skills/tools can actually enhance supervision with any professional who is open to them. One way of using drama is to represent the therapy material or relationship brought to the supervision with projective objects/figures or through role-play.

(p. 163)

This is followed as a theme in the consideration in Chapter 3 of action methods and the exploration in Chapter 5 of the theatre model's influence in supervision, and where case examples show how scripts and dramas are used by supervisor and supervisee. Looked at in this way a play about AIDS can form a touchstone and inspiration for the aesthetics and process of clinical supervision:

So, like our play extract, we were beginning with a kind of void, a darkness into which the life of the group emerged. A recurrent theme became staying with what was going on, and a metaphor for that 'staying with' was, for me, the idea of breathing, to ground experience, and bring energy. In our sessions, I was constantly aware of the pace of our work.

(pp. 90–1)

The language and process of image and enactment in dramatherapy supervision is explored in Chapter 8 and their relationship to psychodrama where, for example, trainees are exploring in the practicum what it is like to be in a hospital:

After *role reversing with the image* by initially taking the role of the image, and then *doubling the image*, the student chose someone to *mirror the image*. The purpose of this exercise was to encourage the students to concretise their feelings and thoughts regarding the concept of hospital and explore what might be underneath their initial impressions of this particular hospital in which they found themselves.

(p. 134)

The book also looks at the kinds of contexts which supervision connects with. Chapter 7 looks at the different cultural contexts and situations within which dramatherapy is practised. It includes a consideration of areas such as prejudice which supervision engages with:

In the triadic relationship of supervisor, supervisee and client the experience of racism can influence the dynamic. It tends to arise early in the establishment of the therapeutic relationship or resurface later to give expression to conflicts within that relationship.

(p. 114)

It also looks at the ways in which different systems within which therapy is practised relate to the presence of dramatherapy and of supervision. Issues relating to the relationship between supervision in dramatherapy and that of other professions are considered. In an age of political rhetoric about interdisciplinarity and multiprofessional working, Chapter 9 examines the tensions and benefits in the relationship between generic and specialist training and practice. As the author Hubbard observes: 'I was apprehensive about undertaking training aimed at a multiprofessional group, wondering what understanding of clinical supervision, if any, the other students might have, and how this would correspond to my own (p. 148).

Another aspect of interdisciplinary is explored in Chapter 10, as Carr and Ramsden examine the connections between education and therapy in relation to supervision, and explore the ways in which the presence of dramatherapy in a non-therapeutic setting, and of supervision in a situation where it is not part of the existing way of working, can be a challenge, catalyst and opportunity. They ask:

> How does supervision of dramatherapy operate in a non-clinical context? To what extent are schools exploring the supervision process with their staff or ignoring it, making its presence invisible? Does supervision have a role at all in educational settings? Can teachers be supervised using a dramatherapy supervision model?
>
> (p. 167)

This includes an examination of the ways in which there are processes and phenomena common within most forms of supervision, and also areas which are particular to specific clinical settings, or where phenomena are encountered in particular ways which can offer new insights into general processes. So, for example, we look at what can occur within forensic work. Stamp, for example, sees her experience of dramatherapy supervision in Chapter 12 in this way:

> There is always an element of voyeurism in supervision, which is especially strong in forensic work. The supervisor can find themselves unwillingly witnessing deeply disturbing and traumatising offences, at one remove, through the role of supervisor. This can be more traumatic for them than the dramatherapist if they are not familiar with this work, and do not have a relationship with the patient to mitigate this picture of them.
>
> (p. 207)

As with Carr and Ramsden, Blackman, in Chapter 11, takes us into questions brought about by a particular context. Her chapter responds to issues her clients with learning disabilities demand of her, and her supervision:

> How can clinical supervision support a dramatherapist to:
>
> - go about developing reflective thinking within her client with learning disabilities?
> - recognise when lack of thinking gets into the system and affects the therapeutic relationship?
> - ensure that she does not collude with not recognising invisible losses?
>
> (p. 185)

We see in these questions the ways in which supervision brings together the supervisor, the therapist and the client in an intimate and essential form of contact. As Chapter 3 suggests:

> The nature of supervision in dramatherapy concerns a chain of connection which joins the client and their situation as brought to the therapy, with therapist and supervisor. This process has been located as primarily benefiting the client coming to therapy . . . One of the key elements of this benefit concerns the ways the connections to the client are made within supervision by the practising therapist. The work with the client is brought into connection with a range of processes contained in the supervision space and relationship.
>
> (p. 49)

This book examines these connecting processes in dramatherapy and explores how they form the core of how the quality of the clinical work of the dramatherapist is enhanced by supervision.

A particular feature of some of the chapters is the inclusion of both supervisor and supervisee perspectives, as well as providing a base line for future supervision research. This is crucial because, although the benefits of supervision are a frequently expressed opinion, they are based on very little hard data. There have only been ten peer reviewed empirical studies in the last 15 years (Lambert 2004). The most consistent evidence points to a reduction in reported stress levels and burn-out. One study suggests improvement in knowledge and skills, as well as decision making. Dramatherapists indicated in the research discussed in Chapter 2 that they considered supervision a crucial aspect of practice throughout their professional lives. To quote two dramatherapists:

> Supervision enables me to work with my clients in the following ways: more spontaneously, in greater depth, with regard to the specific emerging needs of my clients, to ensure adequate closure while taking into account my personal process.

> If I did not receive clinical supervision it would affect my practice in the following ways: loss of clarity about the process, lack of challenge of my way of working, no exploration of the countertransference, less safety for my clients.

Whilst still stressing the need for research into the benefits and limitations of supervision, we hope this book will add to the necessary data to evaluate supervisory quality in relation to both client and therapist benefits.

References

Kadushin, A. (1992) *Supervision in Social Work*, 3rd edn, New York: Columbia University Press.
Lambert, M. J. (ed.) (2004) *Bergin and Garfield's Handbook of Psychotherapy and Behaviour Change*, 5th edn, New York: Wiley.
Lave, J. and Wenger, E. (1991) *Situated Learning. Legitimate Peripheral Participation*, Cambridge: Cambridge University Press.
Peters, D. E. (1967) *Supervision in Social Work. A Method of Student Training and Staff Development*, London: George Allen & Unwin.

Chapter 1

The state of the art of supervision

Review and research

Phil Jones

Introduction

Supervision is connected with all aspects of dramatherapeutic work. Grant (1999) has described the core of supervision to be the act of a therapist presenting their work to a supervisor. It is an ongoing process, normally conducted throughout the practising life of a therapist, and concerns and consists of a complex set of relationships. Grant sees supervision as 'an opportunity for clients to get the best help possible', as well as aiding the professional development of the therapist (Grant 1999: 7). In her comments we already see client, therapist, supervisor and profession brought into relationship with each other through the act of supervision. Supervision has become closely allied to professionalisation, and in the UK is a necessary component of state registration. As Chesner, for example, has pointed out in relation to dramatherapists in the UK:

> The profession in Britain has reached a point . . . where there is not only a list of practitioners and trainees but a register of dramatherapy supervisors. These have been trained in a BADth accredited course and themselves make a commitment to be supervised on their supervision as a further level of professional quality assurance.
>
> (Chesner 1999: 41)

The following gives a sample of some of the key relationships connected to supervision in dramatherapy:

- between therapist and client
- between supervisor and therapist
- between the settings that offer therapy and their staff and users
- between training institutions and trainee therapists
- between regulators of the standards and practice of therapy and those delivering and consuming therapy.

Looked at in this way, supervision forms a framework to enable a specific kind of *contact* between all of those involved in therapy. This chapter will introduce this contact. It draws on literature and research undertaken by myself and Dokter (see Chapter 2) to look at the different ideas about what supervision is, exploring what different schools of thought consider to be the nature of the supervisory process.

For other discussions of professionalisation, see pp. 68–70

The chapter examines the different contexts of contemporary dramatherapy supervision: the different situations within which it is practised. This includes a consideration of the role of supervision in the life of a professional and the different ways in which therapists encounter supervision in different settings. It looks at the definition of supervision – what it is seen to be, and what it is not. It includes an overview of the aims and outcomes of supervision. Dramatherapy is practised within a number of different frameworks or models (Jennings *et al.* 1994; Read Johnson 1999; Andersen-Warren and Grainger 2000; Landy 2001; Jones 2005; Langley 2006). This chapter refers to research undertaken by myself and Dokter into how dramatherapists see these models in relation to the nature and function of the supervision they receive. Most importantly, the chapter outlines some of the thinking, evidence and debates about whether, and how, supervision benefits the client coming to therapy.

For other discussions of models in dramatherapy, see pp. 59–60

The different contexts of supervision

The introduction to this chapter stressed the nature of supervision as relating to contact. The literature on supervision from different professions describes supervision in a variety of ways but the theme of *contact* is a constant. *The Register of Psychologists Specialising as Psychotherapists: Principles and Procedures* talks of ongoing supervision and professional development as a requirement of practice and justifies this by attributing to supervision particular value in terms of the kind of contact it enables: 'to the development of honest and satisfactory ways of establishing and maintaining constructive therapeutic alliances with clients and relationships with colleagues' (Psychotherapy Implementation Group 2005: Principle 4). McNaughton *et al.* (2006) cite the UK Department of Health definition of contact in clinical supervision as a 'formal process of professional support and learning which enables individual practitioners to develop knowledge and competence, assume responsibility for their own practice and enhance consumer protection and safety of care in complex clinical situations' (UK Department of Health 1993, cited in McNaughton *et al.* 2006: 211). McNaughton *et al.* stress contact in a different way from their citation of the Department of Health. They contrast the task of line management supervisory accountability with clinical supervision, and see 'the aim of supervision is to develop a trusting and collaborative relationship, enabling counsellors to feel safe and supported enough to reflect on all dimensions of their practice' (2006: 211).

Whilst contact can be said to be the essence of supervision, the nature of this contact clearly varies. So, for example, supervision can create contact between supervisor and therapist to enable the therapist to reflect on their practice. It can create contact between a professional body, overseeing standards of therapeutic practice in order to protect clients, and a clinic or private practice offering therapy. In this way, supervision can be part of the processes that enable a client to be assured that the therapist they are working with is receiving support adequate to maintaining a quality of delivery. Supervision can be used as part of line management where one worker offers supervision to another as part of 'administration of the line functions of an organization; administration of activities contributing directly to the organization's output' (www.thefreedictionary.com/line+management). Already, through these brief examples, we can see that supervision creates meaningful and varied contacts, and that these can have different functions. This brief overview has used terms such as 'reflect', 'overseeing standards', 'receiving support' and 'protection'. Such variety reflects the richness and importance of supervision. However, this diversity and range can also create tensions and dilemmas.

The different kinds of connections, contact and function of supervision can work easily and well together, but they can also produce friction for those involved. The tensions can represent dilemmas such as whether a supervisory relationship can contain both monitoring of standards and support for a therapist, for example. Jacobs and Jacobs (1996) talk about the importance of separating line management from clinical supervision, saying that supervision for therapists, 'is not, as in some professions, the equivalent of line management . . . strenuous efforts (are made) to separate line management and supervision . . . carried out by different people . . . to talk about patient or client work without any anxiety that she or he will be reprimanded for not working well enough' (Jacobs and Jacobs 1996: 1). Another tension concerns the nature of supervision over the lifetime of a therapist's work. Some have questioned the necessity of supervision beyond the training stage. Behr summarises this view in the following way: 'it is an open question whether supervision should be construed as an essential element of the work routine, or a luxury for which a few can afford either the time or the money and which belongs indispensably to the student role'

(1995: 17). Others have asserted the essential need of continuing supervision throughout the life of the professional (Jacobs and Jacobs 1996; Blackwell 2005).

The literature and our research (Jones and Dokter 2008) indicate that the use of, and need for, supervision can vary during the life of a therapist. So, for example, it can initially be part of the training process and of the support and assessment within areas such as a training placement. Later, it can take the function of support within continuing professional and personal development for the therapist. For some this journey will evolve into their training to become a supervisor. Aspects of this changing role within the life of a dramatherapist will be featured through the book, illustrating the need for flexibility in relation to the developing practitioner.

For other discussions of training and supervision, see pp. 44–5 and 68–82

The role of supervision also relates to professional identity. Behr has talked about this in a particular way, in relation to the transmission of knowledge, ways of working and approach: 'Supervision . . . becomes a way of transmitting an accumulated body of knowledge and expertise from one generation of therapists to the next. It is a vehicle for the "oral tradition" of the school of psychotherapy it represents' (1995: 4). In the research, 96.1 per cent of respondents agreed or strongly agreed with the statement that supervision is 'useful to keep me connected with my discipline and profession'. The points made above relate to this, but concern this process over time – the change from neophyte to fledgling to maturing therapist. Supervision relates to professional identity in other ways. It has played, and plays, a role in the broad establishment of the profession through the development and maintenance of standards in setting benchmarks for training and for national criteria, and in creating a space for the professional associations to articulate what is necessary to therapists in their ongoing work. It can be part of the way therapists maintain a sense of their professional identity and fuel their creative and personal development within their work. The complex relationship between professional body and therapist, between the supervision space and the holding and development of professional identity, will be a feature of much of the discussion of dramatherapy supervision in this book.

Just as dramatherapy has expanded to work with an enormous range of clients in different settings: from school to prison, from private practice to national and regional health systems, so supervision is connected to very different working contexts. The research undertaken in relation to this book gave a picture of the following diversity (terminology is that used by respondents): mental health day care, forensic settings, mainstream and specialist education, settings for elderly people, family and adoption services, adults with learning disabilities in day and residential centres, medium secure hospitals, settings for people living with brain injury, centres for people with eating disorders, work with people dealing with addictions and freelance private practice with referral and self-referral from the National Health Service, education and the general community.

The clients and settings ask of therapist and supervisor alike to engage with great differences in knowledge and experience. This range concerns areas as different as the diagnosis of schizophrenia, the understanding of child protection legislation, the impact of poverty on well being or the relationship between the justice and health systems. This book looks at issues arising from such diversity and examines some of the ways in which practitioners of therapy and supervision work with it.

In a similar way, dramatherapy embraces a wide range of theoretical approaches and models. There is not one way of practising dramatherapy, nor is there one theoretical approach. So, supervision has needed to develop a capacity to encounter and work with these differences. These include dramatherapy practised from a Jungian perspective, influenced by cognitive behavioural therapy or rooted in arts approaches allied to conflict resolution work. This book explores the ways in which supervision models and approaches have attempted to respond to such diversity.

Supervision in dramatherapy is emergent – it is developing new ideas and approaches (Tselikas-Portmann 1999; Lahad 2000). It both engages with new and existing ideas about supervision and reflective practice from other fields such as clinical psychology or participatory arts and is engaged in creative ideas from the theory and practice of dramatherapy itself. This book participates in the emergence and debate about theory and method of supervision in dramatherapy, both in the individual chapters and in the research into supervision which the editors conducted with the support of the British Association of Dramatherapists.

What is supervision? What is it not?

Supervision in dramatherapy is not a static field, with ideas, methods and forms that are petrified in stone. The field as a whole is rooted in creativity, exploration and imagination. This book looks at the ways in which supervision is *being created*. Some have argued that creativity emerges from a number of interacting factors such as imagination, tension and the combination of different factors into new wholes (Muller-Thalheim 1975; Jones 2005). This approach can be useful in examining dramatherapy supervision – to see it as a developing field of thought and practice combining such factors as imagination and tension, the production of new wholes.

In essence, supervision can be seen as one worker meeting with another to enable them to reflect on their practice. As referred to above, though, the theoretical grounding and practice of supervision varies. This ranges from psychoanalytically orientated supervision (Sharpe 1995) to cognitively based approaches, from transcultural models (Behr 1995) to those rooted in peer work (Blackwell 2005). The values of group or individual supervision have been discussed and compared (Sproul-Bolton *et al.* 1995) and of work rooted in accurate note taking (Langs 1994) compared to those emphasising the role of creativity and fantasy (Maclagan 1997).

For other discussions of approaches to supervision, see pp. 21–31 and 120–22

Supervision can be defined in a number of ways. The act of defining it reflects issues such as ideas about client needs and rights; the intentions behind creating the definition by the bodies involved in developing, offering and using the process. These include different political ideas about governing and overseeing health provision, and differences such as those referred to earlier regarding the theoretical orientation of therapy. Butterworth and Woods (1999), for example, have explored the relationship between supervision and clinical governance. Edwards (1997) has explored the relationship between supervision and the legacy of psychoanalytic thinking. Coleman has emphasised the importance of the value of supervision in relation to factors such as examining cultural factors and assumptions and of racism in therapeutic work (Coleman 1999). Spy and Oyston (1999) have looked at the ways in which issues concerning disability need to be attended to in terms of areas such as prejudice, medical and social models of disability and concepts of client empowerment.

Literature has often approached supervision by defining it through parallels and differences with allied fields of activity or endeavour. Dryden (1996), for example, uses parallels and differences between the act of psychotherapy and supervision. She asserts that psychotherapy supervision and practice have many features in common. These are summarised in Box 1.1.

Box 1.1 Common features of psychotherapy supervision and practice

- The therapist/supervisor is an agent of change.
- Both involve a dyadic interaction.
- Both require mutual active participation of those involved.
- Both are discovery orientated.
- Both are experiential.
- Both are carried out over an extended period of time.
- Both 'embrace the view that an open, trusting and collaborative relationship between participants is essential for . . . success'.

(Drawn from Dryden 1996: 203–6)

Table 1.1 Differences between therapy and supervision (developed from a reading of Dryden 1996)

Therapy	Supervision
Therapy aims at helping clients achieve greater self-understanding.	Supervision focuses on the supervisee learning and developing as a professional.
Therapy aims at the client developing more functional ways of dealing with problematic experiences.	A fundamental goal of supervision is 'to develop through their transactions with the supervisor, an increased self-understanding and a broader perspective on issues to do with their work as psychotherapists' (Dryden 1996: 204).

Processes in supervision and in therapy are seen as similar but not identical. Dryden (1996) defines the difference as involving a number of different factors. Table 1.1 presents her framework, in order to help clarify this key relationship.

This book, and later sections of this chapter, explore the issues identified in Table 1.1 in more depth. One broad definition which UK dramatherapists developed runs as follows:

> Dramatherapy supervision is a formal and mutually agreed arrangement. The British Association of Dramatherapists recommends that Dramatherapists discuss their work regularly with someone who is an experienced and competent Dramatherapist and familiar with the process of Dramatherapy supervision. The task is to work together to ensure and develop the efficacy of the supervisee's Dramatherapy practice. It is also aimed at the development of a critical reflective practitioner, who is committed to on-going professional development as a Dramatherapist and the continued development and practice of the profession . . . Supervision . . . is also known as . . . consultancy supervision, clinical supervision or non-managerial supervision. It is an essential part of good practice for Dramatherapy. It is different from training, personal development and line management accountability.
>
> (BADth 2006: 1–2)

Within this definition you can see some of the concerns and issues raised earlier, for example, the relationship between two workers, the connection to reflection and the centrality of bringing benefit to the client. The Association has also chosen to define supervision by saying as much about what it is *not* as what it *is*. This is not uncommon, as pointed out earlier, and it can be a useful starting point for us to consider how this definition positions itself. Table 1.2 presents BADth's material on supervision in a different way in order to see these oppositions more vividly.

Table 1.2 Dramatherapy supervision as defined by BADth (2006)

Supervision is	Supervision is not
Formal and regular. Mutually agreed. An essential part of good practice. Involves discussion and reflection.	Informal and occasional. An assigned relationship without choice. Part of line management. A relationship based on delivery of knowledge or information from one party to another.
Involves a supervisor who is an experienced and competent dramatherapist. Involves supervisor and supervisee working together with agreed aims.	Delivering an organisational management agenda as part of the process.
These aims are defined as being to ensure efficacy; to develop efficacy; to develop a critical, reflective practitioner. Involves a commitment to ongoing professional practice.	Incidental to the core engagement with change in the client's experience of dramatherapy. An add-on, not part of processes beyond immediate case discussion such as the therapist's continuing understanding of their work, the processes of dramatherapy as a whole and the way individual experiences with clients affect the way the supervisee develops over time as a dramatherapist.
Connects to developing a therapist who is committed to the continued development and practice of the profession as a whole.	Disconnected from the ways that discoveries made can enable the supervisee to contribute to the development of the field of dramatherapy as a whole.

Table 1.2 highlights some key oppositions within the definition. It shows that the Association asserts the need for regular contact, and that it is not enough for the supervisor to be experienced in supervising clinical therapeutic practice. The Association draws a clear line between supervision of line management related matters and the supervision of therapeutic process. The picture in the field is that supervision is paid for by employers for some therapists, but that others pay for it themselves. However, whether employers or therapists pay for the supervision, the division was emphatically reflected in our research: 100 per cent of respondents stated that their line management supervision and their supervision of dramatherapy were separate and were given by different professionals (see Figure 1.1).

The Association also sees the process of supervision as not being only connected to the direct work at hand: to the specific benefits to clients in particular piece of work that is being brought to supervision. Rather they choose to link supervision to *the identity of the dramatherapists themselves* and, on an even wider scale, to the development of the whole field or discipline. They do this by asserting that part of the role of supervision is to

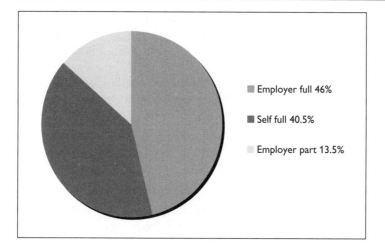

Figure 1.1 Funding supervision. *Does your employer fund your supervision?*

engage not only with the case material at hand, but also with the development of the individual dramatherapist. The Association sees this as developing the dramatherapist's ongoing insight into the methods and processes they work with, and how they work as therapists. Our research revealed a picture of supervision which 'in many ways' supports this aim and assertion, in that all but two of the respondents said that their supervision included attention to professional development, with 66.7 per cent saying that their supervision paid attention to developing new ways of working or adapting techniques to function in new ways and 90.1 per cent reflecting on the philosophy of their own practice.

Table 1.2 illustrates that the basic definition, apparently straightforward and basic, is full of assumptions. These relate to the questions we formulated earlier such as: 'Does supervision benefit the client in dramatherapy?' Or 'How is the relationship between supervision and the idea of 'good practice' seen?' This book explores these assumptions, examines how this definition relates to other definitions of supervision and sees how it relates to the theory and practice of dramatherapy supervision. How is dramatherapy supervision currently conducted? What issues are alive in the developing field of dramatherapy supervision?

Overview of the aims and intended outcomes of supervision

The aims of supervision can be looked at from a macro and a micro level. The macro level concerns the general aims which supervision has when looked at across the field of dramatherapy as a whole. The micro level concerns the kinds of aims that are negotiated within the specific encounter between individual dramatherapists and supervisors. The following broad aims are derived from the BADth Standards of Ethical Practice (2006: 1–3):

- To discuss, reflect on and monitor work regularly.
- To reflect the volume of clinical work and experience in the frequency of supervision.
- To ensure that the needs of the client are being addressed.
- To monitor the effectiveness of therapeutic interventions.
- To work together to ensure and develop the efficacy of the supervisee's practice.
- To develop a critically reflective practitioner.
- To explore the implicit and explicit dynamics that may occur between client and supervisee, supervisee and supervisor, supervision and the clinical/organisational context.
- To enable supervisee and supervisor to work constructively together and include supportive and challenging elements.
- To enable supervisees to recognise and value diversity and difference.
- To pursue equality of opportunity through the development of good practice and ensure the 'basic values of dramatherapy and drama-therapy supervision' are underpinned by anti-discriminatory practice.

The following are examples from specific aims cited in the literature, and from the research conducted for this book, which illustrate the micro level of concerns in supervision. They include, for example, the specific aims developed between individual dramatherapists and individual supervisors. It also gives an indication that a number of respondents in the research indicated that their needs for supervision changed over time.

All the respondents to the research agreed or strongly agreed that supervision was 'central' to their practice, and necessary to them *throughout* their career. It was not seen as something needed by the fledgling therapist, but not needed once practice was established. As the following figures illustrate from responses in the research, 90.2 per cent strongly agreed that supervision is central to their practice (100 per cent when 'agreed' and 'strongly agreed' are combined), see Figure 1.2; with 84.3 per cent strongly agreeing with the statement that it is essential throughout their career (100 per cent when 'agreed' and 'strongly agreed' are combined) in Figure 1.3; and 72.5 per cent in Figure 1.4 even strongly agreeing that they see no reduction in the need for supervision as they become more experienced as drama-therapists. Fewer (66.7 per cent) saw supervision as a place for keeping them connected with the profession and discipline, though 'again' this was 96.1 per cent when 'agreed' and 'strongly agreed' categories are combined, as Figure 1.5 shows. This response could suggest that aspects of this are taken care of elsewhere (in Association organised events or through

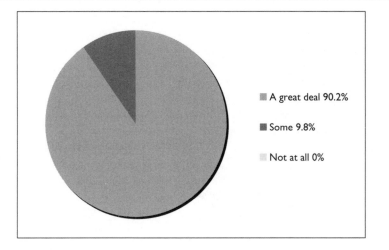

Figure 1.2 Perceptions of the uses and limitations of supervision. *To me supervision is central to my practice. Please indicate your level of agreement: 1 = Not at all 2 = Some 3 = A great deal.*

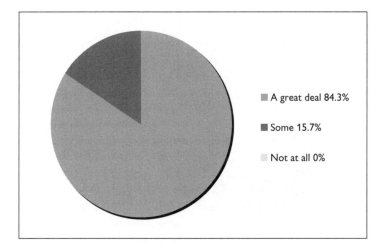

Figure 1.3 Perceptions of the uses and limitations of supervision. *To me supervision is necessary throughout my working career. Please indicate your level of agreement: 1 = Not at all 2 = Some 3 = A great deal.*

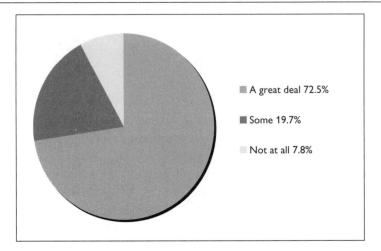

Figure 1.4 Perceptions of the uses and limitations of supervision. *To me supervision is something that I would need less as I grow confident. Please indicate your level of agreement: 1 = Not at all 2 = Some 3 = A great deal.*

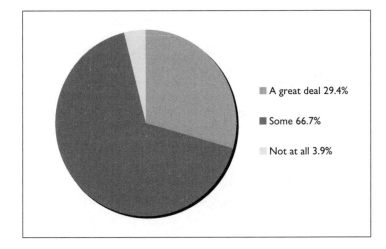

Figure 1.5 Perceptions of the uses and limitations of supervision. *To me supervision is useful to keep me connected with my discipline and profession. Please indicate your level of agreement: 1 = Not at all 2 = Some 3 = A great deal.*

continuing professional development), or that this area of need changes over time, or that there is more of an emphasis upon supervision as a place for maintaining the reflective space – as the comments summarised below and in Chapter 2 'perhaps' indicate.

However, the aims of supervision in the time immediately after initial qualifying training, compared to the developing professional post-qualification, was a difference identified by a number of respondents:

> 'Initially I think, yes, it does help enormously to have someone who reflects the same orientation and shared ideology. However, drama-therapists tend to continue training, and other theoretical backgrounds influence one's view of the self and the nature of the work. In my case integrative psychosynthesis has become linked to my practice of dramatherapy.'

> 'My supervisor and I both trained at Hertfordshire at a similar time, although I have since added different training. I feel this helps our understanding. I chose my supervisor for her work with current clients (children and families).'

A recently qualified dramatherapist, for example, shows a similar position in saying:

> 'In my own opinion, I feel that because I am a newly qualified drama-therapist it is important to me as a practitioner to receive clinical supervision from a clinical supervisor who relates to my own practice and who has a diverse range of knowledge, theory and practice, that continues to expand my own personal development and learning.'

Another differentiates between the time immediately after qualifying and later needs in the following way:

> 'This was important early on in my career and when developing par-ticular areas of practice. Currently the organisational dynamics need to be considered, so I looked for a supervisor who could pay attention to that as well as working with complex client case material.'

This demonstrates another theme, which is that supervision can be changed in order to fulfil a perceived need in the therapist for a specific area of expertise in the supervisor (Sharpe 1995). Sharpe asserts that it is essential for supervisors to be aware of 'and to have had considerable experience with' the patients which the supervisee or trainee therapist is working with, and of the external contexts in which the trainees work. The literature and our research are divided on this issue. Some see the supervisory act as not necessarily needing the supervisor to be familiar with the client group or clinical setting the supervisee is working with. The emphasis is on the act of supervising the therapist's process, irrespective of the differences of clinical setting. Looked at in this way, the supervisee will bring material specific to the issues brought by a particular client group, but the supervisor does not need expertise in a particular client group to conduct effective supervision. For others, knowledge of a particular client group is a key part of what the supervisor offers within the supervision. This issue was seen in different ways within our research. One facet concerned the supervisee's needs in relation to working with a client population that was unfamiliar to the supervisee:

> 'My current supervisor is not a dramatherapist but has a great deal of expertise in mental health which is more valuable to me in my current practice than any other consideration. She is a trained psychotherapist and mental health professional and I am able to bring any concerns to her.'

Supervision was seen to be important to the therapist and client in a number of different ways. The following respondents give an overall view that echoes themes in many of the responses in the research to the request to complete the sentence '*Within my clinical context supervision is especially important because*':

> 'Within my clinical context supervision is especially useful because it enables me to think with my supervisor about the processes, relationships and dynamics emerging from the work. Offers me a space to express, reflect and distance myself from group. Illuminates subconscious influences at work and ways of making this conscious in future sessions. Offers me invaluable professional support.'

> 'Within my clinical context supervision is especially useful because it provides an objective view and different insight into the work and the therapeutic/supervision triad, opening up new avenues for reflection.'

Both reflect many of the responses that stressed the importance of support, additional reflective space and the consideration of different perspectives on the practice. As one response succinctly summarised:

> 'Within my clinical context supervision is especially useful because it enables me to continually reflect on, and refine, my practice'.

Overview of the forms and models of supervision

As this picture begins to reveal, supervision can be offered in different forms or models. Different forms might be between group, pair or individual supervision. Different 'models' of supervision refers to the approach to ways of working or therapeutic orientation taken in the supervision. The research revealed that dramatherapists see their choice of supervision as being influenced by 'models'. Examples of the ways they saw this might include a model that draws on a 'psychodynamic approach' or one which uses a 'psychodramatic approach'. This section gives an idea of the ways in which dramatherapy supervision takes place. The variety of forms or models of supervision have some basic ways of working which are common, but have others which are specific to them.

The research showed that most dramatherapy supervision takes place on a one-to-one basis whereby the supervisee and supervisor meet together face to face. Group dramatherapy was also used, which involves the supervisor working directly with a small number of dramatherapists at the same time. Attention is allocated between the therapists, and supervisees develop insight into their practice through reflecting on their own and each other's work. In these forms there is a clear role difference between the supervisor and supervisee. Peer supervision is an alternative form, and can occur in one-to-one or group situations. This involves mutual supervision between dramatherapists where the role relationship differs from those described so far. One way of describing this peer form is that 'there is no essential difference in experience or membership grade between supervisor and supervisee' or that they 'recognise each other as peers and that, therefore, the supervision is mutual and reciprocal, each taking on both roles' (BADth 2006: 4).

The Association also refers to the ways in which internet supervision can be used. One form involves real time technology such as MSN messenger as the main focus of communication, where other information such as text and video information is drawn on. The other form uses tools such as email or an online forum as the means of communication. These different forms are seen to suit different practitioner needs and levels – for example, the needs of a newly qualified dramatherapist will be different from someone who has been practising for a number of years. Supervision is often provided within an interdisciplinary framework: this means that the supervisor can come from outside the field of dramatherapy. Examples of such a supervisory relationship were common within the practice revealed by the research. The interdisciplinary relationship was exclusively between dramatherapy and other forms of therapy. These included dramatherapy supervisees working with supervisors who were identified by them as coming from other disciplines such as psychoanalytic psychotherapy or psychodrama, for example.

All forms of dramatherapy supervision include regular contact, developing the processes and relationships involved over time. All work within a professionally based code of ethics and code of practice. These include positions on issues such as confidentiality, safety in terms of ethics and areas such as the setting of boundaries in areas such as professional conduct, for example, ensuring that the supervisor takes action if they are aware that the supervisee's practice is not in accordance with the BADth's Codes of Practice and that a supervisory relationship does not involve financial or sexual exploitation.

Within dramatherapy supervision different approaches are taken in relation to theoretical orientation and the methods used within the session. Theory and method connect. The following gives an introductory sense of the range of this difference and illustrates the ways in which theory and method result in different experiences for the supervisee and supervisor. Examples of these differences include:

- the theoretical orientation of the way dramatherapy is seen: for example, a specific model of dramatherapy might inform the way practice is reflected on within the supervision. An example of this might be dramatherapy informed by the Sesame approach which has a Jungian orientation, compared to a dramatherapy approach rooted in role model.
- the theoretical orientation of the way supervision is seen and worked with: for example, a specific model of supervision might underpin the way sessions are conducted.

This issue of the perceived therapeutic 'orientation' of the supervisor was identified by dramatherapy supervisees in selecting and working with supervisors. A minority of the respondents indicated that they would not consider supervision from a supervisor with a background indicated as being too different, or which would cause difficulty in understanding change or therapeutic processes used in dramatherapy, or in familiarity with the clinical context, for example:

'I think [orientation] is important, to an extent. I would not like to have a supervisor trained at Sesame as I believe this is very different to my training, as I found out when co-working with a Sesame trained therapist. I do, however, think it is also important to have a supervisor who has experience of working with a similar client group as the one I work with. I practice within forensics, and my supervisor has no experience of this, and it can be difficult, as we have both acknowledged.'

Others, however, emphasized the value of contrast between supervisor and supervisee's background and approach. The following are from three different therapists, all reflecting this position in different ways:

'I think it is important for a therapist to work with a supervisor that can relate to their orientation. But equally I think it is important – for the therapist's development – to be challenged by the supervisor, by introducing/suggesting different ways of working.'

'I feel my supervisor has an understanding of my Sesame training as she has experienced it, but as neither of us solely use this in our practice, I am glad to have the opportunity to refer to other approaches.'

'My long-term work with the same supervisor felt enriching because of the differences in our trainings and orientation. She was able to put forward an alternative perspective and understanding of what was happening in the client work.'

Others seek out supervision from different supervisors at the same time, seeing complementary needs which are seen not to be satisfied by one individual:

'It has been important for me to have a supervisor with knowledge of dramatherapy, also another supervisor with expertise in adoption, fostering and detailed knowledge of attachment/trauma.'

This seems to indicate that some dramatherapists seek supervision for dramatherapy process and method from one kind of supervisor, and supervision in relation to the specific client population from another:

'I have two supervisors and a pair supervisor [supervision with another practitioner as co-supervisee], all of them with different approaches (one psychodynamic, the other with a systemic approach and the third one rooted in transactional analysis theory). Each gives me different perspectives.'

However, this may well have implications for resources, as one respondent commented:

'Because of the range of my work I do not have a supervisor more experienced than me in ASD, and this is becoming an issue for me since I do not "co work" in this area any more, and the school would not pay for extra supervision.'

The range of models in dramatherapy supervision, as this material drawn from our research indicates, is wide. The literature also reflects this with references ranging from Jenkyns' use of the 'six modes' of supervision

(Jenkyns 1997) defined by Hawkins and Shohet (2000) to comments by Lahad about difference:

> It is not so easy to start supervision with supervisees who have already been to several supervisors in the past, most of whom are 'talking left brain supervision'. They come for your supervision but they expect to get the same outcome or, as Minuchin (1974) describes it, to dance the same dance.
>
> (Lahad 2000: 17)

Here Lahad asserts that for him as a supervisor there can be a difference between the way the dramatherapist sees the supervisory space and the supervisor. He frames this difference as potentially problematic and allies this to difference in method and paradigm: using talking, and an approach identified by him as 'left brain'. The image he uses, of dancers seeking to find a way of dancing, reflects a theme present for many of the respondents, that of how best to engage together: What languages? What processes? What models? This issue can be seen in the following excerpt from Jenkyns' writing about supervision.

Jenkyns creates a moment from a supervision session using a script format. The fictionalised example involves a therapist who has brought a piece of clinical practice concerning a woman who left a dramatherapy session. The supervisor has asked the therapist whether she wants to work 'symbolically or through talking' (1997: 194). After a verbal description of the background and discussion of the therapist's response to the client, the therapist says:

T: I felt this overwhelming sense of anger which I felt she was projecting into me. But immediately after I felt irritated with her and those feelings seemed to be mine. I didn't say anything, but it was after that she said she was going.

S: What do you make of those feelings now?

T: I'm not sure. I just can't work out what's her and what's me.
'At this point the supervisor suggests they work with two chairs, one to represent the therapist and the other to represent Mrs H. Using the two chairs the therapist re-enacts the session . . . In the reconstruction the therapist suddenly realizes why Mrs H. might have terminated the session. She de-roles the chairs and resumes her conversation with her supervisor' (1997: 196).

Later, in the reflection, the therapist explores her perceptions and her own response, for example, saying on her own childhood, how the client had evoked something in her 'she reminded me of something I didn't want to be reminded of, and it was something about which I've got a lot of anger' (Jenkyns 1997: 197).

For other discussions of script in supervision, see pp. 85–97 and 160–61

In reflecting on this interchange, Jenkyns refers to ideas about counter-transference and says 'it is our own process which we must constantly monitor and rigorously analyse' (1997: 202). She refers to 'issues of merger and separation', and the ways in which the relationship between the client and her family are paralleled in the relationship with the therapist, and in the therapist's own feelings about her own family life and emotional responses. She talks about one of the supervisor's tasks being 'to help the therapist refrain from compensating for her own unconscious envy of the client's needs being met by over-protection of Mrs H' (1997: 202), for example. The idea strongly represented by her is that the supervisor's role is to assist the therapist to engage with processes which are seen as being 'unconscious'. A chain of connection is present here – between unconscious material linking client, therapist and supervisor, between dramatherapy session and supervision session. This connection is seen as being at the core of the work: 'one of the central tasks of the supervisor [is] to "hold" the therapist enough to help her "hold" the client, to help Mrs H. be the child she needs in order to become the adult she wants to be' (1997: 202). The supervisor is seen to need to be 'rigorous in monitoring her own process particularly as it happens within supervision . . . where the dynamics of the therapy session are often replayed' (1997: 203).

Such concepts are shared elsewhere in dramatherapy literature. In working with clients who hear voices and are living with psychotic experiences, Casson uses the concept of countertransference, in saying that as a therapist he experienced feeling 'overwhelmed,' and that he 'needed supervision to understand what was happening' (2004: 139). Like Jenkyns, he uses the term 'holding' and 'containment', drawing on psychoanalytic thinking in relation to supervision: 'I felt baffled, frightened, "out of my depth" . . . it was at times like this that supervision sustained me: as I felt held so I could hold on holding the person in therapy . . . Such holding provides a container that counters the possibility of being overwhelmed' (2004: 140).

For other discussions of countertransference, see pp. 99–110

The issue of difference in orientation arose in many of the accounts of supervision within our research. Some respondents' replies indicated that they were very aware of the specific model which their supervisor worked within, for example:

'I have used three different supervisors, the first used the Sesame approach – supervision used the dramatherapy medium, sometimes role-playing clients, sometimes using creative processes, never solely talking. My second supervisor was a dramatherapist and also a counselor who used the person-centred approach and other methods. The third was a psychodramatist, which was not entirely ideal, and was talking based.'

Another commented:

'I have recently changed supervisors from psycho-analytical to drama-therapist. Analytical approach included references to scientific based findings on neuro-psychological research. Dramatherapist offers a deeper understanding and relevance in connection with the psycho-dynamic work.'

Here we see the ways in which a particular framework is brought to the supervisory process. The discussion of therapy here contains ideas that are specific to a particular model of understanding the therapeutic process and the processes that make supervision effective:

• transference and countertransference processes
• a chain of connection between client, therapist and supervisor rooted in feelings, memories and associations, connected to ideas of the unconscious
• the need for the supervisor to use the space and relationships in supervision to maintain a 'rigorous awareness' to these phenomena in order to help reveal and work with them, and that their visibility will assist in the task of the supervision
• the idea that the therapy space and the supervisory space and relationship are linked to ideas of 'holding'.

These are not axiomatic within all therapy, but are seen in both the longer extract from Jenkyns (1997), and the briefer excerpt from Casson (2004), to be consensual ways in which therapist and supervisor work both to examine the therapeutic processes within the dramatherapy and to fuel their examination of the practice in supervision.

The research reflected that these ways of using supervision were widespread. The emphasis was often upon supervision as an arena to reflect upon the transference and countertransference process:

'Supervision enables me to work with my clients in the following ways: with new insights and energies and greater clarity about any transference/countertransference issues.'

'My practice would be impoverished without dialogic reflection gained in supervision. It might also be possible for boundaries [esp. within the area of transference/countertransference] to become blurred.'

'Becoming aware of transference and counter-transference issues; having more insight as to what the underlying issues may be.'

All but one respondent agreed with the statements that supervision was useful to look at the therapist's own experience, that it enabled the therapist to look at their 'own process', to assess and look at the progress of clients and to evaluate the work. The supervisor–therapist–client triad was seen as important in maintaining perspective on, and awareness of, the clinical practice:

'It provides an objective source of expertise and a listening ear who is able to identify and assist with issues because they are distanced from the work.'

'Supervision is especially useful because it provides an objective view and different insight into the work and the therapeutic/supervision triad, opening up new avenues for reflection.'

'It enables me to think with my supervisor about the processes, relationships and dynamics emerging from the work. Offers me a space to express, reflect and distance myself from group. Illuminates subconscious influences at work and ways of making this conscious in future sessions. Offers me invaluable professional support.'

The idea of 'holding' was also reflected in the analysis of the use of supervision made by most of the respondents:

'Knowing I can process with someone who understands both the clinical and personal demands and effects of my work, who cares about me as I care about my clients and who is there to "hold" me, helps me continue my hold on my work and my clients.'

'It is my space to reflect on my work in a supportive environment.'

'Supervision is especially useful because it keeps my working practice safe for me and for my clients.'

This illustrates the ways in which supervision may draw on a particular model or approach to dramatherapy but also that, within the research, certain processes were common to many of the accounts of the usefulness and nature of supervision. Different people saw the issue of the variety of models in different ways. Some stressed aspects of the orientation of their training, others the model of therapeutic change drawn on:

'I wanted to have supervision with someone who uses movement particularly, as this is at the centre of my drama and movement therapy practice as a Sesame therapist.'

'I think it is important that there is a similar approach to supervision and clinical work, and, where this is eclectic, an understanding of different paradigms is essential.'

'"Orientation" for me is not linked to training background so much as my orientation as a therapist and the context that I find myself working in.'

However, overall, there was an emphasis on the need for the supervisor and supervisee to be able to reflect or complement each other's approach. Within the research 77 per cent said that they felt it was important that therapist and supervisor shared an understanding of the supervisees' therapeutic approach. A further 7.5 per cent said that it was a useful feature, with only 15 per cent saying that it did nor matter, or that a difference of approach was something to be positively looked for.

Conclusion

This chapter has given an overview of the ways in which contemporary dramatherapy supervision is currently seen. It has looked at the variety and tensions present within supervision. If, as I said at the beginning of the chapter, supervision at its simplest involves one worker reflecting on practice with another, then we have identified the ways in which this can be interpreted. The main focus is the ways in which supervision can benefit the client. However, this is seen through different lenses. Therapists offer different approaches to change and development in dramatherapy, using different frameworks to identify how change takes place and to see how they work with dramatherapy. As identified early in this chapter, the following statement indicates a view common to many dramatherapists:

'My individual supervisor is from a group analytic background, my weekly peer s/vision is within a multi-disciplinary psychological services team, and my quarterly peer s/vision is within a ritual theatre model framework.'

This is that dramatherapists look to the framework of their supervision for different ways of looking at therapeutic process, the model of drama-therapy, and the nature of their clinical setting. The nature of the thera-peutic space and relationship, the language of drama and the conception of therapeutic change can be conceived of differently within supervision. Some factors, however, are common across many accounts: these include the notion of the value of the perspective of distance which supervision offers and the concept of holding, for example. This book explores some of these different and common ways, the variety of opportunities they can help to create and the value to client and therapist alike.

References

Andersen Warren, M. and Grainger, R. (2000) *Practical Approaches to Drama-therapy*, London: Jessica Kingsley Publishers.

Behr, H. (1995) The integration of theory and practice, in M. Sharpe (ed.) *The Third Eye: Supervision of Analytic Groups*, London and New York: Routledge.

Blackwell, D. (2005) *Counselling and Psychotherapy with Refugees*, London: Jessica Kingsley Publishers.

British Association of Dramatherapists (BADth, 2006) *Code of Practice*. Online. Available HTTP: <http://www.badth.org.uk/code/supcode.html> (accessed 15 July 2007).

Butterworth, T. and Woods, D. (1999) Clinical governance and clinical supervision: working together to ensure safe and accountable practice. A briefing paper. Manchester: University of Manchester.

Casson, J. (2004) *Drama, Psychotherapy and Psychosis*, London: Brunner-Routledge.

Chesner, A. (1999) Dramatherapy supervision: historical issues and supervisory settings, in E. Tselikas-Portmann (ed.) *Supervision and Dramatherapy*, London: Jessica Kingsley Publishers.

Coleman, H.L.K. (1999) Training for multi-cultural supervision, in E. Holloway and M. Carroll (eds) *Training Counselling Supervisors*, London: Sage.

Department of Health (1993) *A Vision for the Future: Report of the Chief Nursing Officer*, London: Department of Health.

Dryden, W. (1996) *Research in Counselling and Psychotherapy: Practical Applica-tions*, London: Sage.

Edwards, D. (1997) Supervision today: the psychoanalytic legacy, in G. Shipton (ed.) *Supervision of Psychotherapy and Counseling: Making a Place to Think*, Maidenhead: Open University Press.

Grant, P. (1999) Supervision and racial issues, in M. Carroll and E. Holloway (eds) *Counselling Supervision in Context*, London: Sage.

Hawkins, P. and Shohet, R. (2000) *Supervision in the Helping Professions*, 2nd edn, Maidenhead: Open University Press.

Jacobs, M. and Jacobs, R. (1996) *Review and Response, In Search of Supervision*, Maidenhead: Open University Press.

Jenkyns, M. (1997) Gender issues in supervision, in S. Jennings (ed.) *Dramatherapy Theory and Practice 3*, London: Routledge.

Jennings, S., Cattanach, A., Mitchell, S., Chesner, A. and Meldrum, B. (1994) *The Handbook of Dramatherapy*, London: Routledge.

Jones, P. (2005) *The Arts Therapies*, London: Routledge.

Jones, P. and Dokter, D. (2008) *British Association of Drama Therapists Supervision Research Findings*, Cheltenham: British Association of Drama Therapists.

Lahad, M. (2000) *Creative Supervision*, London: Jessica Kingsley Publishers.

Landy, R. (2001) *New Essays in Drama Therapy*, Springfield IL: Charles C. Thomas.

Langley, D. (2006) *An Introduction to Dramatherapy*, London: Sage.

Langs, R. (1994) *Doing Supervision and Being Supervised*, London: Karnac.

Maclagan, D. (1997) Fantasy, play and the image in supervision, in G. Shipton (ed.) *Supervision of Psychotherapy and Counselling*, Maidenhead: Open University Press.

McNaughton, K., Boyd, J. and McBride, J. (2006) Using CORE data in counselling supervision: an initial exploration, *European Journal of Psychotherapy and Counselling* 8, 2: 209–25.

Minuchin, S. (1974) *Families and Family Therapy*, Cambridge MA: Harvard University Press.

Muller-Thalheim, W. K. (1975) Self-healing tendencies and creativity, in T. Jakab (ed.) *Transcultural Aspects of Psychiatric Art*, Vol. 4, Basel: Karger.

Psychotherapy Implementation Group (2005) *The Register of Psychologists Specialising in Psychotherapy: Principles and Procedures*, Leicester: BPS.

Read Johnson, D. (1999) *Essays on the Creative Arts Therapies*, Springfield IL: Charles C. Thomas.

Sharpe, M. (1995) Training of supervisors, in M. Sharpe (ed.) *The Third Eye: Supervision of Analytic Groups*, London and New York: Routledge.

Sproul-Bolton, R., Nitsun, M. and Knowles, J. (1995) Supervision in the National Health Service, in M. Sharpe (ed.) *The Third Eye: Supervision of Analytic Groups*, London and New York: Routledge.

Spy, T. and Oyston, C. (1999) Supervision and working with disability, in M. Carroll and E. Holloway (eds) *Counselling Supervision in Context*, London: Sage.

Tselikas-Portmann, E. (ed.) (1999) *Supervision and Dramatherapy*, London: Jessica Kingsley Publishers.

Websites

http://www.badth.org.uk/code/supcode.html, accessed July 15 2007.
www.thefreedictionary.com/line+management, accessed July 15 2007.

Chapter 2

Researching contemporary supervision

Method and findings

Ditty Dokter and Phil Jones

Introduction

The opening three chapters of this book draw on research into UK dramatherapists' use of supervision. The origin of the research had two components. The first was a response to the lack of structured investigation into the general experience of supervision within dramatherapy. The second was connected to the needs of the British Association of Dramatherapists. The Association wanted to obtain data concerning the ways in which supervision was being used by its members. This was in order to represent the profession's needs, and to establish members' current situation in relation to areas such as funding, frequency and methods used. The Association supported the development and undertaking of the research into its members' experiences.

Background

Previous literature on dramatherapy supervision has consisted of theoretical reflection (Landy 1999), on guidance in conducting supervision (Lahad 2000) and on case studies or the inclusion of illustrative anecdotes from people's experience (Jennings 1999; Tselikas-Portmann 1999). The strength of this approach was that it contributed to the emerging field of theory and practice of supervision in dramatherapy by examining the ways in which supervisors and their accounts of supervisees were articulating how and why they chose the methods used, and identified the potentials of supervision within dramatherapy though their individual accounts. However, this body of literature was largely based on the authors' immediate experiences – mostly from the perspective of a supervisor. Even when drawing upon accounts of their own experiences as a supervisee, this was described and perceived through the lens of their current position as supervisor or trainer. Hence, the analysis was based in the perspective of the supervisor, influenced by individual supervisor caseloads and specific supervisory experiences. The perspective was naturally confined to the authors' professional contacts, to the people who had chosen to come to them for supervision, or to those they had trained. The authors of the research drew on this literature and on the broader field of supervision in allied fields such as psychotherapy, art therapy and counselling, to develop a set of themes, issues and questions. These aimed to investigate the nature of theory, the practical factors affecting the general provision of supervision and the way supervision was conducted. In contrast to the existing literature, however, our research aimed to undertake a structured investigation into a wider population than that gathered by authors basing their writing on their own caseload, professional contacts and individual case examples.

The British Association of Dramatherapists collaborated with the authors on the research. Their concern was communicated as a desire to gain a snapshot of what was occurring within the UK in order to respond to practitioner needs identified within the research. In addition, the Association wanted to establish how dramatherapists articulated their uses of supervision. The authors responded to this by developing a set of questions linked to the Association documentation on the purpose and form of supervision (BADth 2006), to establish whether this articulation matched the experiences of practitioners. The research questions were:

1   How is supervision accessed by dramatherapists?
2   What are the main areas of content in dramatherapists' supervision of their clinical practice?
3   How do dramatherapists see the methods used in the supervision of their clinical practice?
4   How do dramatherapists see the relationship between supervision and their work?

Developing the research approach

The act of researching supervision raised questions about the nature of the research's attention: how best to reach *into* the experience of supervision. Given that the experience was a live interaction between two or more people, what qualities could be accessed by different research methods, and what would not be accessed by different methods?

A number of approaches were considered, drawing on different traditions and methodologies. One approach, for example, could have been to monitor and analyse actual supervision sessions. This way of researching could have involved supervisor and supervisee monitoring their work within each session, building up a profile over time. This approach would have enabled the research to gain in-depth, detailed accounts of specific supervisors' work, but would have needed considerable resources to document and analyse the data. Another approach would have been to tape record or video sessions and engage in an analysis of these sessions. The advantage of this method would have been to create insight into specific experiences of supervision, and would have given substantial information about the conduct and experience of supervisor and supervisee. It would also have enabled the researchers to examine the actual supervision work rather than respondents' opinions or interpretations of what occurred within supervision. The research could have involved interviews. The advantages of this would have been the gathering of rich data. For example, this would have enabled the research to follow the perceptions, opinions and attitudes of respondents. It would also have allowed the respondent to clarify communication, for example, in dealing with any ambiguities within the questions asked. The disadvantage of this would have been that it would necessitate travel, time and resources in conducting, recording and analysing the interviews. Given the constraints of resources, this would have reduced the range and scope of the gathered data. It was also felt that a base line of the current state of UK dramatherapy supervision needed to be achieved, in order for further in-depth research to take place.

The method chosen was that of the questionnaire. A questionnaire was designed and electronically sent out to members. In addition, hard copies were made available. The ethics procedures complied with the British Association of Dramatherapists' guidelines and the Research Ethics of Leeds Metropolitan University. Anonymity was guaranteed. Forms were completed using members' numbers, data would be kept for a precise period of time, and the material stressed the necessity of not using any identifying data for settings or clients. Permission to withdraw at any time was given and the uses of the data were made clear to respondents. The use of questionnaire as a research method has a number of particular qualities:

- Data can be gathered from a range of comparable sources.
- The researcher is able to contact large numbers of individuals easily and effectively.
- Problems regarding access due to geographical factors are minimised.
- Specific groups of interest can be selected and involved.
- Data can easily be coded and interpreted.
- It is comparatively easy to standardise the data collection, in that the respondent is asked the same questions in the same way; hence it can be seen as a reliable method of researching opinion and experience.
- It can be anonymous, completed in privacy, so that questions are more likely to be answered 'honestly' (Bynner and Stribley 1978; Foddy 1994; Grainger 1999; De Vaus 2001).

The disadvantages of the questionnaires include the following:

- The format can make it difficult to examine complex material or issues.
- The depth of answers can be more limited than other methods and hence it can be difficult to gather rich or detailed information.

- As the researchers are not present, they are not able to clarify questions.
- The researchers have to assume that the meaning of the questionnaire is the same to them as to the respondent (Bynner and Stribley 1978; Foddy 1994; Grainger 1999; De Vaus 2001).

Resource was a key factor in developing and undertaking the research, and in analysing the data. The questionnaire method used meant that factors limiting access and representation, such as geographical reach and availability of respondents' time, were reduced as potential problems. The material needed to be easy to interpret, given the uses that BADth wanted to make of it. In addition, a speedy, accessible way of conducting research was necessary to engage busy professionals.

A concern was that the use of email might mean that those who were not computer literate would not access the questionnaire. However, BADth uses email to communicate with its members and, given that we were dealing with a graduate, trained population this was felt to be an appropriate method. In addition, hard copies were made available by request and at a national conference.

The validity of the research can be looked at in different ways. The response rate was low in terms of viewing the data as a 'representative' sample – 20 per cent of the total membership completed the questionnaire. The literature cites that a 20–25 per cent return of questionnaires is the norm and 'probably something that most researchers would happily settle for' (De Vaus 2001: 27). However, researchers have pointed out that a low response rate might mean that the material is unrepresentative of the general population. It could be that the opinions of a highly motivated section of the sample are obtained, rather than those who are disaffected or, for example, the views accessed are of people with strong opinions who take the time and trouble to answer the questionnaire (Foddy 1994). To improve validity, a variety of perspectives can strengthen the data, providing richer material to research supervision. The approach gathered material in different ways, drawing on different research traditions. These methods attempted to reflect the nature of the information required. Hence, validity was considered from both a quantitative and qualitative perspective. We were concerned with the nature and richness of the data, as well as the number of responses. The approach taken relates to Grainger's definition of 'hybrid design' combining quantitative and qualitative perspectives. Grainger defines this way of working as:

> Using elements of both of these models in order to be as comprehensive as possible or because measurement does not provide all the information required and descriptive material is needed as well. Because qualitative research is more concerned with describing processes than

demonstrating results, these hybrid designs tend to be more qualitative than quantitative, numbers being used to quantify ideas or impressions and render them more systematic.

(Grainger 1999: 37)

Our approach reflected Grainger's comments in being concerned both with identifying processes best encountered with a qualitative approach and with phenomena that could best be gathered from a quantitative perspective. So, for example, data on the frequency of attending supervision was most effectively gathered numerically. Material on the relationship between employer and supervision was most effectively established through multiple choice. Respondents' reflections on their perceptions of the value of super-vision needed to be gathered by a method which would allow a higher degree of individual responses, such as seed sentences. The shortcomings of the different perspectives used in a questionnaire format reflect Grainger's comments, in that the numerical data was limited in the kind of information it yielded. The research using closed questions to obtain data on attendance, for example, did not uncover the respondents' reasons for the supervision frequency. In relation to multiple choice questions, the limitations con-cerned restricting the choices available to respondents. In all cases the criteria drew on published literature and accounts. The research provided a space for respondents' specific responses to the offered choices. Some questions were 'open ended' and required the respondent to write their own words in reply to a question, or to complete a seed sentence. The advantage was that this created opportunities for individualised, richer material (Robson 1993: 243). However, the limitations of such questions and seed sentences are that some might be dissuaded from responding to the ques-tionnaires because of the extra time and effort needed to complete complex data (compared to a simple checklist or multiple choice). In addition, the data gathered in seed sentences is less rich than that accessed through interview based methodologies.

The response

The questionnaire was divided into different sections. The first asked for details regarding the practical supervision arrangements for the respondent. These included the profession of the clinical supervisor and the relationship of the supervision to the respondent's work setting, for example. Questions included whether the supervisor was employed in the same organisation as the supervisee, whether the respondent's main employer funded super-vision, and whether supervision was supported inside 'or outside' work time. Other practical factors included the frequency and duration of the sessions. The work relationship with the supervisor was also covered. The

Table 2.1 Dramatherapist experience (supervision research)

Years since qualifying	1	3	5	7	9	11	13	15	17	19	21	23
Numbers of therapists	5	12	9	10	4	5	5	6	3	2	3	3

approach here was quantitative, with all questions requiring answers that involved ticking boxes or giving numerical answers. The sample of the respondents all practised and were supervised in the UK. Table 2.1 shows their years of experience as dramatherapists.

Dramatherapist experience

To contextualise the research sample within the general dramatherapist population we present the results from the BADth equal opportunities survey, which had a 60 per cent response rate (Dokter and Hughes 2007) (Figure 2.1). Dramatherapy training in the UK started at the end of the 1970s. This response shows that approximately 8 per cent of dramatherapists have practised for more than 20 years, an additional 10 per cent have been practising between ten and 20 years, while a third has been qualified within the last ten years. Six per cent of dramatherapists indicated that they were retired. Forty per cent of the population did not respond to the survey, but there is no indication that the make up of that 40 per cent is significantly different from the rest of the sample.

For the purpose of this research we did not ask questions about the nature of dramatherapists' employment contracts, but the results of the equal opportunities survey conducted in the same year as this research (Dokter and Hughes 2007) are shown in Table 2.2 and Figure 2.2.

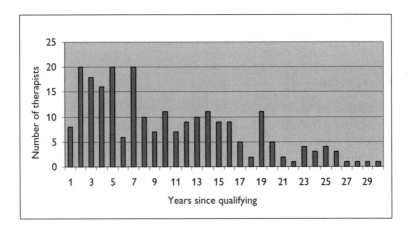

Figure 2.1 Length of experience of dramatherapists

Table 2.2 Dramatherapist employment patterns

Category	Respondents
Employed dramatherapist	58 (24%)
Employed/self-employed dramatherapist	36 (15%)
Self-employed dramatherapist	92 (37%)
Employed different title	33 (13%)
Other/voluntary	10 (4%)
Not practising/retired	15 (6%)

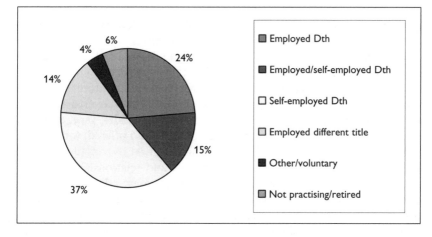

Figure 2.2 Dramatherapy employment

The frequency of supervision for most of the sample was fortnightly (45 per cent), with 20 per cent each receiving weekly or monthly supervision. The remaining 10 per cent of respondents varied. Half of the respondents received supervision within their place of work, while the other half obtained clinical supervision external to their employment. As mentioned in Chapter 1, for all dramatherapists, managerial supervision was separate from clinical supervision, as recommended by BADth guidelines, but only half of the respondents received managerial supervision. This may be related to the employment pattern of dramatherapists, where 50 per cent work on a self-employed or voluntary basis. That pattern of employment may also influence whether dramatherapists or their employers pay for their clinical supervision.

A question asking respondents to describe the professional identity of their supervisor showed that 75 per cent were supervised by dramatherapists. It is interesting to note that approximately half of those have an additional professional identity, for example, psychotherapist, occupational therapist, social worker or psychologist. Twenty five per cent of dramatherapist supervisors are psychotherapists from a variety of orientations. The variations include arts psychotherapy, gestalt, Jungian, psychodynamic, psychodrama and group analysis.

For other discussions of the identity of dramatherapy supervisors, see pp. 54–61

The second section of the questionnaire addressed the respondent opinions about supervision. This section aimed to define aspects of the way supervisors and supervisees worked within supervision practice. The aim was to range from macro areas such as government policies to the micro level of specific client responses within the therapy and the therapist's own process. This gave a range of areas of attention drawn from the literature and offered space to add areas not offered in the questionnaire. These covered areas such as ethics, philosophy of practice, issues concerning gender, race, disability, age and sexual orientation. Technique areas were also offered, for example, assessment methods, and whether attention was given to adapting or developing dramatherapy techniques. The process and relationship of therapy was also included – for example, the client–therapist relationship, evaluation and assessment, and specific client reponses. Professional and organisational matters were also listed. These included professional development and organisational dynamics. Other areas included exploration of the therapist's own life experiences in relation to their practice and countertransference feelings and processes along with the processes at work within the supervision itself (see Box 2.1).

Box 2.1 Sample questionnaire illustration: Question 5

The responses have been arranged with the most frequently featured first, the least last.

5.   We are trying to gain some general sense of the kinds of attention given within supervision. If you feel you want to say more specifically what *you* mean by a category, or its presence irritates you because the nature of this task is broad and you want to make it more specific – please make a note in the space below the categories. We are not interested in frequency here – it really is whether you *ever* pay attention to these areas.

	RESPONSE % YES/NO
Specific client responses to dramatherapy	100/0
The client–therapist relationship	98.4/1.6
Your professional development	96.1/3.9
Issues concerning age*	92.3/7.7
Issues concerning gender*	92.2/7.8
The relationship between organisational aims and those of your dramatherapy work	92.2/7.8
Philosophy of your own practice	90.2/9.8
Your countertransference	90.2/9.8
Ethical issues	88.4/11.6
Issues concerning race*	86.3/13.7
Issues concerning client or therapist's cultural differences or expectations and the medium of drama*	86.3/13.7
Organisational dynamics and your general experience as a worker outside of the dramatherapy	86.3/13.7
Organisational dynamics and how they relate to the dramatherapy itself	86.3/13.7
Referral	86.3/13.7
Your own life events and their relationship to your practice	86.3/13.7
Assessment methods	84.2/15.8
Feedback from clients on your practice	84.2/15.8
Issues concerning disability*	82.4/17.6
Your relationship with your supervisor	80.4/19.6
The evaluation of your own supervision	78.5/21.5
The processes at work within the supervision	76.5/23.5
Issues concerning sexual orientation*	74.51/25.49
Adapting specific dramatherapy techniques you already know from your basic training	66.7/33.3
Developing new dramatherapy techniques (either ones you create yourself, or ones you have learned in development post basic training)	66.7/33.3
Government policies relating to the area of your practice (e.g. health policies, or education policies)	66.7/33.3
Evaluation methods	59/41
Evaluation results	51/49

* These concern any aspect of this content area – from issues within the client process, to the therapist's experience – we are interested here in the nature of attention in relation to themes covered, rather than the nature of the specific experience.

Commentary on Question 5: kinds of attention in supervision

It is interesting to note where dramatherapy supervision tends to focus and which areas receive little attention. Most attention is paid to the client–therapist relationship, the therapist countertransference and the dramatherapist's professional development. Least attention is paid to evaluation of practice. Half of the respondents said that evaluation (especially the more formal evaluation of practice) was not discussed in supervision. One-third of the respondents did not address government policies, the development of dramatherapy techniques, or the nature of the supervision relationship. The research gave a picture of the amount of attention paid to equal opportunities, assessment and referral and organisational dynamics. The picture of attention paid to the social divisions within society gave a varied picture. In terms of gender and age, 8 per cent said this was never given attention. Regarding race and disability, for example, up to 15 per cent of the respondents did not cover these areas in their supervision, with this rising to 25 per cent concerning sexual orientation.

For other discussions of race and culture, see pp. 111–27

A third area concerned the way in which the supervision is conducted. A key issue here was whether the supervision was conducted purely by talking or whether active methods were used to explore the therapist's work. This area included whether areas such as role play, play with objects, storytelling or movement were used. It also asked whether specific issues such as group dynamics or individual clients were explored using dramatic techniques and whether the supervisors themselves entered into processes such as movement or role. Both of these areas used a quantitative approach to drawing out data (see Box 2.2).

Box 2.2 Sample questionnaire illustration (a): Question 6

Please indicate which statements most represent your experience:

Comments:	PERCENT INDICATING YES
The supervision is conducted entirely by talking with no drama	49.0%
The supervision uses drama techniques every session	1.9%

The supervision uses drama techniques on occasion	41.7%
My supervisor takes part in the drama as an active participant	11.7%

(Full details of Question 6 responses, see Box 3.1, p. 52.)

Commentary on Question 6: the experience of supervision

It is interesting to note issues such as that whilst 75 per cent of the respondents are supervised by dramatherapists, half of all respondents receive purely verbal supervision, while 40 per cent occasionally use drama techniques within the supervision. If drama is used, projective techniques such as object sculpts and creating images are prevalent. The dramatic work is mainly used to depict the individual or group dynamics in the therapy, as well as the therapist's feelings towards the clients (countertransference). This area of the research is discussed in more detail in Chapter 3.

For other discussions of action methods in dramatherapy supervision, see pp. 85–98 and 130–45

A fourth area looked at matters relating to the respondent's experience or attitude towards specific connections between theory and practice in supervision. Issues here included whether the respondent felt that their supervision was linked to a particular model – either of supervision, or of therapy, or of dramatherapy. The literature indicated that some people might say that the supervision sessions are rooted in a psychodynamic approach, or that the approach to dramatherapy within supervision is linked to the 'Sesame approach', or 'ritual theatre model' or is 'eclectic', for example (Jennings 1999; Tselikas-Portmann 1999). The research sought to establish the nature of this issue within the respondents' experience and perceptions of supervision.

For other discussions of models and approach in supervision, see pp. 120–22 and 148–65

Commentary on Questions 7 and 8: orientation

Question 7 asked the respondents to identify their supervisor's orientation. The main orientations identified were eclectic (29 per cent) and psychodynamic (50 per cent). Other orientations identitified were specific to dramatherapy such as Sesame and theatre model, but also social constructionist, gestalt and humanistic/Rogerian. Almost half of the respondents identified a combination of orientations in their supervision (46 per cent), but did not identify this as eclectic. The difference seems to be that the orientations are clearly delineated.

Question 8 asked the respondents how important a similar or different orientation between supervisor and supervisee was to them. The response was evenly distributed between those who preferred their supervisor to have a similar orientation to themselves and those who felt they benefited from the differences. We found that the level of experience of the dramatherapists coloured the response. Early on in their career dramatherapists preferred a supervisor from the same orientation: 'This was important early on in my career and when developing particular areas of practice.' However, for another respondent the clinical experience of the supervisor was more important than their orientation: 'I feel that because I am a newly qualified practitioner it is important to receive clinical supervision from a supervisor who relates to my practice and has a diverse range of knowledge, theory and practice, to expand my personal development and learning.'

All respondents emphasised that understanding each other's paradigms was very important in establishing a working relationship between supervisor and supervisee. When there is a difference in orientation, there can be a difficulty in having to interpret, echoing the struggle of the lone dramatherapist in a setting with a different orientation:

'I do feel it helps to share orientation so that the struggles I encounter are recognized by the supervisor. Our process together helps me to unearth the roots of the struggle, which are personal and helpful for my clients. My practice needs to be untangled without finding another non-shared language of interpretation and meaning making.'

At times the dramatherapist seems unclear about orientation:

'I am unsure about my own theoretical approach as a dramatherapist, never mind the supervisors, so I feel confused by this. My trainings were eclectic, a bit of this and that but no strong clarity on approaches.'

It is interesting to consider such issues in relation to an item within the research that asked about the relationship between supervision and the adequacy of training (Figure 2.3). Although the majority of respondents' responses concerning the possibilities and limits of supervision did not feel that they needed supervision to supplement inadequate training (6 out of 51 yes; 9 out of 51 some; 36 out of 51 not), the orientation of practice may be

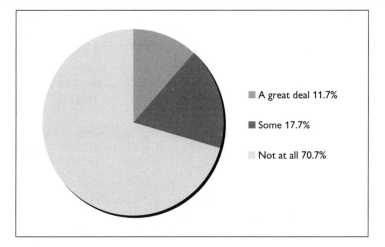

A great deal 11.7%

Some 17.7%

Not at all 70.7%

Figure 2.3 Perceptions of the uses and limitations of supervision. *Please indicate your level of agreement: 1 = Not at all 2 = Some 3 = A great deal. To me supervision is useful as I feel my training did not adequately equip me to practise and the supervision is functioning in part as training.*

an area for attention in supervision, given that the term 'eclectic' may be a way of naming uncertainty.

This is not the case for all though and eclectic can also indicate a valuing of diversity. Approximately 50 per cent of respondents really valued the challenge from a difference in orientation:

'My practice is eclectic, with a base of integrative arts. On the whole, I think it is important for the supervisor to have some knowledge and understanding of the therapist's own orientation. However, a different approach can not only bring into awareness aspects which might otherwise remain hidden but also serve to develop and widen the skills of the practitioner.'

'I work very differently in my own work as a supervisor, where my approach is person-centred and uses drama at all levels. I have had supervision in the past where my supervisor has used creative methods. My current supervisor is not a dramatherapist but has a great deal of expertise in mental health which is more valuable to me in my current practice than any other consideration. She is a trained psychotherapist and mental health professional and I am able to bring any concerns to her. She has experience of dramatherapy and has a good understanding of the processes involved and encourages me to work creatively within our sessions if that's what I need to do. I feel our sessions provide me with the chance to raise any issues, personal as well as professional, and a grounded confidence in my practice.'

'It can be helpful to receive support from somebody who has a very different training, as I believe good supervision should not be an essentially "cosy" process.'

'In fact, another orientation might help inform the practice of other perspectives hence continue learning and develop thinking.'

Occasionally the respondents emphasised the importance of the creative medium:

'I wanted to have supervision with someone who uses movement particularly, as this is at the centre of my drama and movement therapy practice as a Sesame therapist. It felt important to be able to use movement as part of supervision, besides talking and role-play/drama, rather than exclusively a cognitive approach. It feels important to combine and balance all the functions of thinking, feeling, sensation and intuition both in my work of course, and in supervision. So it's important to be able to express myself in supervision using the means I offer to my clients.'

The value of talking in supervision for a dramatherapist was also stressed: 'I appreciate a talking approach in my supervision as the rest of my work is so active and physical.'

Conclusion

The research enabled a structured investigation of the nature of supervision in the field of dramatherapy in the UK. Material was gathered on patterns of use, and on the practical provision of supervision. These areas included the frequency attended, the funding of therapists in relation to supervision and the professional identity of supervisors. The research provided insight into a variety of different areas of dramatherapists' experience.

The research showed that dramatherapists draw on supervisors from a broad range of professional identities. The tendency is not for dramatherapists only to seek out supervisors who are also dramatherapists. The research showed that dramatherapists do not choose supervisors from one particular orientation. There was no tendency, for example, to choose supervisors who were classified in one particular way – for example as a 'psychodynamically orientated supervisor'. The clear picture here was of a diversity of identities. The respondents gave 21 different identities to the question 'What is the profession of your clinical supervisor?' ranging from Jungian analyst to art psychotherapist, from dramatherapist to CPN counsellor. Writing about the relationship between the orientation of supervisors and those of supervisees, Edwards (1997) refers to ways of thinking that see differences between supervisor and supervisee in this area as problematic. This position asserts that in situations where very different theoretical models are being utilised in order to make sense of the material presented in supervision, the mismatch between supervisor and trainee may as Pilgrim and Treacher observe, be 'potentially very damaging' (1992: 125). This is not the picture that the research created in relation to dramatherapy. The analysis of data such as the responses to Question 8 shows that the experiences and views of dramatherapists vary. The research indicated that there were factors which affected views and opinions in this area. These included the experience of the dramatherapist, their proximity to the completion of their training, the nature of the client group being worked with, the therapeutic paradigm of the clinical setting and geographic availability, for example.

The results gave a picture of areas that were commonly included within dramatherapy supervision. These included client responses, the client–therapist relationship, countertransference, professional development, the relationship between organisational aims and those of the dramatherapy practice, philosophy and issues concerning gender and age. Other areas were not so commonly considered in dramatherapy supervision. These included evaluation methods, evaluation results, government policies relating to the area of the therapist's practice, the processes at work within supervision, the dramatherapist's relationship to their own supervisor and the evaluation of the supervision.

The results also created a clear sense of the methods used in the supervision of dramatherapy clinical practice. For example, as discussed above 49 per cent of supervision is conducted with no drama or action methods, using talking alone. With just over 41 per cent using some drama on occasion, the most used action-based process is object-related work. Authors such as Maclagan (1997) have argued for the importance of active engagement in the arts and fantasy within supervision. The research revealed a significant lack of use of arts processes within dramatherapy supervision. The responses indicated a variety of reasons for this. Some dramatherapists' experience was that their supervisor was not trained or comfortable in using arts processes. Others did not want to use arts processes, feeling that they needed a space away from active methods within supervision, whilst others felt this access to creativity through arts media was central to their experience and choice of supervisor.

A piece of research such as this does not aim to have an 'answer' or 'conclusion'. As the research questions indicated, the approach was to create a project that would yield material to create a sense of dramatherapists' perceptions and experiences of supervision. What can be concluded is that the field creates diversity for itself: a diversity in background, orientation of supervisors and a range of methods. It is worth noting that 100 per cent of the respondents agreed or strongly agreed that supervision is central to their practice, and necessary to them *throughout* their careers within all the forms that supervisors and supervisees are creating together.

References

British Association of Dramatherapists (BADth, 2006) *Code of Practice*. Online. Available HTTP: <http://www.badth.org.uk/code/supcode.html> (accessed 15 July 2007).

Bynner, J. and Stribley, K. (eds) (1978) *Social Research Principles and Procedures*, London: Longman.

De Vaus, D.A. (2001) *Research Design in Social Research*, London: Sage.

Dokter, D. and Hughes, P. (2007) *Analyses of Drama Therapy Equal Opportunities Survey*. Online. Available HTTP: <http://www.badth.org.uk> (accessed 15 July 2007).

Edwards, D. (1997) Supervision today: the psychoanalytic legacy, in G. Shipton (ed.) *Supervision of Psychotherapy and Counseling: Making a Place to Think*, Maidenhead: Open University Press.

Foddy, W. (1994) *Constructing Questions for Interviews and Questionnaires: Theory and Practice in Social Research*, Cambridge: Cambridge University Press,

Grainger, R. (1999) *Arts Therapies Research: A Dramatherapist's Perspective*, London: Jessica Kingsley Publishers.

Jennings, S. (1999) Theatre-based dramatherapy supervision: a supervisory model for multidisciplinary supervisees, in E. Tselikas-Portmann (ed.) *Supervision and Dramatherapy*, London: Jessica Kingsley Publishers.

Lahad, M. (2000) *Creative Supervision*, London: Jessica Kingsley Publishers.

Landy, R. (1999) Role model of dramatherapy supervision, in E. Tselikas-Portmann (ed.) *Supervision and Dramatherapy*, London: Jessica Kingsley Publishers.

Maclagan, D. (1997) Fantasy, play and the image in supervision, in G. Shipton (ed.) *Supervision of Psychotherapy and Counselling*, Maidenhead: Open University Press.

Pilgrim, D. and Treacher, A. (1992) *Clinical Psychology Observed*, London: Routledge.

Robson, C. (1993) *Real World Research*, Oxford: Blackwell.

Tselikas-Portmann, E. (ed.) (1999) *Supervision and Dramatherapy*, London: Jessica Kingsley Publishers.

Chapter 3

From role to play

Research into action techniques in supervision

Phil Jones

Introduction

This chapter focuses on the uses of drama within dramatherapy supervision. It reviews the nature and extent of the use of methods such as role play and object and image-based techniques, as well as examining the ways in which creativity relates to the process of supervision. The consideration includes a review of the research undertaken by myself and Dokter into dramatherapists' experience of supervision and examines the ways in which supervisors and supervisees use the space.

The nature of supervision

The relationship between form, content and relationship

The nature of supervision in dramatherapy concerns a chain of connection which joins the client and their situation as brought to the therapy, with therapist and supervisor. This process has been located as primarily benefiting the client coming to therapy (Butterworth and Woods 1999). One of the key elements of this benefit concerns the ways in which the connections to the client are made within supervision by the practising therapist. The work with the client is brought into connection with a range of processes contained in the supervision space and relationship. These connecting processes are at the core of how the quality of the clinical work of the therapist is enhanced by supervision. The processes have been formulated in a range of ways. Rice *et al.* (2007) in their review of supervision literature identified them as involving the development of knowledge, competence and skills in order to provide best care. The processes they list include the ongoing connection between practitioners and skilled supervisors; a supportive environment; the facilitating of reflective practice; enhancing the self-esteem of the supervisee; and supporting personal and professional development. Other research into supervision has emphasised the importance of reflecting on the relationship between social location, lived contexts and the clinical encounter and the need for mentoring the 'next generation' of therapists (Taylor *et al.* 2007) or cultural sensitivity (Butler 2004).

There can be seen to be three main components in the nature of the 'connection' identified at the start of this chapter, as revealed by the literature (Borders 2006; Rice *et al.* 2007) and by our research. The first is that it is a reflective space, the second relates to protection and the maintenance of protection; the third is that it is a space for professional development and enquiry into the mode of therapy. This is common to dramatherapy and to most supervision within the helping professions. However, a question with which this chapter will concern itself is whether supervision in dramatherapy can use particular approaches rooted in the language and process of drama, and whether these offer specific value to the supervisee. Lahad states as a basic position within his approach to supervision that:

> One very important thing for me is that I am at the service of my supervisee. This means that we will rarely do anything that does not respond to her needs or that is not in our agreed contact.
>
> (Lahad 2000: 17)

However, the ways that the supervisor can be 'at the service' was seen to be a tension within the research. One of the key issues identified both within the literature and within our research was whether the supervisor prioritised certain ways of working within the supervision sessions over others: for example, using words alone compared to active methods. Within the literature Langs, for example, has talked about supervision being 'a living process that must unfold within a carefully defined frame and set of guidelines, but in natural fashion' (1994: 132). However, the method advocated by Langs has as its centre the use of detailed written case notes. This is seen as essential within this method as such detailed notes reduce the 'distortions, repressions, denial and other kinds of errors and lapses' that 'render the spontaneously recalled material' relatively useless and unusable (1994: 132). The emphasis is on what Langs calls the 'most accurate recall possible' (1994: 132) and that such recall is by detailed noted recollection.

Others would challenge the placing of this way of creating a connection between the clinical situation and the supervisory space, seeing it as too restrictive and emphasising the act of a certain kind of recall over the exploratory, the imaginary, the associative. Maclagan, for example, has talked of the value of creativity in supervision, that fantasy is a 'resource to be tapped' (1997: 63). Mollon's writing about supervision as a creation for a 'space for thinking' (1997: 24) directly contrasts with Langs' views, in asserting that in supervision 'thinking is not linear, logical "left brain" cognition, but a kind of free-associative mulling over, perhaps more characteristic of right-hemispheric functioning. Wishes to understand quickly, to appear competent, or to compete with peers or with the supervisor can all interfere with this thinking space' (1997: 33). Such ideas foreground the use of free association, for example, of recall through the relationship between remembered or associated feeling and clinical event rather than through written event recall alone. Some have emphasised the value of artistic process in supervision's capturing and exploring the clinical encounter (Jennings 1999; Lahad 2000).

A theme within dramatherapy literature and in our research reflected a tension between modes which consisted purely of talking and those that combined verbal and artistic expression and exploration. Some respondents within the research valued supervision that was verbal, for example, saying:

'I am a newly qualified dramatherapist and have recently secured dramatherapy work, therefore I consider the talking approach effectively covers a wide area of my dramatherapy practice and meets all my needs effectively, within the given time scale for each clinical supervision session.'

Some saw the exclusive use of verbal language as an asset, whilst others, however, as we will see, felt that action-based work in supervision offered particular kinds of experience which were essential to their work:

'Most of the psychodynamic and counselling supervisors have not used action methods in supervision within my work. However in my freelance work I have a dramatherapist as supervisor and this orientation has provided a richer experience and a more varied approach to the work. I would conclude that it is important to have a supervisor with the flexibility/willingness to use action methods as well as words.'

For other discussions of different models of supervision, see pp. 120–22 and 148–65

The emergence of a pool of appropriately trained and qualified supervisors, their backgrounds and their availability, are all factors within the form of supervision which dramatherapists can access. The diversity of the background and qualifications of therapists in a relatively new and emergent field is something that Chesner (1999) refers to, as she comments on the impact of dramatherapy supervisor training courses in relation to the use of action-based approaches in supervision:

Such courses have begun to contribute to the availability of appropriate specialist supervision for dramatherapists. They have brought a creative and action-based dimension into the supervision of practitioners from other backgrounds and furthered the awareness and recognition of dramatherapy within the wider professional world.

(Chesner 1999: 41)

For other discussions of supervision training, see pp. 104–5 and 146–65

The reflection in supervision takes place as supervisee and supervisor work together to encounter the clinical situation, but the extent of creative or action-based methods within supervision varies. The way reflection occurs varied within different approaches to supervision of dramatherapy practice revealed by the research (see Box 3.1). The following gives a brief summary of points from the research relating to this:

1   All supervision involved the supervisee verbally describing their clinical situation in terms of the aims and form of dramatherapy activities and the narrative of the client's engagement with the activities.
2   All supervision involved the supervisee considering the individual responses of clients.
3   Some supervision involved the supervisee looking at their own emotional responses to the material within the sessions and seeing the therapist's emotional responses as an important aspect of trying to understand the therapeutic processes occurring within the session.
4   Some supervision draws on a psychodynamic approach which sees the relationship between supervisee and supervisor as representative of dynamics and processes at work within the therapy session. Looked at from this perspective, this forms another way in which the supervisee represents what has occurred in the clinical setting, through the transference and countertransference between supervisee and supervisor.
5   Some supervision involves the supervisee representing and exploring the therapy session through arts processes such as role and object play, storytelling, movement and music.

Box 3.1 Sample questionnaire illustration (b): Question 6

Please indicate which statements most represent your experience:

Comments: PER CENT INDICATING YES

Overview
The supervision is conducted entirely by talking
with no drama   49.0%

The supervision uses drama techniques on occasion	41.7%
The supervision uses drama techniques every session	1.9%
My supervisor takes part in the drama as an active participant	11.7%
Method/content (presented in descending order of positive responses)	
We use object work	43.13%
We use image making	35.29%
We use movement	25.49%
We use role-play	23.5%
We use storytelling or myth	15.68%
We use music	7.84%
Kinds of content using action methods (presented in descending order of positive responses)	
We depict individual clients using drama	41.17%
We explore my feelings within the work using drama	31.37%
We explore group dynamics using drama	25.5%

In what ways can drama feature in dramatherapy supervision?

The uses of action within reflection

There are a number of ways in which dramatherapists use active methods in dramatherapy supervision. As a way of introducing these, the following are summaries of the two ways that our research indicated were the most used active approaches in dramatherapy supervision: the use of object play and the creation of images. Objects are used in dramatherapy supervision in the following ways:

- to play without any set agenda to see what themes and issues emerge in relation to the issues brought to the supervision
- to use objects to depict a situation from clinical practice, for example, a moment from a session or the dynamics at work in a group
- to use objects to create a representation of a client's feelings or life situation
- to use objects to depict the supervisees' own feelings or issues

- to re-create or explore an activity in a session or to try out a development of a technique in order to test the experience
- to depict aspects of the supervision process.

Here the emphasis is upon the use of objects as a narrative technique, as a way of using dramatic projection to explore an encountered situation or set of feelings, or to explore a technique where the supervisee actively represents a moment of play within a clinical session by playing within the supervision. Objects might also be used to explore aspects of the processes at work within supervision.

For other discussions of object work, see pp. 109–10 and 133–34

Images might be used in dramatherapy supervision in the following ways:

- to use materials to explore themes, issues, feelings or situations without a set agenda or direction
- to use image making through activities such as a spectrogram to create diagrams to form and explore issues such as the relationship between therapist and client, the client's life situation, group dynamics
- to use images to express and explore areas with a given theme or focus such as transference and countertransference
- to use images to explore aspects of the supervisory process.

The emphasis is upon images as a way of expressing and exploring material. The idea is that the creation of imagery can access issues and processes in a way that words alone could not. The notion is that they can hold and work with material in a manner that assists supervisee and supervisor to gain insight into the work.

Both of these show the ways in which particular active methods can be used. However, another way of looking at the idea of active creative avenues of approaching supervision concerns a position which emphasises a playful 'attitude'. The next section broadens the discussion to examine this.

Active methods: internal playfulness

It is interesting to think about the kind of division created by analyst Patrick Casement. He talks about the way he has developed as a supervisor and that, increasingly, he tries to create a certain kind of supervision as well as specific ways for the 'internal supervisor' to develop:

> I try to show a more playful use of internal supervision, wanting to create the atmosphere of a sandpit (playing with different shapes) rather than that of a court room; but a continuing tension between these two attitudes is still evident . . . outgrowing a longstanding wish to be more sure can only be achieved gradually and with difficulty.
>
> (Casement 1990: 13–14)

The idea of the internal supervisor is that the process of supervision is not confined to the sessions between supervisor and supervisee. Over time the knowledge, experience and reflective relationship developed between supervisee and supervisor is internalised by the supervisee. The idea is that the supervisee draws on this within their live practice, as well as in the supervision space. The quote from Casement is provoking to think about in relation to dramatherapy supervision in a number of ways. First, it is interesting to note a theme, which Casement as an experienced supervisor notes, in his metaphor between legal language and play 'attitudes'. He relates this to a tension between a desire to achieve a state of surety within supervision, and remaining in a playful relationship with the material. I see this in two ways. The first way is that his words reflect the need to be alert to moving too quickly to try to focus on one reading or interpretation of what has occurred in the therapy brought to supervision. The second way I see this concerns the difference between analyst Casement's use of sandpit as a metaphor and the way a supervisor might actually use sandplay within their supervision. In relation to my first comment, Casement emphasises the value of remaining open to possibilities and meanings. He is talking about the act of supervision itself and the way it should be internalised by the supervisee: it should be playful. In saying that the function of supervision concerns playfulness, Casement refers to Winnicott's notion of therapy being the overlap of the patient and the therapist's play areas (Winnicott 1971: 54). He says:

> I regard playing as one of the functions of the internal supervisor, and it is through this that the therapist can share in the patient's creativity. It is also here that he can discover a balance between what he knows of the nature of the unconscious and the pitfalls of premature assumption.
>
> (Casement 1997: 36)

Here the supervision space is seen to be allied to the therapist's own creativity and the ways in which it relates to the client's. Playfulness, from this point of view, can be said to be a frame of mind, an attitude, and that words as much as active techniques can hold this attitude. This takes me to my second comment on metaphoric and actual playing. We could say that Casement, as an analyst, was using the sandpit as a metaphor, not actually expecting playing with sand and toys to be a part of his supervision, just as all the supervisees in his two books do not ever use sandplay as a part of their therapeutic language. However, most dramatherapists might more readily acknowledge the uses of the active language of play through actual play or playfulness in drama. The active engagement with play and drama, after all, is seen as central to the efficacy of dramatherapy. So, it becomes interesting to ask whether dramatherapists make use of this active engagement with play through action and drama in supervision, and whether this might be appropriate and useful?

Does it matter whether this playfulness is present through words alone in dramatherapy supervision? What pictures does our research give of whether dramatherapists are actively using the media of play and drama in their supervision? Why might this be important? Within the literature Casement is relatively unusual in his emphasis on playfulness and creativity. It is more usual to find supervision featuring the following:

> The activities involved in group supervision as described in the literature have a variety of ends. These can be didactic; they can serve the purpose of situation analysis (individual, community, family or group); they can aim at enhancing either personal or group development; and they can focus on organizational matters and the relationship between supervisor and supervisee.
>
> (Arkin *et al.* 1999: 50)

This comment within the literature is typical, in that creativity in attention or in the content of the supervision is not referred to. Is this the same for dramatherapy supervision?

All models of dramatherapy emphasise the centrality of creativity and the expressive processes of drama to its efficacy for clients (Jennings 1997; Landy 2001; Langley 2006; Jones 2007). One issue that the research undertaken for this book revealed is that the use of the media of drama in clinical supervision varies very widely. It would be wrong to simply ally creativity with active methods. The literature on dramatherapy supervision locates creativity and drama as key components of the therapy space which the supervisee refers to, but this need not be realised through drama based techniques in the supervision space. Indeed, many of the therapists in the research indicated that, though they were aware of issues concerning having a supervisor who was skilled in enabling access to arts media, this was not necessarily a priority in their choice of supervisor and use of supervision:

> 'I work very differently in my own work as a supervisor, where my approach is person-centred and uses drama at all levels. I have had supervision in the past where my supervisor has used creative methods.

My current supervisor is not a dramatherapist but has a great deal of expertise in mental health which is more valuable to me in my current practice than any other consideration. She is a trained psychotherapist and mental health professional and I am able to bring any concerns to her. She has experience of dramatherapy and has a good understanding of the processes involved and encourages me to work creatively within our sessions if that's what I need to do. I feel our sessions provide me with the chance to raise any issues, personal as well as professional, and a grounded confidence in my practice.'

Some emphasised a direct need not to work with creative methods in the supervision space:

'I find it helpful to have a psychotherapist as a supervisor as he brings to my work a more in-depth understanding of the psychological processes at work. I appreciate a talking approach in supervision as the rest of my work is so active and physical. Occasionally I find that my supervisor and I are coming at an issue from different directions due to the different orientations – but on the whole I find it positive.'

Others, as noted earlier in this chapter, in contrast, made clear that the supervisor being able to work with creative process was central.

I want to return to the material described earlier concerning the use of drama in dramatherapy supervision. Of respondents 49 per cent said that their dramatherapy supervision stays completely verbal, never using enactment or arts-based processes. Just over 41 per cent said that their supervision only engages with drama occasionally, with just under 2 per cent saying that their experience was that drama featured in every session (Figure 3.1).

This could be due to a number of factors. One issue might be the capacity of the supervisor to facilitate work using drama and play. A significant number of those providing supervision were not trained dramatherapists or arts therapists. The research indicated that supervisors included group analysts, psychoanalytic psychotherapists, psychological therapists, Jungian analysts and analytic psychologists. The respondents using these supervisors were less likely to engage in active methods than those with dramatherapy or psychodrama trained supervisors. However, it cannot be assumed that just because a supervisor is not trained in the use of dramatic media that the space cannot feature drama-based work. Dramatherapists cannot be assumed to be passive in the face of supervisor's experience or background. In addition, most literature on supervision stresses the development and importance of mutuality. Hence, it would be possible to assume that most dramatherapists, if they wished to, could introduce dramatic expression into

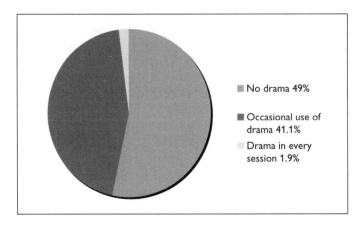

Figure 3.1 The use of drama in dramatherapy supervision

their supervision. Another factor could be that the model of supervision might not be one that recognises the role of active engagement with play or drama. Another might be that the dramatherapist herself wishes to stay within verbal reflection.

For other discussions of the role of the dramatherapy supervisor, see pp. 68–82 and 187–91

The uses of enactment within supervision

Of the dramatherapy supervision sessions using active methods, the most likely techniques, as mentioned at the start of the chapter, were the use of objects and images. Other techniques included story and myth work, with 15 per cent of respondents reporting working with these forms. Just over 25 per cent used movement and 23 per cent used role play. Of the respondents 11 per cent said that their supervisors joined in with the creative activities, with 89 per cent reporting that they remained outside the processes. So supervisors taking on roles within role play, for example, or engaging in movement work, were rare. The picture is one where a significant proportion of sessions use objects (43 per cent) and images (35 per cent), occasionally drawing on other methods.

The research gave a clear picture of how these active methods were used. Two were indicated as involving the depiction of activities and moments from the dramatherapy, the other involved the depiction of the feelings of the therapist. A significant minority used arts media specifically to look at the dynamics of the session.

A number of authors have considered the importance of supervision in reflecting on the therapist's perceptions of the client experience (Casement 1997; Gilbert and Evans 2000; Hawkins and Shohet 2000; Rice *et al.* 2007). One key theme is the concept of parallel process. Evans and Gilbert (2005) draw on the ideas of field theory (Lewin 1952) to look at supervision. They cite field theory's conceptualisation of the individual being interrelated to their environment: the internal world of feelings and thoughts and the external world of their lived context. This was reflected by a number of respondents in that the connectivity and interrelation of supervision in expressing and exploring helpful connectivity was cited:

'If I did not receive clinical supervision . . . I would become insular. My ability to reflect on the multi-layered processes within the clinical relationship would be limited by my own perceptual framework.'

As Evans and Gilbert state, in this way:

The context or field is a dynamic and interrelated system in which every part influences every other part . . . in psychotherapy and in supervision there is thus a co-created field of mutual reciprocal influence between client and psychotherapist in the former, and between psychotherapist and supervisor in the latter.

(Evans and Gilbert 2005: 134)

Thus, an interaction is created between 'the current nature of the therapeutic relationship, together with the personal histories of the client, psychotherapist and supervisor will each impact on the field' (p. 134). Events are seen as multicausal and reciprocal. One respondent echoed this multilayered concept:

'Knowing I can process with someone who understands both the clinical and personal demands and effects of my work, who cares about me as I care about my clients and who is there to "hold" me helps me continue my hold on my work and my clients.'

The use of objects, role play and sculpting can be an effective way to encounter this connectivity. The dramatherapy literature argues that enactment, dramatic projection into objects and methods such as role reversal enhance and deepen client participation in engaging with material from life brought into the therapy space (Jennings 1997; Johnson 1999; Landy 2001; Jones 2005; Langley 2006). It can be argued that the therapist and supervisor playing the role of the client, or depicting their perceptions of the client in improvisation can lead to an enhanced exploration of this 'connectivity'. The personal histories of those involved can be expressed and explored through the improvisatory qualities of dramatic media. Perhaps what matters most here is that playfulness occurs, and that this is internally held.

The space between: action as reflection in supervision

This section explores the benefits to therapist and client of insight, learning and the need for perspective which supervision can offer. It looks at the ways in which action methods can contribute to this process. I want to return to the findings of the research in a different way here. I will now consider the issue of active techniques in relation to the comments made earlier in this chapter on the three components of the way connection is made between the clinical situation and the supervision space: the first that it is a reflective space; the second related to maintenance and protection; the third that supervision is seen as a space for development.

In addition to specific processes the research indicated that many dramatherapists saw supervision functioning in a way that related to their professional identity and their maintenance and development as professionals. The research pictured supervision as containing a space for the dramatherapist to connect with their professional identity. This occurs in a number of ways. The majority of dramatherapists saw the supervision space as a place to reflect on the techniques they trained with, developing insight into their efficacy, and a majority saw supervision as a place to work creatively in developing new ideas and ways of working. A very high majority strongly agreed or agreed that their experience of supervision was one of creativity. Some saw this to do with a creative attitude, whilst others saw it as specifically to do with expression and processes to do with the arts. As one respondent said, supervision is a place to develop 'use of story, arts and drama (including writing my own stories, plays) in a way that addresses and resolves problems effectively'.

The nature of the reflective process varies according to the model of supervision informing the work. Clarkson and Aviram have said that 'supervision . . . is perceived through the prism of one's theoretical framework, beliefs and attitudes' (1998: 275). One of the key themes in the research was the importance of supervision in providing a certain kind of distance and perspective. One respondent sums up a number of themes relating to this:

'It sustains my own internal supervisor and therefore helps me to keep in mind the distancing which is essential with this client group while still enabling me to participate closely in the work, e.g. in role play. Clients engage in much issue-based improvisation and I believe that by maintaining the ability to step into role at any time the therapist offers valuable support. Past experience shows me that it is also essential for part of one's mind to remain disengaged which is where the internal supervisor helps.'

Within this process of reflective engagement and disengagement, the goal of reflection is common to most of the respondents: to enable the therapist to enhance their work through this is seen to be at the heart of the endeavour. The ways in which this occurs can vary. One reading of the research is that the concerns of the reflective task are common, with areas such as:

- ethics
- philosophy
- concerns with gender, race, disability, age, sexuality
- referral
- assessment
- client responses
- therapeutic relationship
- countertransference
- organisational dynamics
- professional development (for full details of these research findings, see Chapter 2).

All indicate a commonality of concern. The research did not reveal a widely different set of reflective concerns. The use of active methods does not mark a different set of concerns than those supervisions that were entirely verbal. Rather they show a different route to identical reflective concerns.

Maintainance and protection

In their research into how supervisors saw the nature of supervision, Clarkson and Aviram (1998) gained data on their perceptions of their role and the supervisory space. The analysis of the data identified the areas most indicated by the supervisors as defining their role and their experience of supervision. Those most frequently identified concerned what Clarkson and Aviram have described as responsibility, teaching and education, the supervisor–supervisee–client triangle, guidance and growth promotion and procedures, ethics and practice. The largest category of statements concerned what they call 'structuring' orientated attention, relating to 'statements referring to process, monitoring, transference and countertransference, confrontation' (1998: 281). A key part of this, centred on the ways in which the supervisor and supervisee work, concerns the maintenance of professionalism. Within the discourse around supervision and professionalism created by dramatherapists in the UK through their professional association, 'protection' is seen to be at the forefront of this area. The first statement in the BADth document on supervision after the contextualising of the document concerns protection:

> The purpose of supervision is to protect the interests of the Dramatherapy client, the supervisee, their agency, the general public and the Dramatherapy profession. Supervision balances these needs but generally presumes that those of the client take precedence.
>
> (BADth 2006: 1)

For other discussions of professionalisation, see pp. 68–70

Looked at in this way protection can be seen as a key feature of the active methods used within dramatherapy supervision. A number of respondents echoed this, as referred to in Chapter 1, for example:

> 'I would lose the ability to keep a constant eye on my physical and psychological well being in accordance with our professional registration requirements.'

> 'Within my clinical context supervision is especially useful because it keeps my working practice safe for me and for my clients.'

The identified focus on using drama to explore the client's experiences can be seen to try to enable the therapist to explore and examine the client experience, to help focus on the effect of the therapy for, and on, them. The other main identified use of active methods was representing the therapist's own feelings. This can be seen within the 'protection framework' as a way for the therapist to explore their own issues and countertransference. This is in order for them to be as clear as possible that they are not working through their own issues within the therapy, for example. In addition, active methods can be used to help the therapist explore their own responses to the clinical material. This allows space to express, and also to connect, with personal material that might need to be taken to their own therapy. A number, as practising artists themselves, saw the need for creative expression as a part of the natural language of their exploration of such material in supervision:

> 'I wanted to have supervision with someone who uses movement particularly, as this is at the centre of my drama and movement therapy practice as a Sesame therapist. It felt important to be able to use movement as part of supervision, besides talking and role-play/drama, rather than exclusively a cognitive approach. It feels important to combine and balance all the functions of thinking, feeling, sensation

and intuition both in my work of course, and in supervision. So it's important to be able to express myself in supervision using the means I offer to my clients.'

Development, enquiry and research

A number of the respondents emphasised the role of supervision in maintaining and developing their professional identity. In part this concerned a space to connect with their role as dramatherapist, in part it concerned supervision's reflective space enabling them to look at professional issues such as ethics and philosophy. For many, though, emphasis was placed on the role of supervision as a place that attended to a separate but related area concerning their creativity, for example:

> 'Without supervision I would become less flexible in my ways of thinking, would see a narrow understanding rather than a broader one (someone else's eyes) have less creativity and be less emotionally aware.'

Alongside this was a majority who found supervision as a place to develop their knowledge of the techniques and methods of dramatherapy. I want to link this notion of supervision as a place for developing insight and knowledge into method, with the concept of supervision as a place for action research.

Goss and Rowland connect supervision with the development of the professional and link this to research. They connect it to the concept of reflective practice. They create a continuum between large scale random control tests (RCTs) and approaches that help therapists to develop evidence-based practice where 'complex study designs are often inappropriate or impractical for practitioners to undertake themselves', saying that gathering the evidence base 'does not comprise only large-scale, headline making studies' (Goss and Rowland 2000: 196). They connect ways in which practitioners can enhance their involvement in evidence-based health care (EBHC) and 'contribute to the culture of evaluation' (2000: 196). They propose a series of areas of enquiry that include reflective practice and supervision/case discussion, undertaking routine audit and evaluation of work and small-scale, possibly qualitative, research. They see all these as part of a range of areas of work which exist alongside more formal ways of research such as site collaboration in large multi-centre randomised controlled trials (2000: 196–97). They describe supervision as part of a *culture* connecting enquiry and research:

> Supervision entails establishing good standards of practice; developing a practitioner's knowledge and skills and working with his or her response

to the process of conducting the therapy . . . although many psychological therapists who receive such supervisory support would not consider it a form of research, it is capable of routinely generating significant
quantities of evidence of clinical relevance. Those professionals who are
required to participate in regular consultative case supervision have, at
the very least, a valuable means of quality control.

(Goss and Rowland 2000: 197)

Clarkson and Aviram (1998) also emphasise that 'the end of the divide
between clinical supervision and academic research can begin to be made as
the work of doing and reflection becomes integrated' (1998: 293). The
connection here emphasises the role of supervision as developing an aspect
of the therapist's skills and competencies to do with the nature of their
reflective process. In addition it validates the nature of the information
processed within supervision and sees it as a site for generating data that
can be used in research. It also views supervision as developing the therapist
into a reflective practitioner engaged in action research.

Our research showed that attention within supervision mirrored this
perception, in that the picture of supervision space was one where concerns
to do with reflective practice were strongly represented. In essence, one way
of seeing the following material is to depict supervision as a place where the
therapist develops skills and attentions parallel with those needed for action
research. Looked at in this way, the supervisee's scrutiny of their work
through their use of the media within dramatherapy can be seen to be allied
to action research. The therapist can bring the processes within their
dramatherapy practice into the analysis which supervision can provide.
The active creative exploration through actual enactment within supervision adds to the ways in which insight into the method and its effects is
researched.

'If I did not receive clinical supervision it would affect my practice in
the following way . . . I would stick to some tried and tested ways of
working rather than branching out to try new things.'

In this way, the supervision space can be seen as somewhere in which the
therapist can be creative, can play and use drama techniques, and can
research their therapeutic practice. Box 3.2 shows the extent of dramatherapists' representation of supervision as a place for creativity and as a
place to help them not become stale, to develop their familiarity with
techniques and to develop new ways of working. Respondents were offered
a series of criteria concerning their attention within supervision. Box 3.2
indicates the extent of areas pertinent to Goss and Rowland's (2000)
positioning supervision within a continuum connecting to action research.

Box 3.2 Sample results from Question 5

Question 5 concerned the kinds of attention given in supervision. The results below give positive responses to the areas being worked with in dramatherapy supervision:

	RESPONSE % YES/NO
Issues concerning client or therapist's cultural differences or expectations and the medium of drama*	86.3/13.7
Assessment methods	84.2/15.8
Adapting specific dramatherapy techniques you already know from your basic training	66.7/33.3
Developing new dramatherapy techniques (either ones you create yourself, or ones you have learned in development post basic training)	66.7/33.3

(For full results for Question 5, see Box 2.1, p. 40)

This data and way of looking at supervision can be understood in a number of ways. One way is to see a part of the role of supervision as developing the professional dramatherapist. The content, concerns and work within the supervision can be seen as developing the dramatherapist as active researcher and as creative individual. This sees the kinds of attention and the skills in analysis in areas such as assessment and evaluation as enhancing and building the individual. Another way is to see supervision as a space for processing and gathering data that can potentially be used to contribute to the evidence base in the ways which Goss and Rowland propose. At a formal level this can be linked to gathering data within research-led investigation, where supervision supports the research process by providing an arena to complement the work. At an informal level the kinds of concerns the research has shown to be within much dramatherapy supervision can be firmly allied to what they describe as influencing the work of the individual practitioner and contributing to 'the culture of evaluation' (2000: 196). Hence, the sample responses from Question 5 in the research show that substantial attention is being given to areas such as developing and adapting techniques, to considering the nature of assessment, and to the client's and therapist's issues relating to cultural differences and expectations regarding dramatherapy. These can easily be seen to operate within the ideas of research as outlined above and can place supervision as a key arena of enquiry within the field. The presence of active work within the supervision session is a key element of this action research.

Conclusion

Casement has talked about the internal supervisor and the ways in which the patient supervises the therapist in the following way:

> During the course of being supervised, therapists need to acquire their own capacity for spontaneous reflection within the session, alongside the internalized supervisor. They can thus learn to watch themselves as well as the patient, now using this island of intellectual contemplation as the mental space within which the internal supervisor can begin to operate.
>
> (Casement 1997: 32)

A key part of this concerns the way in which the supervisees construct themselves within the supervision space. This relates to the ways in which they use the space to create links with the client, their lives and the therapeutic encounter, to the emerging and developing professional identity of the therapist and to their enquiry into the impact and efficacy of their medium – dramatherapy. This chapter has illustrated some of the ways in which active methods can play a key role in the performance and efficacy of supervision. It has shown how through the use of objects, images, role and play therapists can deepen their engagement with their practice, enhance their capacity to imagine the experience of their client and to heighten their journey as developing reflexive practitioners: all of which brings benefit to the client in therapy.

References

Arkin, N., Freund, A. and Saltman, I. (1999) A group supervision model for broadening multiple-method skills of social work students, *Social Work Education* 18, 1: 49–58.

Borders, L.D. (2006) Snapshot of clinical supervision in counseling and counselor education: a five year review, *Clinical Supervisor* 24, 1: 69–113.

British Association of Dramatherapists (BADth, 2006) *Code of Practice*. Online. Available HTTP: <http://www.badth.org.uk/code/supcode.html> (accessed 15 July 2007).

Butler, S. (2004) Multicultural sensitivity and competence in the clinical supervision of school counselors and school psychologists: a context for providing competent services in a multicultural society, *Clinical Supervisor* 22, 1: 125–41.

Butterworth, T. and Woods, D. (1999) Clinical governance and clinical supervision: working together to ensure safe and accountable practice. A briefing paper. Manchester: University of Manchester.

Casement, P. (1990) *Further Learning From the Patient*, London: Routledge.

Casement, P. (1997) *On Learning From the Patient*, 2nd edn, London: Routledge.

Chesner, A. (1999) Dramatherapy supervision: historical issues and supervisory settings, in E. Tselikas-Portmann (ed.) *Supervision and Dramatherapy*, London: Jessica Kingsley Publishers.

Clarkson, P. and Aviram, O. (1998) Phenomenological research on supervision: supervisors reflect on being a supervisor, in P. Clarkson (ed.) *Counselling Psychology: Integrating Theory, Research and Supervised Practice*, London: Routledge.

Evans, K.R. and Gilbert, M.C. (2005) *An Introduction to Integrative Psychotherapy*, Basingstoke: Palgrave Macmillan.

Gilbert, M.C. and Evans, K.R. (2000) *Psychotherapy Supervision: An Integrative Relational Approach*, Maidenhead: Open University Press.

Goss, S. and Rowland, S. (2000) *Evidence Based Practice: A Guide for Counselors and Psychotherapists*, London: Routledge.

Hawkins, P. and Shohet, R. (2000) *Supervision in the Helping Professions*, 2nd edn, Maidenhead: Open University Press.

Jenkyns, M. (1999) Training the supervisor-dramatherapist: a psychodynamic approach, in E. Tselikas-Portmann (ed.) *Supervision and Dramatherapy*, London: Jessica Kingsley Publishers.

Jennings, S. (ed.) (1997) *Dramatherapy: Theory and Practice 3*, London: Routledge.

Jennings, S. (1999) Theatre-based dramatherapy supervision: a supervisory model for multidisciplinary supervisees, in E. Tselikas-Portmann (ed.) *Supervision and Dramatherapy*, London: Jessica Kingsley Publishers.

Johnson, D.R. (1999) *Essays on the Creative Arts Therapies: Imaging the Birth of a Profession*, Springfield IL: Charles C. Thomas.

Jones, P. (2005) *The Arts Therapies*, London: Routledge.

Jones, P. (2007) *Drama as Therapy*, London: Routledge.

Lahad, M. (2000) *Creative Supervision*, London: Jessica Kingsley Publishers.

Landy, R. (2001) *New Essays in Dramatherapy*, Springfield IL: Charles C. Thomas.

Langley, D. (2006) *An Introduction to Dramatherapy*, London: Sage.

Langs, R. (1994) *Doing Supervision and Being Supervised*, London: Karnac.

Lewin, K. (1952) *Field Theory in Social Science*, London: Tavistock.

Maclagan, D. (1997) Fantasy, play and the image in supervision, in G. Shipton (ed.) *Supervision of Psychotherapy and Counselling*, Maidenhead: Open University Press.

Mollon, P. (1997) Supervision as a space for thinking, in G. Shipton (ed.) *Supervision of Psychotherapy and Counselling*, Maidenhead: Open University Press.

Rice, F., Cullen, P., McKenna, H., Kelly, B., Keeney, S. and Richey, R. (2007) Clinical supervision for mental health nurses in Northern Ireland: formulating best practice guidelines, *Journal of Psychiatric and Mental Health Nursing* 14: 516–21.

Rowland, N. and Goss, S. (2000) *Evidence-Based Counselling and Psychological Therapies: Research and Applications*, London: Routledge.

Taylor, B., HernAindez, P., Deri, A., Rankin, P. and Siegel, A. (2007) Integrating diversity dimensions in supervision: perspectives of ethnic minority AAMFT approved supervisors, *Clinical Supervisor* 25, 1–2: 3–21.

Tselikas-Portmann, E. (1999) *Supervision and Dramatherapy*, London: Jessica Kingsley Publishers.

Winnicott, D.W. (1971) *Playing and Reality*, London: Tavistock.

Chapter 4

Training supervision in dramatherapy

Ditty Dokter

Introduction

This chapter outlines the history of supervision in the field of dramatherapy within the UK. Some of the models of providing supervision in dramatherapy training are discussed. This is followed by a discussion of some of the issues inherent within training concerning the form and nature of supervision. These include a consideration of the benefits of group or individual supervision, whether supervision should be provided within the training programme, or external to it, the separation of managerial and clinical supervision in placements, and the issues and dynamics around assessment in the supervisory relationship.

The outcomes of a placement research project conclude the chapter. This research project examined work experience learning and the importance of team holding for the student. Case examples are used from two supervisees of the author (Derby and Manchester training courses), as well as contributions from placement managers and supervisors at Roehampton University.

Historical background

Supervision was not part of dramatherapy training when I trained in the UK a quarter of a century ago. It has been interesting to observe and be part of the changing role of supervision in dramatherapy training and practice over those 25 years. The development of supervision started in 1983 and went hand in hand with the development of professional recognition and registration (Chesner 1999; Gersie 2007) Discussions between various dramatherapy executive members and trainers led to the establishment of supervision workshops and a supervision subcommittee of the British Association of Dramatherapists (BADth) in 1983. The aim of the work was to design and deliver appropriate supervision during dramatherapy training as well as for ongoing clinical practice; to design and deliver training courses for dramatherapy supervisors; and to promote the role of supervisors in assisting the career development of their supervisees. The validation of dramatherapy training by the Council for National

Academic Awards (CNAA) in 1989, and subsequent national registration with the Council for Professions Supplementary to Medicine (CPSM) in 1991, now the Health Professions Council (HPC), seemed to recognise the importance of supervision in dramatherapy practice and professional development. Between 1990 and 2007 the number of BADth registered supervisors has tripled from 20 to 69 in the context of a membersip of 400 fully registered dramatherapists. Over the years various supervision training programmes have been offered, varying in length from one to two years. Training was offered as continuous professional development by universities who also offered dramatherapy registration training. Other trainings were specifically developed (Jenkyns 1999). The main training at the beginning of the twenty-first century is the Creative Arts Therapies Supervision (CAST) training. This was developed by Sesame trained practitioners, who were consequently trained in the psychodynamic dramatherapy supervision model developed by Marina Jenkyns (1999).

For more discussion of this psychodynamic model of practice, see pp. 99–110 and 138–40

These slowly added to the number of recognised supervisors. Recognition refers to the fact that the professional association has recognised these people as adequately trained and experienced to act as supervisors. Before 2005 supervision registration depended on recognition via a grandparenting clause, or through the completion of a BADth registered supervision training. New supervision registration criteria were formulated in 2005. These recognise a wider variety of routes and trainings to becoming a BADth registered supervisor. Some of the other chapters in this book provide examples of both routes (Jenkyns, Chapter 6 and Hubbard, Chapter 9). In the past non-dramatherapists have provided supervision for dramatherapy trainees. Some of this was for practical reasons; the number of dramatherapist supervisors is small and geographically limited. As someone who was supervised by psychotherapists as well as dramatherapists, I can testify to the complexities of communicating and exploring my arts-based therapy through words within a supervision using verbal language.

For other discussions of professionalisation, see pp. 181–82

The level of dramatherapy registration moved from postgraduate diploma to masters degree in 2004. In validating courses, the HPC requires that all supervision of practice within the qualifying training is provided by dramatherapists. This has created some difficulties for those trainees living in geographical areas where there are few dramatherapists and, therefore, even fewer dramatherapists who are also qualified to offer supervision. A recent survey showed that 35 per cent of dramatherapists live in Greater London (Dokter and Hughes 2007). Smaller concentrations can be found in South West England, the North East and West, where other training courses are or were situated. Scotland and Wales have only 2 per cent of the dramatherapist population, and Northern Ireland only 0.2 per cent (Dokter and Hughes 2007). Proposals were formulated in 2007 to create a UK network of dramatherapy supervisors with annual and regional meetings to facilitate further supervisory development within the profession (Gersie 2007). This is more of an attempt to facilitate further professional development than being formally linked to Health Professions Council requirements.

Theoretical context

Clinical supervision originates in the traditional 'apprentice' model, adopted by the medical profession in the nineteenth century. This approach to supervision has subsequently been mirrored by that taken by psychoanalysts in the early twentieth century, by social work practitioners as early as 1911 and by occupational therapists in the 1960s. Currently there are over 30 different models of clinical supervision, with very different professional, practice and theoretical backgrounds to each. These include models that have been described as developmental (Hawkins and Shohet 1989), discipline bound (van Ooijen 2000), cyclical (Johns 1997) and matrix (Davies *et al.* 2004).

My theoretical framework for dramatherapy supervision is based within psychoanalytic psychotherapy and group analysis. These forms of psychotherapy stress working with the unconscious and recognise how past relationship patterns tend to become re-enacted in present relationships. The interesting aspect for me has been the transferral of these ideas in recent years to other fields such as nursing (Bishop 2007) and other health professionals, where clinical governance has stressed the importance of clinical supervision in the wider health professions context (Stuart 2007). Gersie (2007) relates the development of dramatherapy supervision to psychodynamic psychotherapy and social work supervision during placements.

For other discussions of psychoanalysis and group analysis in relation to supervision, see pp. 138–39 and 170

Supervisee perspective: I consider the clinical supervison style to be based upon a reflective and analytical model of practice. The process of clinical supervision assists and develops my reflective apprenticeship.

(Trainee reflective log 2006–7)

Pedder (1986) describes clinical supervision as a process of professional development which is more than education and less than psychotherapy. The problem with this statement is: if clinical supervision is less than psychotherapy, does that mean that being a good enough clinician is sufficient qualification for being able to provide effective supervision? Within the arts therapies there is no consensus about this. BADth requires specific supervisory training and experience in order to be a recognised supervisor. The British Association for Art Therapists, however, only requires a certain amount of post-qualifying clinical experience. However, if supervisors need additional training, what are the specific educational skills they need (Scanlon 2000)?

A model frequently used in dramatherapy supervision training is one where the supervisor is taught to operate on a variety of modes within a process model of supervision (Hawkins and Shohet 1989). This approach to supervision has been described as developmental. It emphasises the educational elements of clinical supervision to help the professional develop from novice to independent craftsman (van Ooijen 2000). Hawkins and Shohet's (1989) six modes of supervision include reflection on the content of the session, reflection on therapist strategies and interventions, along with an exploration of the therapy process and therapeutic relationship. These three modes are part of reflection-on-action (Schon 1987), through which a practitioner learns skills from recalling past actions and/or preparing for future action, also called experiential learning. The reflection-on-action involves more conscious problem solving, which is one aspect of supervision (Scanlon 2000). However, there is a need to move beyond this to reflection-in-action. This is a practice-led epistemology in which practical know-how, though informed by theoretical knowing, is grounded in a third subjective domain of experiential knowledge (Heron 1992). Schon (1987) argues that the truly skilled practitioner is one who is able to engage in a 'reflective conversation with the situation'. Casement (1985) echoes this when stating that theory must help moderate the helplessness of not knowing, but theory should remain the servant not the master. Practitioners need to learn to what extent their practice is rooted in an informed application of theory (Turkel 1990), and to what extent in intersubjective discourse (Brown 1994). Hawkins and Shohet (1989) see supervision facilitating reflection-in-action through a focus on the therapy process as it is reflected in the supervision process. This occurs through the other three modes of supervision: focus on the therapist countertransference, focus on the here-and-now process as a mirror or parallel of the there-and-then process; and through a focus on the supervisor's countertransference.

For other discussions of countertransference, see pp. 99–110 and 159–62

Scanlon (2000, 2002) provides a useful developmental structure to show how the trainee can develop from reflection-on-action to reflection-in-action within the training supervision group. The supervisor needs to draw attention to the way in which the new supervisee arrives in the supervision group, identifying emergent patterns to enable the supervisee to make meaningful links between the experience of being in the supervision group, anxiety about facilitating their placement group and his or her personal history. The way the supervisee selects their clients is also indicative of their 'valency' (Bion 1961). Bramley (1979) describes valency as the tendency of the therapist to be attracted by a basic assumption style of group leadership towards a dynamic with which the therapist feels comfortable. The therapist looks for clients who fit their way of operating in the world, reflecting Bion's three basic assumptions towards group conflict resolution: fight/flight, pairing and dependency (1961). An example of a valency towards 'fight/flight' occurs when the therapist selects acting out, challenging clients, who are able to confront. A valency towards 'pairing' may be indicated by the therapist searching for clients 'who go well together', while valency towards dependency may be seen by a therapist selecting needy clients 'who deserve help'.

Once the supervisee starts the therapy, anxiety often becomes a major theme within supervision. The supervisee may bring a jumble of unconscious images, impressions and fantasies, which are both personal and a reflection of the unconscious ways of relating in the therapy itself. At this stage of supervision, the supervisee often does not know what is happening and the main job of supervision is to provide an optimally frustrating and sufficiently holding/containing environment within which this anxiety can be safely thought about (James 1994). The difficulty is that the trainee often experiences the anxiety as a narcissistic wound, because in the rest of their professional life they manage with skill and confidence. They may defensively resort to this other professional identity (Behr 1995). In a supervision group the supervisees may feel rivalrous or competitive and may avoid exposing their vulnerability. The supervisor needs to address these potentially destructive dynamics (Mander 1991).

For other discussions of group supervision, see pp 76–8 and 177

Supervisee vignette 1

I found the relationship with my supervisor tricky, as I sometimes felt that she used a rather didactic and forceful manner with me. For a long time I did not bring this to supervision and I struggled to bring anything at all. Then one day she said she was leaving in four weeks and I would have a new supervisor. I explained that this was fine and not a problem, but I said this before I had given myself a chance to think.

Over the final four weeks I felt I had nothing to lose and brought up our relationship difficulties. We began to wonder together what they might be about. She wondered if I saw her as a persecutory figure and in some ways that sat well. After all, it was the supervisor that held my final mark for the placement. Before long this supervisor left and I thought all these feelings would go with her. But they did not, and although my new supervisor was not forceful or didactic in her approach, I realised that I was still bringing feelings of inadequacy, fear of judgement and anger at the power imbalance that I felt.

I decided that this time I would be honest and after about three sessions brought up the relationship difficulties. We began the exploratory process. I began to acknowledge that the change in supervisor had not felt as fine as I originally stated. It was okay and essential to recognise this with my supervisor and myself. This turning point opened a floodgate, which then allowed me to explore all the difficult and negative feelings I had about the supervisory relationship. Subsequently I began to bring myself into the space.

(Trainee reflective log 2006–7)

Having survived the initial anxiety the supervisee can be usefully directed to reflection-on-action in the form of the first three supervision modes. The next step is to proceed towards reflection-in-action, pure description of what happens and a focus on the interventions chosen that can leave the therapist 'out of the space' (as described by the supervisee in the above vignette). The dramatic media within dramatherapy supervision can facilitate some of this process (Lahad 2000), but attention to the parallel process of the supervision session is crucial. The majority of respondents in our supervision questionnaire (Jones and Dokter 2008) gave 'psychodynamic' or 'eclectic' as their supervision orientation, even though as practitioners dramatherapists are more likely to be humanistic/client-centred or theatre based in orientation (Karkou and Sanderson 2006). However, even client-centred oriented dramatherapy supervisors pay attention to parallel process in the supervisor countertransference (Lahad 2000: 17–18). What this parallel process can reveal about the client group dynamics (Voorhoeve and van Putte 1994; Lahad 2000) and the organisational dynamics (Schneider and Berman 1991; Obholzer and Zagier Roberts 1994) has been discussed by a variety of authors in a variety of clinical contexts.

For other discussions of parallel process, see pp. 177–78 and 181–82

Supervisee vignette 2
I was taking part in the group supervision at the university. I was describing my client to the group, but as I was talking I was struggling to remain clear and not jump

about with my sentences. As I was nearing a stumbling end, my supervisor reflected to me that, as she was listening, she was feeling really irritated and she wondered what that was about. I was really taken aback and quite shocked and hurt by this statement, and was not sure what to say. As I sat with these feelings I began to think about my feelings towards my client. Some of the feelings I had allowed, like sadness. However, just as in the supervisory relationship, I had not allowed any negative feelings. My client irritated me. The fact that she disabled herself, carrying a stick, saying she could not do things, really irritated me. Why had I not allowed these feelings to surface?

(Trainee reflective log 2006–7)

As the supervisee becomes better able to reflect-in-action on the parallel process occurring in the supervision session, they become better able to transfer this experience back into the clinical space itself. Transitionally, the supervisory discourse develops between the external reality of the supervision group and the internal supervisor of the trainee (Casement 1985). The need to overcome superego conflicts and develop a benign internal supervisor is an important aspect of this process (Olivieri-Larsson 1993). The enhanced capacity for internal dialogue, transferred back into the clinical context, allows the supervisee to reflect-in-action and keep open the reflective space in the therapy itself (Hinshelwood 1994).

For other discussions of the internal supervisor, see pp. 60–1

Supervisee vignette 2 (continued)

In supervision we began to examine the reasons for my irritation. I could link it directly to my experiences of disability and the cosseting nature of my family. I had spent most of my adolescence and early years removing my disabled label, literally and metaphorically, in a persistent, independent manner. In contrast to this, I saw my client disabling herself and becoming increasingly dependent. My supervisor pointed out the contrasts and similarities between myself and my client.

External or internal training supervision?

Historically, the different dramatherapy training courses in the UK have operated different models of training supervision. Some favoured in-house group supervision, others asked trainees to find supervision externally, mostly on an individual basis, frequently paid for separately by the trainee. Supervision might be in a group or individual format. Cost and availability of supervisors are one factor in the selection of a supervisor by the supervisee.

The difficulty about in-house supervision can be the multiplicity of authority roles that a supervisor, who may also be a tutor, can hold. Especially in the area of assessment it is important to consider that one person may mark the essay, provide the supervision assessment and perform the three-way placement visit, where trainee, placement manager and university tutor meet to discuss progress. On the other hand, supervisors who are also placement managers often combine managerial and clinical supervision roles, which also raises an issue around multiple authority roles. The supervisee who describes her experience in the two vignettes received the supervision from a supervisor who was also her placement manager, and who was also the head of the dramatherapy clinical department. Multiple authority roles influence the student experience, as illustrated in vignette 1. The supervisee quotation at the beginning of the chapter stems from a trainee for whom I was an external supervisor in her final training placement and who I have continued to supervise in her post-qualifying year. The initial authority struggles had been worked through and there are no other conflicting authority roles.

For other discussions of supervision and training placement, see pp. 130–45

Supervisee perspective

The process of clinical supervision ensures that my benign internal supervisor is lovingly maintained. When critical incidents occur during dramatherapy sessions, I need supervision to address internal conflicts. My benign supervisor was hijacked and my internal authoritarian supervisor sought control when I 'lost it' and found myself shouting at a client. My supervisor acknowledged my thoughts and feelings, asked me to reflect on and learn from the experience. We also focused on group themes which related to the incident, including homophobia, subtleness and vulnerability.

Vignette of related incident

In session 4, seven adolescent clients attended. A new sound was created for freezing and the word was 'Liverpool', given by the boys as a group decision (this was a first, the boys made a decision together as opposed to individually).

To use up energy and to encourage the young people to participate, we played 'sock tag'. During this exercise a girl subtly tripped up a boy (co-facilitatior spotted the incident, I did not). He reacted quickly by punching her hard in the stomach. I was shocked and shouted at him, 'You do not do that!' I had to hold him because he wanted to atack the girl again. She kept saying, 'Sorry.' He finally hid himself behind a pile of chairs and I told him to rejoin us when he was ready. At the last game of sock tag he joined in. To confront conflict, sparring together without touching, a 'hate and love machine' performance was created. The girls found it difficult to work against one another, the boys found it difficult to work together, but all achieved it. The following week all clients attended again and it was a break-through session in acknowledging feelings and conflict.

(Trainee reflective log 2006–7)

The supervisee struggled to maintain a benign, internal, observant third eye. The fact that she had a well-established trust with the supervisor, who had no additional authority roles beyond that of supervisor, might have made it easier for her to raise and discuss an incident where she was concerned about her effectiveness as a therapist. If one of the functions of supervision is for a trainee to find their own authority and develop their own benign internal supervisor, it is important that the multiple authority roles of the supervisor are considered.

BADth has, from the outset, advocated separation of clinical and managerial supervision functions. This addresses the authority issue, but does not address the issue of clinical accountability for the work. Although dramatherapists are expected to be autonomous, they are still accountable for their work to the organisation and clients they are working with. A manager who is not a dramatherapist is unlikely to clinically supervise the work. The clinical supervisor may not be a member of the organisation where the student undertakes her placement. To compensate for needing to know about clinical content because of accountability, the student may receive two different perspectives on their clinical work. Although enriching, this can also create splitting. Supervision can be provided externally to both the placement and the training. In-house group supervision may be provided within the training. Supervision may be provided within the placement. Whichever of these options is chosen, the liaison between supervisor, placement manager and trainer around managerial responsibility and clinical accountability needs to be ongoing during the placement. Later in this chapter I will discuss the outcomes of a placement learning research project, which indicated the importance of this across different professions, as well as sharing some reflections from placement managers, trainers and supervisors.

Group or individual supervision?

The question whether to provide individual or group supervision is linked to the development of the trainee and the nature of the clinical practice they are undertaking. I adhere to the principle that group supervision is the best model to supervise group practice, particularly when looking from a psychodynamic supervision perspective at parallel process in supervision (Hawkins and Shohet 1989). Group dynamics are more likely and more clearly re-enacted in group supervision. From an educational perspective a supervision group may also be most useful; students learn by listening to and contributing to one another's reflections during supervision. This can also argue for group supervision of individual practice (Scanlon 2002). The supervisor needs to facilitate the group-as-a-whole parallel process rather than focusing on the individual in the group.

In group supervision, the presence of other supervisees makes the dynamics of the parallel process different from those in individual supervision. The matrix of the supervision group itself is made up of each supervisee's countertransferential responses to each of the groups they facilitate. At its best, the discourse in the supervision group becomes reciprocal reflection-in-action. The supervisees think about their reactions to the group, remembered in the parallel process, while the supervision group – including the supervisor – attempt to interpret what is revealed in the discussion about the supervisee and their group (Scanlon 2000).

One difficulty of group supervision during training is the level of competition with, and fear, of exposure in front of colleagues (Mander 1991; Olivieri-Larsson 1993; Scanlon 2000). Fear of groups can be expressed through anti-group fantasies of ideal togetherness in individual therapy/ supervision and a concept of the group being treated as if it were a cake that everyone needs or deserves an equal slice of. This denies the possibility of learning from each other and views other group members purely as siblings, in rivalry for the attention of the supervisor/carer (Nitsen 1996). The supervisor may need to allow for this rivalry by initially carefully structuring group supervision for equal individual presentation and reflection time (reflection-on-action). In later stages, the supervisor can allow a more organic non-directive approach (reflection-in-action). Group members may indicate at the beginning of a session whether they need more or less space, or follow one another in a more free associative style. The structuring of group supervision thus varies depending on the learning needs and stage of the trainees.

A slow open model of group supervision, with a mixture of more and less experienced practitioners (Behr 1995; Scanlon 2002), allows for heterogeneity in exchanges between supervisees at different stages of anxiety and development. However, practicalities around provision and geography usually mean that a homogeneous group of trainees receives supervision for a limited period in direct parallel with their placement. A certain amount of collusion around themes can thus be expected. Avoiding exposure can allow an individual member to hide in group supervision. Some group members may be very busy contributing to other people's reflections, while avoiding personal exposure of their own practice. The anxiety state related to not knowing what is happening and fear of flooding the supervision group may create a feeling in certain group members that there is not enough room for their material.

Novice therapists may need more time to enable them to start working out what they need to present in supervision. At the University of Hertfordshire we experimented with peer supervision or supervision 'buddy' meetings prior to the weekly group supervision, to enable the flooding about practice to be somewhat more processed before the actual supervision. Students were asked to complete a supervison preparation sheet and record for prior processing. Such strategies do not contain the unconscious acting out, which will still need to be addressed within the supervision group, but they do allow for greater containment prior to the supervision group.

Supervision group size and the length of time available both need to be considered for group supervision. A maximum size of three to four trainees in a session of one and a half to two hours has been found to be a minimum requirement if supervison is to be adequate. Some trainings provide larger groups within the training and also rely on complementary individual supervision provided in the placement. Findings from placement research later in this chapter show that this requires close working together of the individual and group supervisor to prevent splitting. A number of authors have suggested that an optimum size is four to six supervisees. Scanlon (2002), when discussing optimum supervision group size, advocates considering how many clients need to be kept in mind, as well as the number of supervisees. The more clients being brought to the supervision group, the more the supervisee may end up presenting what she or he thinks is problematic and veering in the direction of reflection-on-action, rather than reflection-in-action.

Another issue concerning group supervision is its ability to facilitate trainees in developing collegial co-operation. Individualised supervision can be very useful in studying parallel process in individual practice, as well as allowing for close monitoring of that practice, but it can foster a climate of interprofessional rivalry (Hahn 2002). Given that dramatherapy trainees tend to come from a variety of professional backgrounds, the multidisciplinarity of group supervision provides a good training ground for multidisciplinary working; one of the core skills which the Health Professions Council requires (HPC Benchmark 2005).

Authority and assessment

One of the aims of training supervision is to assist the trainee to develop their practice. Clinical placements help a trainee to develop and consolidate their identity as an arts therapist (Teasdale 1993). There are, however, inherent tensions in the supervisory relationship (McCann 1999). It can be easier for a trainee to form a relationship with the client than with the placement organisation or the supervisor (Schneider and Berman 1991). Part of this is related to the fear of having to perform, to be intellectually and professionally honest, and yet to be graded/evaluated by the organisation and the supervisor. These difficulties can become bound up with the difficulties about being a student and being a professional worker in the placement. Group rather than individual supervision can be an instrument to balance the authority and assessment functions of the supervisor. It can move away from the traditional supervisor/trainee and teacher/ student models often employed by the supervisee in their initial expectations about supervision (Sharpe and Blackwell 1987). Mutual assessment models, where students are asked to provide peer assessment of each other, as well as self-assessments, can aid the moving away from dependency on external authority towards identifying and developing an internal authority and self-reflexive practitioner.

Supervision quality control

In the above model, even though it involves sharing assessment to develop the supervisee's own authority, the supervisor does hold an external assessing function. This relates to whether the trainee meets the skills levels required by the HPC in order to complete their training successfully. This assessment is cumulative; over the years of training and between trainers/tutors, supervisors and placement managers. However, each of these parties holds the responsibility for identifying and challenging unsafe practice, and asking a student to stop practising when that practice becomes a danger to the client. Although in training the assessment function of the supervisor is explicit, I would argue that it remains implicit at all levels of practice.

Within qualifying training the trainee's questions about their own suitability to practice can be projected on to the organisation they are working with, the placement manager or supervisor they are working with, and on any practice they may be observing. In addition, the supervisor may feel called to monitor the suitability of the training and practice the supervisee participates in. Channels of communication need to be in place to allow for this, but an awareness of parallel process in supervision is crucial in order not to collude with the trainees' narcissistic retaliation about their anxieties and feeling deskilled.

A different orientation between training and supervisor can feed into this splitting between supervisee and supervisor on the one hand, and the tutors/ training on the other hand. Both training and supervisor can collude in writing off a placement for unsafe practice. The difficulty around this is how to identify and separate actual unsafe practice from projections. A thorough system of auditing tends to be in place for both placement and other areas of training. The training organisations can be held to account on that basis. All therapists are held to account through their codes of practice, whilst universities also have policies concerning safety to practice. It can be important for all parties to familiarise themselves with these systems (Stuart 2007), but also to have good communication strategies in place to enable any of the parties to contact the other if there are concerns.

Currently there is no separation between the roles of training supervisor and clinical supervisor within BADth. Given the already increasing bureaucratisation, I would be wary of calling for yet another layer of registration. I would like to call though, on the basis of quality control, for continuous professional development monitoring of supervisory practice, such as is now put in place for clinical practice.

For other discussions of professional development, see pp. 11–12 and 146–47

Fourway contracts: supervisor, trainee, training and placement

In 2002 an interfaculty research project aimed to compare aspects of placement learning for artists, arts therapists and teachers (Dokter *et al.* 2002). Its aims were to examine tutor strategies that facilitate student learning in placement/work experience settings. For the purpose of the project three stages were identified: preparation for placement; supervision during placement; and debriefing post-placement. A review of the literature had shown a similar identification of these three stages (Parker and Emmanuel 2001). The research design included the study of placement handbooks and meetings to identify placement stages and common issues. This was followed by a survey of placement providers, students and tutors. The final stage included focus groups involving art and design, arts therapies and education tutors. The survey had a response rate of 37 per cent. Two-thirds of the respondents were from education, approximately a quarter from the arts therapies and a small proportion of artists. Of the respondents a tiny percentage were tutors, the majority being students and approximately one quarter were placement providers.

The findings of the 2002 interfaculty research project revealed a number of issues relating to supervision provision in a training context. In order for the preparation for placement to be effective, suitable settings needed to be found, ideally with trained supervisors working in the placement setting. Students needed to be prepared for placements through training and the development of placement-related skills. They also needed pre-placement visits and an organised induction.

The research project revealed that ongoing supervision, once the student was in placement, was perceived to work best if there was close collaboration between university tutors/supervisors and placement supervisors. The supervision needed to be regular and consistent, with good communication between supervisee and supervisor. Support needed to be available on both emotional and organisational matters.

The post-placement debriefing needed to offer an opportunity for review of and feedback about the whole placement experience by the student and staff involved. A final assessment by staff was crucial and needed to be based on honesty, accuracy, constructive criticism, with a listing of strengths and weaknesses.

The research found that the highest level of satisfaction by students was with the ongoing supervision experience whilst students were on placement. Comparison between the responses of artists, teachers and arts therapies students revealed that the therapists showed the highest levels of satisfaction regarding support available for finding suitable placements. Designated university placement tutors helped students to find placements. The placement tutor's contacts with the work field proved to be influential for student satisfaction (Dokter *et al.* 2002).

Feedback gathered on a 2007 placement managers and supervisors day at Roehampton University echoed the findings on a purely dramatherapy basis. Their feedback drew on their provision of 60 placements, in a variety of settings (health and education in particular). The following issues emerged. What worked well for the students was the range of hands-on experiences that were on offer over the three years. They learned to form good relationships within multidisciplinary teams and how to present reports for a non-dramatherapy audience. The preparation for placement worked well, including the pre-placement visits and induction and there was good liaison between the different parties. Difficulties can occur in splitting between placement, supervisor and university, dual roles (placement manager and co-worker, placement manager and supervisor, university tutor and placement manager), in matching the suitability of the placement to the level of student experience, in ensuring accountability within the placement and in organisational complexities (space, time, team changes or restructuring). One post-placement difficulty centred around the cumulative assessment of skills achieved over three years of placement experience. Although the HPC benchmark stipulates graduating skills needed, the trainings need to identify individually at which level they expect which skills. For individual placement managers and supervisors it can be difficult to obtain an overview.

Conclusion

Training supervision in dramatherapy has become well established over the last 25 years. A multiplicity of models and practices contributes to a rich diversity, but may need some more thorough review for their effect on training and practice. Given the importance of supervision for student learning and subsequent practice, continuous professional development for supervisors is advocated. Supervising trainees involves certain complexities around authority and assessment. A close liaison is needed between trainee, placement, supervisor and training in order to provide a supportive learning environment for the development of a benign internal supervisor. The latter also allows a critical reflexive evaluation of practice, which benefits dramatherapy clinical governance. The following quote from our research as described in Chapter 2 summarises many aspects of this:

Supervisee perspective

For me, clinical supervision is a continuum of learning, a protective measure. It prevents burn out, supports good practice and is a 'given' in a pro-active commitment to change. It prevents me from being isolated in my profession, because at present, I am the only qualified dramatherapist in my city.

Acknowledgements

I wish to thank Linda Laletin, Jane Lasseter and the supervisors and placement managers of Roehampton University for their contributions to this chapter.

References

Behr, H. (1995) Integration of theory and practice, in M. Sharpe (ed.) *The Third Eye: Supervision of Analytic Groups*, London: Routledge.

Bion, W. (1961) *Experiences in Groups*, London: Tavistock.

Bishop, V. (2007) *Clinical Supervision in Practice: Some Questions, Answers and Guidelines for Professionals in Health and Social Care*, 2nd edn, Basingstoke: Palgrave Macmillan.

Bramley, W. (1979) *Group Tutoring: Concepts and Case Studies*, London: Kogan Page.

Brown, D. (1994) Self development through subjective interaction: a fresh look at ego training in action, in D. Brown and L.M. Zinkin (eds) *The Psyche and the Social World: Developments in Group Analytic Theory*, London: Routledge.

Casement, P. (1985) *Learning from the Patient*, London: Routledge.

Chesner, A. (1999) Dramatherapy supervision: historical issues and supervisory settings, in E. Tselikas-Portmann (ed.) *Supervision and Dramatherapy*, London: Jessica Kingsley Publishers.

Davies, E.J., Tennant, A., Ferguson, E., Talkes, K.J. and Jones, L. (2004) Developing models and a framework for multiprofessional clinical supervision, *British Journal of Forensic Practice* 6, 3: 237–48.

Dokter, D., Burchell, H., Karkou, V. and Warren, V. (2002) *Evaluating Placement Learning: An Interfaculty Research Project*, Hatfield: University of Hertfordshire Learning and Teaching Centre.

Dokter, D. and Hughes, P. (2007) *Analysis of Dramatherapy Equal Opportunities Survey*, www.badth.org.uk.

Gersie, A. (2007) Diminished work for dramatherapists – a question of supervision?, *The Prompt*, Spring.

Hahn, H. (2002) Helping the helpers, in A. Chesner and H. Hahn (eds) *Creative Advances in Groupwork*, London: Jessica Kingsley Publishers.

Hawkins, P. and Shohet, R. (1989) *Supervision in the Helping Professions*, Maidenhead: Open University Press.

Health Professions Council (HPC, 2005) Benchmark. Online. Available HTTP: <http://www.csp.org.uk/uploads/documents.html> (accessed 30 April 2008).

Heron, J. (1992) *Feeling and Personhood: Psychology in Another Key*, London: Sage.

Hinshelwood, R.D. (1994) *Clinical Klein*, London: Free Association Books.

James, D.C. (1994) Holding and containing in the group and society, in D. Brown and L.M. Zinkin (eds) *The Psyche and the Social World: Developments in Group Analytic Theory*, London: Routledge.

Jenkyns, M. (1999) Training the supervisor-dramatherapist: the psychodynamic approach, in E. Tselikas-Portmann (ed.) *Supervision and Dramatherapy*, London: Jessica Kingsley Publishers.

Johns, C. (1997) Reflective practice and clinical supervision, Part 1: the reflective turn, *European Nurse* 2, 2: 87–97.

Jones, P. and Dokter, D. (BADth, 2008) *British Association of Drama Therapists Supervision Research Findings*, Cheltenham: British Association of Drama Therapists.

Karkou, V. and Sanderson, P. (2006) *The Arts Therapies: A Research Based Map of the Field*, London: Elsevier.

Lahad, M. (2000) *Creative Supervision: The Use of Expressive Arts Methods in Supervision and Self-supervision*, London, Jessica Kingsley Publishers.

McCann, D. (1999) Supervision, in R. Bor and M. Watts (eds) *The Trainee Handbook: A Guide for Psychotherapy and Counselling Trainees*, London: Sage.

Mander, G. (1991) Some thoughts on sibling rivalry and competitiveness, *British Journal of Psychotherapy* 7, 4: 368–79.

Nitsen, M. (1996) *The Anti-group: Destructive Forces in the Group and their Creative Potential*, London: Routledge.

Obholzer, A. and Zagier Roberts, V. (1994) *The Unconscious at Work: Individual and Organizational Stress in the Human Services*, New York: Routledge.

Olivieri-Larsson, R. (1993) Superego conflicts in supervision group analysis, *Group Analysis* 26: 163–68.

Parker, A. and Emmanuel, R. (2001) Active learning in service delivery: an approach to initial clinical placements, *International Journal of Communication and Language Disorders* 36: 162–66.

Pedder, J. (1986) Reflections on the theory and practice of supervision, *Psychoanalytic Psychotherapy* 2, 1: 1–12.

Scanlon C. (2000) The place of clinical supervision in the training of group analytic psychotherapists: towards a group dynamic model for professional education?, *Group Analysis* 2, 33: 193–207.

Scanlon, C. (2002) Group supervision of individual cases in the training of counsellors and psychotherapists: towards a group-analytic model?, *British Journal of Psychotherapy* 19, 2: 219–34.

Schneider, S. and Berman, B. (1991) The supervision group as transitional object, *Group Analysis* 24, 1: 65–72.

Schon, D.A. (1987) *Educating the Reflective Practitioner*, New York: Basic Books.

Sharpe, M. and Blackwell, D. (1987) Creative supervision through student involvement, *Group Analysis* 20, 3: 195–208.

Stuart, C.C. (2007) *Assessment, Supervision and Support in Clinical Practice: A Guide for Nurses, Midwives and other Health Professionals*, 2nd edn, London: Elsevier.

Teasdale, C. (1993) The role of the clinical placement in art therapy training: towards consolidating our professional identity, *The Arts in Psychotherapy* 20, 3: 205–12.

Turkel, J. (1990) Knowledge vs nurture: how views on the mechanism of action of psychodynamic treatment affect the early training of psychodynamic psychotherapists, *Psychoanalysis and Psychotherapy* 8, 1: 29–36.

van Ooijen, E. (2000) *Clinical Supervision: A Practical Guide*, Edinburgh: Churchill Livingstone.

Voorhoeve, J.N. and van Putte, F.C.A. (1994) Parallel process in supervision when working with psychotic patient, *Group Analysis* 27, 4: 459–66.

Chapter 5

A theatre model of dramatherapy supervision

Madeline Andersen-Warren and Anna Seymour

Introduction

Working with theatre processes in the context of dramatherapy offers a unique way of conceiving human relationships. By their very nature, the formal structures of the theatre boundary experience to a particular purpose, whether it be to explore social issues in the 'problem plays' of Ibsen in the early twentieth century or to entertain by deflating social pretentions in the sixteenth century Commedia dell'arte. In this chapter we will offer a view developing from the theatre model of dramatherapy, suggesting the kinds of intervention that can be used in the process of supervision. We will offer two case studies to illustrate these processes linking theoretical concerns with practice.

Theatre and dramatherapy

There are a number of ways in which a theatre model of dramatherapy may operate. We may draw on Jennings' (1992) developmental model of dramatherapy noting that the phases of embodiment-projection-role have their theatrical parallels in the processes of embodiment and identification with character and situation, and the enactment of role within the dramatic framework. We can see clearly with reference to Goffman (1959) that a direct analogy may be made between life and the theatre: in effect 'life is like art'. We may look specifically at the professional roles within the theatre exploring the similarities between the roles of dramatherapist and theatre director (Mitchell 1996; Meldrum 1999; Jones 2007) or the lighting designer wondering about what should be highlighted, what atmospheres are to be created, what gloomy corners are to be framed. These roles may be enacted by the dramatherapist to some degree or they may serve as useful analogies with which to reflect on the therapeutic process.

We may want to work in different genre through identifying that the expressive world of the commedia or melodrama can open up aesthetically boundaried forms for clients with limited movement. We might decide that wresting meaning from a piece of text and experimenting with interpretations presents the opportunity to experience the rewriting of stories and engenders a sense of control and empowerment. The theatre process allows a separation between role and character. Along the continuum of dramatic distancing, the client may work in a fully embodied way, taking account of the feelings, thoughts, motivations, history and dramatic actions of a character. At the opposite extreme, the client may stay with the conception of a person acting a role, in this way more focused on plot rather than deeper psychological processes. Any movement along the continuum of role–character allows for some level of aesthetic distance and enables the possibility of performance. The client may create something that can be witnessed kindly by the dramatherapist who then facilitates the way through the process of derolement.

For other discussions of distancing and role, see pp. 95–6 and 162–63

Theatre and dramatherapy supervision

Working with the theatre offers limitless ways of encountering life issues. In supervision, all aspects of theatre may be used, insofar as they are instrumental in supporting the therapeutic alliance between therapist and client and enable the therapist to process their work. It might appear sometimes that working creatively in supervision is 'luxurious', whereas the reality is that creative methods can often provide economy because of the clarity and containment they offer. We are going to talk about a way of working within supervision process that uses dramatic text or texts that become plays through dramatisation. These texts could be literary or oral. They could range from anecdotal stories to myths, or legend, or fragments from popular culture.

For other discussions of creativity in supervision, see pp. 49–66

At the heart of the process of working with a play is the struggle to understand how to stage it, to relate physicality to interpretation – to understand how both to 'inhabit it' and to be distanced from it – the resonance of metaphor. All of this *theatrical* process can be instrumental in the supervisory process. In supervision it is crucial to identify the tasks at hand. These might involve an examination of role, the context, content or process of the therapy. By analogy, using a theatre model, the supervisor may suggest exploring these issues 'as if' they were within a theatrical framework. This not only allows for distancing from the immediate problems, but may also offer insights, as the supervisee/therapist's role is enriched by seeing the process from a theatrical perspective. The theatrical roles themselves carry different tasks and may uncover fresh avenues to explore. For example, the deputy stage manager in the prompt corner has a copy of the script in front of them, ready to assist the actor who forgets their lines. What might this role provoke in the dramatherapist? Do they perceive that there is a given script for the session? Who wrote the script? What kind of play is it? How does the dramatherapist 'prompt'? Do they 'remain with the script as it is' or allow the actors to improvise? At each point in the theatre perspective a range of questions opens up that could be useful in supervision. When we look at plays, the aesthetics, rehearsal processes and relationships between actors and spaces, we have to identify tasks that are implicit in the therapeutic process and, therefore, the subject of supervision. The supervisor may model like a theatre director: where next to turn their attention, how to prioritise the order of things to do when everything seems important and each element is interlinked. All of this work moves us into the realm of metaphor.

The use of metaphor is at the heart of dramatherapy practice. As Mann writes: 'the power of metaphor rests upon its levels of meaning and its ability to be flexible, poetic and intuitive. Its Greek origin literally means "to carry across", implying a transfer of meaning from one frame of reference to another' (1996: 2). In the supervision process, the frames of reference are multifaceted. Hawkins and Shohet (2000) outline the various processes that may take place during a supervision session. These include the conscious and unconscious dynamics between the supervisor and supervisee, the client and therapist. In addition, the client, the supervisor, and the therapist may be responding to the prevailing social, political and economic conditions and these are brought into the supervision space. During an individual supervision session there are two people in the room but the focus is on the absent client or clients whose frames of reference are being interpreted, or retold, by the supervisee.

A theatrical metaphor can both contain and expand the frames of reference. A theatre-based intervention can expand horizons through an imaginative framework and contain feelings and thoughts through the framing of a scene, act or play. We are reminded of the 'wooden O' described by the chorus at the start of Shakespeare's *Henry V*, a small space which, with the aid of our imagination, can contain the 'the very casques which did affright the air at Agincourt' (Act 1, sc. 1, line 14) as well as the monarch, courts and a vast array of characters and places.

At the same time, there is much that we cannot immediately 'understand' at a cognitive level, in both the theatrical and supervisory processes, and might never understand. There are things which we do and respond to on an intuitive level that resist explanation. The artistic process contains this tension – some complex piece of thinking might be completely unravelled by seeing actors moving in the rehearsal space. There is a paradoxical way in which we might use a theatrical metaphor to explain something that we cannot 'understand' in any other way. This contains ignorance and knowledge so that in consciousness we may have a form to occupy the otherwise inexplicable space.

In the supervision context we are familiar with this tension, and know well the part of the supervisor that wants to know what is going on, and believes that understanding can be pinned down. At the same time, the part of the artist plays and speculates, it allows the presence of multiple meanings. Both parts can be brought into the space, with the confidence that in supervision it is possible to contain this tension and still provide a safe and ethical practice.

But process brings into question the whole issue of models of practice. For example, superficially at least, it seems a lot safer to be able to say I work from a particular 'model' and be able to relate structures of practice, techniques and key theoretical concepts. There are lingering questions about models of practice and these relate to supervision. Anxieties about what dramatherapy *is* abound: for example, is it a psychotherapy or an art form? This distinction often emerges when dramatherapists are asked about their identity as practitioners. Questions of status arise as old arguments surface around the 'hard' evidence of medically oriented clinical interventions versus the more intangible processes of the arts therapies. These issues are important in the broad context but how does this distinction matter in terms of what the dramatherapist actually *does*?

Is dramatherapy promiscuous in its theory and eclectic in its practice? Jennings (1998), for example, provocatively asked whether or not dramatherapy exists? She questions a potential dichotomy between practice and process rooted in an art form and interpreting the art form through a set of theories or the practices of a particular individual such as Rogers or Klein. Her argument is that many dramatherapists have recourse to these theorists to validate their practice. This leads to her central point, namely that it is the thing itself, the theatrical process, that is the centre of dramatherapy. The rest may be importantly related and should be within our consciousness and study, but not as a way of making up for some lack.

For other discussions of models of dramatherapy, see pp. 59–60 and 205–6

The psychiatrist Cox talks about 'being beset by literary metaphors that would not leave him alone' (1992: 28) when working with clients. Tselikas-Portmann addresses this process of internalising the client's processes and converting them into artistic expression in relation to the supervisory relationship:

> She [the supervisor] will need to be able to make use of the art form and to differentiate when an analytical attitude (in its generic sense rather than psychoanalytic) is appropriate to the setting and situation and when a dramatic process will be more helpful in enhancing the supervisee's potential and insight.
>
> (Tselikas-Portmann 1999: 204)

So, the issue for dramatherapy supervision in Cox and Tselikas-Portmann is to pay attention to the interdependency of the artistic, the clinical and the everyday in the dramatherapy process, and where it is appropriate to make a separation of the elements of the process to be able to examine them in more detail.

To explore these issues we now turn to two case studies. The first examines how the dramatherapy supervisor may use a play text as a guiding metaphor, a reference point to contain and inform their thoughts. It demonstrates how the text may support the supervisor, not least in giving palpable form to a sense of unknowing, as in the following example.

Case examples

Introduction to the play Jack

The play tells the story of Jack who commits suicide when his life living with AIDS becomes unbearable. It is written by American playwright Greenspan (1990) for a cast of four actors. There are three female voices, which are only ever visible on stage from the neck up. The faces exist in three spotlights, the actors speak from fixed lecterns – the image is one of 'floating busts'. The one male actor enacts only one monologue and is fully visible. The case study focuses on the first scene.

The opening of the play looks intriguing on the page. The lines for each of the three female actors are written in columns. Sometimes each speaks only a word, very occasionally a whole sentence. Sometimes the actors speak simultaneously, the same or different words. The audience experiences words carefully placed in a dark landscape, an unknown and strangely formless state is evoked. This fog may seem at once bleak and statuesque, as its words carve out a space pregnant with meaning and yet without meaning at all. The play captures the mood of the historical moment, as with dark foreboding the reality of what AIDS would come to mean is insinuated. Out of these fragments a character, Jack, begins to emerge. This is not an easy introduction, as in the self-conscious exposition of the naturalistic drama where contrived speeches seek to provide the backstory of the play. In this drama, the central character emerges in biblical form from nothing, and finally slides back into the darkness in the final moments. His story is told in a way that forces those who witness it to work imaginatively – sometimes filling in gaps, sometimes struggling to interpret the fragments of information on offer. In this sense, the audience becomes co-producer of the drama and is implicated in its contents. The play opens and closes with a breath audibly produced by the actors. This breath punctuates and fuels the action of the play. It enables the beginning and finally is all that is left.

Case study 1: Using the play in supervision with a trainee dramatherapist

She came to the fourth session quite physically locked, sat awkwardly and, when encouraged to begin, said she did want to use the session but felt she didn't want to speak, as if she didn't want to tell me anything. I went into theatre director mode – as the actor in this drama, she had no script as in the actor's worst anxiety dream – she wanted to be in the play but didn't know how to. I offered quite specific instructions and asked 'to the point' questions. First, I asked her to take up more space on the sofa and take some breaths. I breathed too and wondered about our physical relationship, sitting opposite each other albeit at an angle, and if that felt comfortable. She said she wanted to sit on the floor, and for me to sit near her. We experimented, and I ended up sitting by her side, both of us leaning against the sofa. What else did she need? Something to fiddle with – a prop? I produced a basket full of objects, she chose a stone.

'Right, now I'm ready', she said, and began to speak rapidly and disconnectedly about her session with the group that day. I found it hard to listen because I was focused on her and how there was an incongruence between the brightness and forced energy of her speech and what I sensed was underlying. I interrupted and checked – was she sure that she was ready to start and asked her just to spend a moment checking and taking another deep breath? At this moment she breathed and began to weep. She began to explore the stone in her hand and found that it was a broken stone. She related how she felt broken and wondered how she could work with the group.

She had, in her first supervision session, told me about anxiety over her father's health, and he was subsequently diagnosed as incurably ill. Now that fact of his impending death became the backdrop to her work. She had also tried to run a creative group before beginning her training and, in her words, it had completely failed. She had put off starting her creative placement and began her supervision before starting the group with a huge feeling of dread and deep fears of failure.

So, like our play extract, we were beginning with a kind of void, a darkness into which the life of the group emerged. A recurrent theme became staying with what was going on, and a metaphor for that 'staying with' was, for me, the idea of breathing, to ground experience, and bring energy. In our sessions, I was constantly aware of the pace of our work. The supervisee would often want to rush, and often I felt this was part of avoiding what was going on in her supervision and that this, in turn, could be being paralleled in her work with the group. I often wanted to slow down the pace, to clarify what was going on. This sort of process was happening in her group, as she related one particular session where it seemed to me that the group were being given too much material too rapidly and couldn't deal with it. Ironically, she was working with a group of adults with learning disabilities who clearly needed a pace that allowed them to absorb instructions.

The anxiety that she began to speak about quite freely, I could also identify with. I have felt in working with a group that I am in a dark place and stuck. I have also experienced the panic reaction of 'flooding' myself and the group with material to avoid the fear of facing what is going on, and what I might find, to avoid the 'danger' of 'meeting' them. The quality of this drama becomes rather statuesque, ancient, bleak. Deep feelings of ancient fear are present, the landscape may be imposing, the space bleak and lonely. It is possible to feel disconnected 'like a floating bust'.

The playwright Kay quotes fellow playwright Ntozake Shange (1992): 'oppression/makes us love one another badly/makes our breathing mangled'. If dramatherapy is to be liberatory then an awareness of breathing is fundamental. We can focus on breathing in terms of literally facilitating the supervisee 'to breathe', but also considering the metaphor of breath. But what if I made a different kind of intervention, or, indeed, did not intervene at all?

In a further example from scene two of *Jack*, one female voice, instead of three, articulates multiple voices. The performer is confronted with the problem of when, and how, to breathe in order to stay with the dramatic metaphor. The actor, paradoxically, needs apparently not to breathe and, looking at the punctuation of the speech, you will see there are hardly any full stops or commas.

As the supervisor listening to this, I may begin to feel 'breathless' and become anxious. Punctuation and breathing are necessary for the performer to give meaning to language. I may want to intervene as a director to enable the performer. I may want to intervene as supervisor to deal with my own anxiety about staying with the delivery of this story. Yet, if I do stay with it, I am rewarded by the information that is shared, and the fact that the 'supervisee' actually shapes the story and brings it to a conclusion. What seems shapeless and formless to me actually has a shape that emerges, if I allow it space.

In the first scene, there was punctuation, full stops, a scene that ended with a breath which gave voice to the flow of this long speech at the beginning of Scene Two. There is no exact guide of how and when to intervene, but it seems to me that an awareness of the potential structures and aesthetics of the art form can produce a more acute sensibility. This awareness can work with intuitive responses in the moment and inform the process as much as analytical thought.

So we are saying that the roles of actor, theatre director and the internalised dramatic text can assist in the supervision process, in working with metaphor. However, it is important to understand that clients, supervisees and supervisors may work in different metaphorical realms, that there are orders of metaphors and we need to be sensitive to this. Sometimes we are working with metaphors drawn from popular culture that may be unfamiliar to the therapist or supervisor. It is important not to be snobbish in our preferences. Our thinking may be sophisticated, even if the form is not to our taste. Sometimes the metaphor is concretely expressed within everyday reality – for example, 'I feel like a sack of potatoes' – but equally it could be something as abstract as 'emptiness'. If we apply theatre principles we can look at staging the play called *Emptiness*. How large a space does the performance need? What will the actors of *Emptiness* look like? And so on. By staying with the given metaphor but taking this into the dramatic process it begins to have a form that offers containment and the capacity to engage with what is troubling in a concrete way.

For other discussions of using script in supervision, see pp. 160–61

However, what if the form does not emerge? What if the therapist stays with the recounted narrative but feels overwhelmed? The second case study illustrates how the supervisor might work with this.

Case study 2: Creating a play during supervision with a dramatherapist

The following case study illustrates ways in which drawing on a theatrical framework can change the therapist's perspectives about working with a client. The supervisee was finding it difficult to understand the needs of her client. During the assessment period it had become clear that the client had suffered physical and sexual abuse during her childhood and was still troubled by the emotional consequences. Although the therapist had undertaken post-graduate training in this area, she felt unable to establish a working alliance with this client because she felt detached and 'rather stupid' in her presence, and was nervous about interrupting her flow of talk about her history of abuse. The therapist was worried that the client would 'give up on her' as an inadequate dramatherapist. While I suspected that there were parallel processes at play, my impulse was to focus on the feelings of stupidity expressed by the therapist. I suggested that we examined the situation through the legend of Perceval and the Grail, at the point where the foolish knight Perceval first sees the Grail, but is banished from the Grail Castle because he does not question its function of sustaining the wounded Fisher King.

As the room was small our space was limited. We focused on a table top as the playing area. From a selection of small plastic figures, the supervisee chose a brightly clothed monkey to represent Perceval and placed it at the edge of the space. In response to a question about the audience area, she stated that they were seated to the right of the table and we arranged a row of chairs to represent them, and I checked that our play was being devised for a proscenium arch stage. The set was made from layers of lace, velvet and moiré materials draped over the backs of chairs, arranged so the audience viewed the set as the back of the stage. I asked about the genre of the play we were about to create. The supervisee hesitated and then said that she wanted it to be like a Lloyd Webber musical. As she said this, she hung her head and looked embarrassed. When her hesitation and head movement were fed back to her, she explained that this was not a form that dramatherapists are expected to work with. She feared my disapproval as she had not cited an intellectual form of theatre. Rather than interrupting the flow of the creative work to engage in a debate about the validity of this statement, and an exploration of her perceptions of my thoughts about her option, I responded that she was free to opt for any genre.

We proceeded to people the stage with the other characters, scenery and props. The banqueting tables and the Fisher King's bed were made from matchboxes covered with white cloth, and the candles were matches. In contrast to Perceval, the Grail Maiden, the pages in the Grail procession and the Fisher King were all represented by human figures. The Grail was fashioned from gold foil and placed in the hands of the Grail Maiden.

Once the characters had been selected, I asked the supervisee to become the director and playwright, to plot the moves and create the script. I would move some of the characters under her direction and use her script for lines attributed to characters I was manipulating. It was essential to ensure that the play was her adaptation of the story, and remained uncontaminated by any images or scenarios in my imagination. The scene started with Perceval and the Fisher King at the edge of the stage. The king was urging Perceval to eat the delicious food on the table but Perceval remained silent. He remained silent during the grave procession of pages and whilst the Maiden carried the Grail across the stage and exited through a lace curtain. The only sound was the soft humming of the supervisee which formed the background music. We repeated the scene and the humming became louder, creating the atmosphere of a royal procession. However, the supervisee was finding it difficult to maintain her breathing at sufficient depth to produce the volume of sound she wanted. At this point, I almost stepped in to become the voice coach, but reconsidered this role, as I knew that she had considerable experience in this area and I suspected that that this session was primarily about allowing her to reskill herself. I therefore asked her what the company's voice coach would advise. As we were restricted by time, I did not ask her to become the voice coach but just to repeat the instructions and then act upon them, which she did. We repeated the play; the Fisher King's words were just 'Please eat', chanted to Perceval in a monotone while the humming flowed into improvised vocal sounds. At this point the supervisee expressed a sense of stuckness and wanted me to take over as director. I believed this would be counterproductive and contribute to her sense of feeling deskilled. Instead, I asked her who might be in the audience watching the preview. She named several leading dramatherapists and I asked her to take their positions while I interviewed them.

The first interviewed person was quite hostile and referred to the production as 'unimaginative' and wondered whether the director was aware of the opera *Parsifal*. The second was more friendly, but wondered why there was so little script. The third wondered whether we could hear Perceval's thoughts, a suggestion that was well received by the supervisee. (After hearing the first audience member speak I did wonder whether I would need to suggest the supervisee created a character to challenge the audience view, but this did not prove to be necessary.) However, when we returned to the play she was still unable to provide a script for Perceval. I introduced the role of the prompter, and asked the supervisee to sit at the side of stage and feed me the lines. A struggle emerged. Again the supervisee, as prompter, attempted to put me into the leading role by stating that I knew the lines and could just say them. Instead of entering into an argument or debate, I suggested a role reversal and I became the prompter saying 'You know the lines'. The response was 'I do not, I only know I want to know'. Reversing roles, I gave her the line 'I want to know' *as* the line and she took this up as a refrain.

Up to this point, I had defined the roles I had inhabited as those which echoed the supervisee's instructions or, as in the interviewer role, those that served to move the session forward, but without character development or plot instigators. As we now had a starting line, I offered to play the Fisher King as a character, to assist Perceval, rather than to create a character. We therefore created a dialogue in which Perceval sang 'I want to know' and the Fisher King chanted 'I wonder what you want to know?' Perceval started to add lines like 'I want to know what is in the Grail', 'I want to know where it is going' and 'I want to know why you [the Fisher King] are ill'. We then changed roles, so Perceval could receive some answers. The Fisher King replied that the Grail contained healing and imagination and that he was the recipient, but he needed someone to ask about his pain and pay attention to his body rather than his words. To close the play I focused on the procession. The supervisee provided the refrain of 'Can we stop this endless procession? We circle round and round. We want to stop.'

Time prevented us returning to the audience for further comment, so we moved into the reflective period to close the session. The reflections focused on the following areas: the struggle to be a 'proper' dramatherapist which had somehow become interpreted as only working with literary texts, or moving straight into 'exciting' creative work, before building a relationship. Interestingly, an experienced Knight had told Perceval that he should avoid excessive talking, which he had interpreted as the need to remain silent, despite a strong desire to ask the questions.

The supervisee reminded herself that many survivors of abuse found safety in the retelling of their story of abuse, but that the words from the procession had reminded her that the repetition can become meaningless. The usefulness of the 'naive enquirer's' role, 'where/what is your pain?', can be rephrased as an appropriate question for the metaphor to begin dramatherapy.

I did ask whether she had any thoughts about Perceval being represented as a clothed monkey. She replied that this was a 'happy representation' because this was a cheerful image, as the monkey could be agile and funny as well as intelligent. This question, I realised later, came from my own dislike of animals being dressed in human clothing. Our frames of reference had differed here. I had interpreted, incorrectly, the choice as a constrained, unhappy image. At the end of the session the supervisee was able to accept the question as a question, but if I had questioned the choice at the start of the session, I believe she would have perceived the question as a criticism and a confirmation of her lack of skill and judgement. I noted that the monkey representing the therapist when alone on the 'stage' was depicted as intelligent; it was only when the client was represented that the monkey became stuck.

For other discussions of the use of objects in supervision, see pp. 53–4 and 133–34

At the next supervision session, the supervisee reported that she had noticed the client repeatedly touched her stomach while she talked. She fed this back to the client, initially by mirroring the movement, which gained the client's attention, and then with words. She was thus able to engage her in a body-based metaphor about her emotional pain. She continued to work with the client and built a healthy therapeutic alliance with her.

For other discussions of the body in dramatherapy supervision, see pp. 166–68 and 171–72

During the supervision session the supervisee has experienced benefits of working within an aesthetic distance in relation to her client. Landy writes that 'at aesthetic distance one retains the role of the overdistanced, cognitive observer and the role of the underdistanced, affective actor' (1994: 114). In the above example, both client and therapist were in an overdistanced place. The client, as reported by the therapist, was distancing herself from the therapist by repeating her story of abuse over and over again. In this way she stayed within a familiar framework of reference. However painful this was, it was a known and recognisable pain. During this period, she was able to be a distanced observer and participant in the therapy. The therapist felt pushed into the cognitive observer role, which led her into feeling deskilled. It later transpired that both client and therapist were feeling constrained and pressurised by external forces. The therapist's experiences included the need to produce positive results from her work, and a directive to move towards short-term interventions. The client's feelings were influenced by a previous experience of a limit of eight therapy sessions during which she had 'opened up' and then felt 'forced to close down almost at once'.

The therapist's experience of becoming the 'underdistanced, affective actor' during the supervision, coupled with the supervisor's refusal to become the external, all-knowing frame of reference, allowed her to work and play within the metaphorical frame of reference. As the supervisor, I had provided the framework for the play, informed by the references provided by the supervisee. Whether or not it is permissible for the supervisor to provide the text is an ongoing dilemma. It can be argued that the session is unduly influenced by the supervisor's rather than the supervisee's frame of reference and that the supervisee will be constrained by the choice of text. In the above example, I believe that it was permissible to offer a text as a vehicle of exploration in this instance as the supervisee was feeling stuck with the client, and was only able to focus on what she perceived to be her failings as a dramatherapist.

Unlike therapy, the supervision session often needs to be self-contained to enable the therapist to unravel issues, to enable them to continue to work with the client. Recurrent themes and the relationship with the supervisor will be ongoing threads within the sessions, but the sessions themselves will often focus on a particular client or clients. In this particular instance, the therapist's imaginative processes had become stifled and my task was to offer her a structure to reawaken her imaginative impulses, so she could create her own play, which would become adapted or changed into another long-running play created in a collaboration between the client and the therapist.

Conclusion

The following points bring together the themes within our consideration of how a theatre model of dramatherapy can be brought into the theory and practice of supervision. They also draw on both case examples in creating common ideas or suggestions. All aspects of the theatre can be used in the process of dramatherapy supervision. These may include:

- the professional roles of director, lighting designer, stage manager
- the roles of characters in plays, or improvisation or roles taken from many sources
- play texts or texts drawn from many sources that become 'plays' by virtue of being dramatised
- by looking at staging it is possible to explore spatial relationships and how material is contained through concretising its presentation
- the content of plays can provide distancing metaphors which may enable insight
- the witnessing or audience roles may be inhabited by the supervisor and the supervisee
- the theatre or dramatic model in one-to-one supervision allows the supervisee to create all the characters that would be created in group supervision.

This chapter has illustrated the ways in which theatre process may be used by the supervisor actively or through analogy, and can inform the supervisory relationship whilst providing helpful thinking structures, as well as intuitive prompts. Staying within the boundaries of the chosen forms for exploring the supervisee's material can create a containing structure, which can support the relationship between supervisor and supervisee.

References

Cox, M. (1992) The place of metaphor in psychotherapy supervision. Creative tensions between forensic psychotherapy and dramatherapy, in S. Jennings (ed.) *Dramatherapy Theory and Practice 2*, London and New York: Tavistock/ Routledge.

Goffman, E. (1959) *The Presentation of Self in Everyday Life*, New York: Doubleday.

Greenspan, D. (1990) 'Jack', in E. M. Osborn (ed.) *The Way We Live Now: American Plays and the AIDS Crisis*, New York: Theatre Communications Group.

Hawkins, P. and Shohet, R. (2000) *Supervision in the Helping Professions*, Maidenhead: Open University Press.

Jennings, S. (1992) *Dramatherapy with Families, Groups and Individuals: Waiting in the Wings*, London: Jessica Kingsley Publishers.

Jennings, S. (1998) Does dramatherapy exist?, *Dramatherapy Journal of the British Association of Dramatherapists* 20: 2.

Jennings, S. (1999) Theatre-based supervision: a supervisory model for multi-disciplinary supervisees, in E. Tselikas-Portmann (ed.) *Supervision and Dramatherapy*, London: Jessica Kingsley Publishers.

Jones, P. (2007) *Drama as Therapy*, London: Routledge.

Landy, R. (1994) *Persona and Performance*, London: Jessica Kingsley Publishers.

Mann, S. (1996) Metaphor, symbol and the healing process in dramatherapy', *Dramatherapy Journal of the British Association of Dramatherapists* 18: 2.

Meldrum, B. (1999) The theatre process in dramatherapy, in A. Cattanach (ed.) *Process in the Arts Therapies*, London: Jessica Kingsley Publishers.

Mitchell, S. (ed.) (1996) *Dramatherapy Clinical Studies*, London: Jessica Kingsley Publishers.

Shakespeare, W. (1981) 'Henry V', in *The Complete Works of William Shakespeare: The Alexander Text*, London: William Collins.

Shange, N. (1992) *Three Pieces*, New York: St. Martin's Press.

Tselikas-Portmann, E. (ed.) (1999) *Supervision and Dramatherapy*, London: Jessica Kingsley Publishers.

Chapter 6

Transference and countertransference in relation to the dramatic form in supervision training

Marina Jenkyns

Introduction

In this chapter the focus is on the ways in which transference and counter-transference phenomena can be brought to consciousness by the use of the art form drama in the training of dramatherapy supervisors. I shall look first at an example of dramatic space as a setting for projective work in supervisor training and then move on to presenting some of the ways in which dramatic metaphor can highlight transference and countertransference. An important aspect of supervisor training, in whatever modality, is the ability for the therapist to take up the authority of the supervisory role. I shall briefly introduce this concept and show how it can be explored through projective work. (For further elucidation of authority in supervisor role, see Jenkyns in Tselikas-Portmann 1999.) The chapter ends with an example of how the projection on to drama itself is an issue for supervisors to be aware of as a transference phenomenon in supervision practice that, when it occurs and is worked with, can be most helpful in understanding the client's defence system. For those readers unfamiliar with some of the concepts, suggestions for further reading may be found at the end of the chapter.

Dramatherapy metaphor

There is no doubt that a theatre can be a very special place. It is like a magnifying glass, and also like a reducing lens . . . the theatre always asserts itself in the present. This is what can make it more real than the ordinary stream of consciousness. This is what makes it also more disturbing.

(Brook 1968: 110–11)

Three chairs are stacked in the centre of a circle. Ten therapists form the boundary of the circle. The workshop is on the supervisor/therapist/client triad. What are the conditions which allow the metaphor to be worked with in depth? How can we enable the unsurprising, a stack of chairs, to reveal the surprising? How can the circle of the enactment space affect us like Brook's vision of the theatre: to disturb the assumptions we bring with us; to magnify so that we can see better; to reduce the wider picture in order to pay attention to detail?

Before placing the chairs I have had to create the conditions for metaphor to work at depth. To begin with I reinforce the dramatic container provided by the boundary of the circle. I find myself musing, 'The circle is a bit ragged, there are a few spaces, it's a hot day and this is the last workshop, maybe it's not so important to tidy the circle up, seems a bit bossy, after all these are experienced therapists.' As these thoughts brush my mind I verge on coming out of role as trainer about supervision of therapy practice. If I do that the group will not be served, neither will the supervisees of these therapists, nor will the clients. And I will not be able to work effectively. Before we even begin I am working with the art form respecting the conditions necessary for dramatherapy metaphor. So I ask the group to join up the circle, remove notebooks and coffee cups. I am not being pernickety or teacherly or patronising, what I am doing is clearing an auditorium and creating a stage for performance. Just as I have had to enable myself to get into role, I am enabling the members of this workshop to get into the roles they will need to take up in order to learn from this workshop. Their roles will be those of enactor and of audience and witness to their own and others' projective work.

I ask the group to focus on the space, meditate on it for a few minutes. This provides a collaborative energy within the group and focuses them on the first ingredient of the work – the space which will hold the enactments. Then I move out of the circle and return with three stacked chairs which I place in the centre. I am about to unstack them and ask the group to sculpt these chairs as client/therapist/supervisor, but I stop myself. 'No,' I think, 'I'm missing something out.' I realise that to begin working in the metaphor I need to invite the group to connect with the chairs as they are brought in from the 'outside world' of the rest of the room, in order to deepen their engagement with the transferential potential of the metaphor. Once the chairs are in the centre they are already objects to be engaged with; they have metaphoric value. They are the equivalent of Brook's famous observation that a person walks across an empty space watched by another and a piece of theatre is created.

If I were to say that one chair represents a client, one a therapist and one a supervisor the likelihood is that I would obstruct the process of the therapists bringing their unconscious processes into awareness from the beginning. I would get in the way of their projecting whatever they are automatically prompted to do by their unconscious the moment they see the chairs in the enactment space. For at that moment of the objects occupying the centre of the symbolic space, all those sitting on the boundary which defines it will project on to them; in other words the stack of chairs will evoke responses. Thoughts and feelings unique to each person will come from many layers in the individual psyche. If I were to put the words 'therapist', 'client' and 'supervisor' on to them at this stage, then other resonances, which exist simply by the chairs being in the symbolic space, will be blocked. To allow the chairs, undesignated, to speak will result in a greater fund of transferential meaning becoming available for contemplation and analysis.

For some people it is the backs of the chairs that they will see, for some the front and for some the sides. Their view will be instrumental in what the chairs suggest to them, how they feel and think about them and what they project on to them. The fact that the chairs are three in number will have meaning too. That the chairs are stacked will provoke certain responses. Already we can see the complexity of the metaphor. This chapter is concerned with exploring some of the ways in which projective techniques and metaphor can be used to understand transference and countertransference issues in supervising and therefore in supervisor training.

As a trainer I need first to choose my dramatic tools carefully, then I have to decide how to use them. The purpose of the workshop with the chairs is to involve the group in exploring the triadic nature of clinical supervision, the client/therapist/supervisor relationship which is at the core of the work. But I also know that the use of the aesthetic form can bring forth a richness of material. Simply by working slowly with the group and the metaphor, many of the additional themes I may want to cover as trainer will be raised. What I aim to do in this chapter, therefore, is slow down the reader just as I would slow down the group, showing how attention to detail can yield in-depth learning in this context.

The position of the chairs

Projective possibilities evoking transferential material

Let us look at some responses and then at how they might be thought about in relation to transference and countertransference as it relates to the supervisory process:

1   *'I felt cut off because they had their backs to me.'* What might 'having their backs to me' mean to this person? What transferential relationship might she have to the chairs, who or what might they represent to her? As supervisor-trainer I need to think about how she might relate the client/therapist/supervisor triad to this feeling. For example, when later in the work we come to look at specific clinical material, I might suggest that she connects with this thought if it seems useful. Aspects of the dynamic to consider would include wondering if it is an aspect of the relationship between the client and the therapist that is being highlighted

here, coming through the system of the triad, e.g. does the client feel the therapist 'has her back to her'? On the other hand, does the therapist feel the client 'has her back to her'? Third, does the therapist feel the supervisor 'has her back to her', or she to the supervisor? In other words we are able to focus on where this transference to the chairs belongs, in the transferences and countertransferences of the triad and of the supervisory relationship itself. The therapist needs to be invited to explore what 'having their backs to me' feels like for her. Much of this exploration will be for her to do outside the workshop setting – in her own therapy or supervision or other contexts for personal reflection. As facilitator of the workshop I also need to muse on what the phrase might indicate in the here-and-now of the workshop. I need to be alert to her use of the projective object of the stack to express her or the group's less accessible feelings about the present.

2   *'Because the seats were facing me I wanted to go and sit on them but then I would have felt funny sitting on them as a stack.'* Here the therapist talks about feeling invited by the chairs yet unable to take up the invitation. We discuss the differences between her experience and that of the previous therapist. This leads to a discussion on the oppressiveness which the stack seems to convey. One person identifies this with the organisation or institution in which the supervision might take place. Another offers that the system of client-therapist-supervisor feels a heavy weight of responsibility; that she is resistant to approaching it. Yet another says, 'With their sides to me, it made me want to go and separate them, they seemed so squashed up.'

3   *'I'm the eldest/middle/youngest in my family.'* We now begin to focus on the specific transference feelings prompted by the stack of chairs. For example, one man says that he is the eldest of his family, that the sculpt reminds him of this and makes him think about his position in it. Someone else says that it immediately makes her think of client, therapist and supervisor and wonders whether the client is at the top or the bottom. This had resonances for her in terms of her place in the family. Someone else says that they really empathised with the bottom chair, the weight of the institution on them, regardless of the role it might represent, and wondered how this related to her position as the youngest in her family.

Here the group are being alerted to their own family dynamics, their own material which may be tapped into in their countertransference reactions within the supervisory task. The work is preparing them for the attention they will need to pay to the supervisor's countertransference responses. By slowing down simply to look at the metaphor, the group are engaging in some of the most important activities of the supervisor's role – observing; being still and waiting; allowing themselves to see and hear from different angles; holding on to their own responses while they hear other people's; exploring their own projections and where these might be coming from in their own internal world. Long before we begin to work with the chairs we have mined a whole field of supervision technique. In this situation, the metaphor provided by the chairs gives the group the experience of the use of dramatic metaphor in supervision.

So far we have paid attention to what the stack of chairs evokes, but the actual setting up of the chairs has also been important. The group was in a circle; the chairs placed in the centre; they were contained by the group. I told the participants that the circle they bounded was to be the enactment space. Thus a dramatic space, a theatre space, was created. It became charged with meaning, a place for projections contained by members of the group. The roles of audience and witness were established by the physical context. In that space the three chairs have more weight and potential for metaphoric meaning than if they had been put outside the group. Thus, for example, the man who says 'When you put the three chairs there, I was struck by the fact that they were three. There are three in my family and I'm the eldest and I'm very aware of that' is put in touch with a powerful internal dynamic that is particular to him and which he carries within him into his professional role. It will be part of his valency to certain trans-ferences and be an ingredient in his countertransference. This is something that would have been missed out if I had gone straight into labelling the chairs. Now his valency will be available to him when he needs to consider his own countertransference as a therapist and a supervisor in this workshop; it will, in other words, have brought it up on his personal screen. And by sharing that it will be on the group screen too.

A woman takes up this theme. 'I'm one of three too but I'm the youngest and I feel I must be on the bottom chair and as I look at that I feel really squashed. Can I go and undo them?' I say, 'We will move into repositioning the chairs soon but I'd like us to stay with exploring responses to the stack formation before we sculpt them.' This way she cannot rush to undo her discomfort, but can be contained by the group, the circle, the enactment space and my holding the task. In this way she can have the space to get to know that part of her in this particular context. She then has this feeling available to her to deepen her experience and learning in the workshop.

What I have been doing is preparation and focusing; creating an engage-ment with the dramatic aesthetic by the way in which I set up the space, the way I use an object – the stack of chairs– the way I focus on enabling the group members simply to notice the process. The atmosphere in the room is one of intense concentration, in spite of the heat and the time of day. I suspect that if I had simply gone straight to designating a role to each of the three chairs the intensity of the focus would have been missing. I have been warming up the receptors of the unconscious in relation to projective work. What we now have in the room is an awareness of the power and usefulness of using projective techniques in supervision. Even a simple stack of chairs intended to be used for a more specific 'exercise' powerfully taps into the script each therapist carries within them. The preparation has therefore achieved one aim of the training; to create conditions for exploring transference and countertransference in relation to the client/therapist/supervisor triad.

The supervisor

Authority of role

The chairs also provide a useful metaphor for thinking about the authority that the supervisor needs to take up in order to work effectively in role. Elsewhere I have discussed this in relation to supervisor training (Jenkyns, in Tselikas-Portmann 1999) and would again refer the reader to the concept outlined by Obholzer and Zagier Roberts (1994). They draw attention to the need for the role to be authorised from above, from below and from within. The stack of chairs can usefully embody this and it is a helpful image to keep in mind before we unpack the individual chairs.

Authority from above

In dramatherapy the supervisor is authorised by the British Association of Dramatherapists as having met its conditions necessary for registering supervisors. A supervisor thus registered can embark on supervision supported by the legitimacy endowed by meeting the requirement of the authorising body. In this particular field this constitutes being authorised from above.

Authority from below

Here the supervisee must authorise the supervisor. If she or he does not willingly give consent to the supervisor to work, then the relationship and task cannot be engaged with. In the case of the practitioner seeking a supervisor it is important for the therapist to feel comfortable and be able to work with a chosen supervisor. If they do not, they may withold their authorising of that supervisor; in this case the supervisor is disabled from fully occupying the role. Normally a qualified therapist will choose a supervisor and have decided, during initial consultation, that this is a working relationship they are happy to engage in. However, occasionally, perhaps due to the difficulty of location and dearth of available supervisors, the therapist may engage to work with a supervisor from whom they withhold full authorisation. Also, in a training situation where supervisors may be provided without the student's consultation, a similar situation might occur. In such instances we see a lack of authorisation from below. In these cases authorisation must be earned by developing a relationship of trust and mutual respect.

Authority from within

Authority from within is something only the supervisor can give themselves. It is the ability to experience oneself as able to do the work without being undermined by attacking or denigrating inner voices. It depends on having a good-enough sense of self. It requires a particular relationship with internalised authority figures. This in turn originates from our experiences of external authority figures and the extent we have worked through whatever negative aspects of these may have taken up residence in our inner world.

If in this workshop I wanted to look at this in depth, I could take the image of the stack of chairs as representing authority in these three forms. It might be useful to explore, for example, the therapists' relationship to the authorising body. There may be ethical and practical questions which can be thought about through responding to the 'top' chair, to sitting on it, to sculpting it. Similarly the bottom chair can be used to explore the supervisor's relationship with his or her supervisee, or imagined potential supervisee, in terms of actual or fantasised giving or withholding of authorisation from below. The central chair can provide a very rich tool for working on the concept of authority from within as its relationship to the two other chairs can provide a starting point for self-awareness of each therapist's ability to feel good-enough about themselves in the role.

Sculpting the chairs: supervisor role projections explored

Whilst the stack can be used to highlight this formula of authority, it can also serve to look at authority which is projected and can be a way in which the task is disabled. This is the hierarchical notion of supervisor at the top and client at the bottom, with the therapist squashed somewhere in the middle. Elsewhere I have written of the unhelpfulness of the concept of hierarchy, which only encourages projections of superiority in relation to the supervisor from the therapist (Jenkyns 1996). This can leave the therapist maintaining a position of not-good-enoughness and even inadequacy. Challenging these projections is one thing, changing them takes time and work which can be provided by an in-depth supervisors' training course. But even in a workshop such as the one I am describing, such challenge provided by the use of the metaphor can produce real learning. Let us move to the next stage and see how sculpting the chairs can allow an opportunity to explore unhelpful dynamics and projections in the supervisory relationship. This technique can also highlight countertransference responses, which can be beneficial in understanding some of the processes at work in the triad.

Supervisor's countertransference

Training workshop example

A group member arranges the chairs in a way in which the client and therapist are close together and the supervisor some way off. She speaks to this sculpt saying she feels that this is how it is when she is working as a therapist, that she does not really think about the supervisor. Then she stands back and I invite her to get a sense of what her transference is to the supervisor. The picture she has created speaks to her and she realises that she has cast the supervisor in the role of an absent authority figure. She is amazed by what she has done and what it reveals to her. She comments that she needs to pay attention to issues of absence, as they occur in her work with her supervisee. As she looks at what she sculpted, she wonders if the supervisee sees her as absent. Suddenly she says, 'The client my supervisee is bringing at the moment had no father.' This enables me to open up a discussion on the client/therapist/supervisor triad, in terms of the light that the supervisor's countertransference can shed on the client's material. Again, the valency of the supervisor to certain dynamics can be used to enable her to be sensitive to an issue which may not be hers, in the work with the supervisee. She can then pick it up and explore where it might be located in the triad. This becomes available in the supervision to be thought about in relation to the client's issues and process.

From training workshop to supervision session

It is important in dramatherapy supervision training to pay attention to the way in which countertransference reactions of the supervisor can be of the utmost importance. It is equally important to be able to pay attention to the setting up of enactment, in such a way for it to safely maximise the unconscious processes of both therapist and supervisor.

There have been times when I have been asked by non-dramatherapist supervisors to 'be' my client. And I have frozen. I need preparation. I need the boundary of the enactment space, even if it is only a mark in the carpet, I need time to prepare myself for the role. Enactment in supervision can be very powerful, because the transferences are felt by taking on the role of the client. They occur as we embody the character of our client. They do not come through conversation but through embodiment, are felt on the pulse and along the blood. As she witnesses her therapist in role as client, the supervisor's countertransference is triggered. What can emerge here is a powerful feeling in the supervisor, which she can then think about in terms of where it might come from within the triad.

For example, the supervisee is sitting bowed in the designated enactment space of the supervision room. She says nothing. The supervisor may wait to see what emerges and then, if the silence continues, she may address the therapist, 'What do you feel X is feeling now, as you embody her?' Or she may address the client being embodied by her supervisee, herself taking the role of therapist. 'X, I wonder what you might be wanting me to know about, I can feel your sadness and it's really hard for you to speak to me at the moment.' She will chose one rather than the other, depending on what she feels will be most useful to her supervisee at that moment and in the context of the work they are doing together. By choosing the latter intervention, she takes the therapist more deeply into her identification with the client and, if she feels this will be most productive for the therapist, that is the intervention she might choose. So far, she is working to engage the therapist to discover more how the client impacts on her. The therapist's thoughts and feelings will then be available, to be reflected on by both therapist and supervisor. In the enactment the therapist will also be using her observing ego to monitor her way of role playing the client. She may come out of it saying, 'I realise when she's like that I feel really distanced from her, sometimes almost annoyed.' Or she may say, 'God, she's in such a terrible place at times like that, I don't think I'd realised the depth of her despair, I mean, I knew she was depressed but this felt more like despair.' Whatever these or other responses might mean to the therapist, they will be powerful transferences to the client. In other words, they are the therapist's countertransference, and as such they provide important material for the supervisor and therapist to engage with in the supervision session.

In this example the therapist's countertransference that was the focus. Let us look at another scenario in the same session. Let us go back to the moment when the supervisor intervenes and rewrite that. In an alternative scenario she decides to do nothing but wait. She finds herself getting uncomfortable and wanting to intervene. She decides to hold on and discover what she begins to feel. She also waits to see what happens to the therapist in the role play. She knows the therapist will come out of the enactment if she feels she needs to, according to the agreement between them about the use of enactment in the supervision. So she waits. The silence grows, the supervisor begins to feel it's unbearable, but still she hangs on. Eventually the 'client' bursts out with, 'And you just sit there, doing nothing!' The therapist comes out of role and says, 'I just wanted to burst into tears then.' The supervisor feels the cloud of pain she has been 'asked' to hold lift. Between them and the art form something has shifted quite profoundly.

What has happened is that, in staying with the process, the supervisor has deliberately invited her own countertransference into the work in an intensified way, by her engagement as witness in the theatre form. In doing so, she held the powerful painful feelings of the client that the therapist was identifying with. By holding these, the therapist-in-role found the client's voice for her anger. So the anger, the pain, the impotence and rejection are now all in the room, ready to be thought about by supervisor and supervisee.

I believe that this way of working is a very important teaching method in supervisor training, as it enable the trainees not to escape into their heads, but continue to educate their feeling selves as resources in supervision. Such work in training can be done, for example, by role playing supervisor and supervisee while other group members hold the boundary of the enactment space and use their own feeling responses to offer the role players. They can freeze the action and offer their responses. The role players can make use of these or not, as they wish, within the integrity of the roles they are playing and the relationship which has been built between them. It gives the 'supervisors' on the outside the chance to experience the power of the supervisory witness role in producing countertransference affect. This can then be used in the service of understanding the therapeutic work.

Drama as a transference phenomenon in dramatherapy supervision

Finally, I want to look at drama itself as a transference-inducing phenomenon. I suggest that this is an important area to think about, when engaging in training supervisors. Many of their supervisees will be dramatherapy students and therefore in a parallel process of being trainees themselves. The following case example involves a trainee dramatherapist. She has a client who trained as an actor. She has a supervisor who is a dramatherapist who has written about dramatherapy and been in the field for a long time. The trainee therapist projects her authority on to the supervisor. The student's background is less in drama than in the fields related to therapy, in which she has a lot of experience. She feels insecure about her ability to work in the dramatic mode, to use metaphor and be at home in aesthetic engagement. She feels insecure in the subroles a dramatherapist needs to use, especially that of director. She assumes that the supervisor 'knows' and she doesn't. Her transference to her supervisor serves to undermine her already shaky faith in her own ability as a dramatherapist. Much work has to be done in supervision to help her with this. This is not uncommon with trainees, but in this particular case there is another facet to the picture. The client is a woman who trained as an actor, has become depressed and has lost all faith in her own ability in her profession. The trainee therapist, however, because of her own lack of a professional drama background, is anxious that the client may know more than her about drama and feels inadequate. The supervisor's task is to help the therapist to realise that the client may feel inadequate and is doing exactly the same thing as the therapist is doing with the supervisor: the client may be projecting her dramatic ability on to the therapist who she assumes must 'know about drama' because she is a dramatherapist.

This chain of projection up the line becomes clear in the supervision, when the supervisor feels she is not helping the therapist and begins to feel inadequate. The relationships in the triad are all 'positive', there is no resistance on anyone's part of an obvious nature, but somehow the work begins to feel stuck. Gradually what begins to become apparent is that the issue of who is 'better at drama' has become the smokescreen for the client's fear of getting into the emotionally challenging material. The client's transference to the therapist produces in the therapist a feeling of inadequacy. It finds a valency in the therapist who fears she may be inadequate and thus her countertransference to the client is to feel afraid of not having the capacity to help her. She brings this still unconscious dynamic to supervision. The supervisor finds herself struggling to boost the therapist's confidence and withdraw her projections on to the supervisor as the one who knows about dramatherapy. She herself is beginning to feel inadequate because the therapy she is supervising seems to be getting stuck. It is only when she begins to examine her countertransference to her supervisee that the picture begins to be clearer and the defensive structure which the client has unconsciously set up be understood. At this point the therapy becomes unstuck and the client moves into looking at her early life in a way which begins to free her up; she gains confidence in her ability to re-enter the profession as the placement draws to a close. Everyone in the triadic relationship has found that their transference and countertransference reactions have tapped into the deeply inadequate early parenting of the client, which has left the client with incomplete mourning. This has contributed to the onset of depression and a self-image of 'not being any good'.

In this example the art form of drama itself, the theory and practice on which the therapy rests, has become a projective object for all the participants in the supervisory triad. Our own experiences and attitudes, our self-image as practitioners of the art form, our internalised objects which form that image must be attended to in our training of dramatherapy supervisors.

Conclusion

In this chapter I have attempted to highlight some of the areas in which the art form, drama, are essential elements in the training of dramatherapy supervisors in relation to transference and countertransference issues. In the training session one of the things I did was to model supervision practice. One aspect which relates to the use of the art form is that the supervisor needs to draw on one of the dramatherapist's subroles (Jenkyns 1996), namely that of director. The training session/supervision is also like a rehearsal. The principle explored in this chapter can be taken into other projective work with objects. It is important to create the theatre space, even if it is on a piece of paper to create a tiny stage for small objects. The supervisor can then have in mind the therapist, who is in the room with her, and the client who is offstage. The supervisor's role is not only as audience and witness, but also as director who is mindful of the ways in which the rehearsal can be enhanced. One of the ways in which she can exercise her role as director is by focusing, preparing and intensifying the task by attending to detail and slowing down the process. In the charged atmosphere of the 'theatre' of supervision, the projective work can yield a rich harvest. By being aware of her own feelings and transference responses – her countertransference – to the metaphoric work of the therapist, the supervisor has a route into the unconscious processes of the triad, which can then be thought about in the supervision session.

References

Brook, P. (1968) *The Empty Space*, Harmondsworth: Penguin.

Jenkyns, M. (1996) *The Play's the Thing: Exploring Text in Drama and Therapy*, London: Routledge.

Obholzer, A. and Zagier Roberts, V. (eds) (1994) *The Unconscious at Work: Individual and Organizational Stress in the Human Services*, London: Routledge.

Tselikas-Portmann, E. (ed.) (1999) *Supervision and Dramatherapy*, London: Jessica Kingsley Publishers.

Chapter 7

Intercultural supervision

The issue of choice

Ditty Dokter and Roshmi Khasnavis

Introduction

This chapter outlines some key definitions and theoretical frameworks relating to the idea and practice of intercultural supervision in dramatherapy. The chapter draws on a survey of UK dramatherapists' cultural backgrounds and on intercultural issues addressed in supervision (Dokter and Hughes 2007), on research into UK dramatherapy (Jones and Dokter 2008) and a small scale pilot project in a UK trust (Dokter 2006). We then discuss two case studies in depth, analysing the two triadic relationships of supervisor–supervisee–client (Brown and Landrum-Brown 1995) and client–therapist–arts form (Jones 2005) for the intercultural issues raised. The chapter concludes with recommendations for research and conceptual development for intercultural dynamics in dramatherapy supervision. Pseudonyms are used to protect client confidentiality.

Multicultural, cross-cultural and intercultural supervision are all terms employed to study the interaction between people of different cultural backgrounds in a supervision context. Each has a distinct difference in emphasis. 'Multicultural' alludes to the study and practice of supervision in, and for, different cultures. In an earlier study, Dokter researched how UK training impacted on southern European students who returned to their country to practise (Dokter 1993). This did not include an examination of the role of supervision, but found that understandings about the efficacy of dramatherapy as a psychological, functional, occupational or creative medium affected the therapist's being able to translate a UK training to a different national context and impacted on their ability to practise. The cultural preference for, and understanding of, the arts medium provided additional contrasts in perspective.

Multicultural perspectives on art therapy supervision are considered by Calisch (1998). She examines how cross-cultural dynamics impact on the supervisor, supervisee and client. She studies how differences in culture between supervisee, supervisor and client need to be addressed in supervision.

Cross-culturally relevant characteristics of the client, therapist and supervisor can be classified along three axes of difference (Calisch 1998):

1   Differences from the majority population.
2   Differences from one's cultural group – differences may be related to class, date of migration, rural or urban setting (Dokter 1998).
3   Differences in cultural background between the supervisor, supervisee and client.

These differences may create significant barriers to effective supervision, similar to factors that inhibit effective psychotherapy. These include: client anger, resistance and defensiveness, therapist defensiveness, therapist over-identification, supervisee resistance, poor therapist development, supervisor countertransference and supervisor patronisation (Atkinson *et al.* 1993). In the context of intercultural supervision, client anger and resistance related to past experiences of racism and discrimination may be particularly relevant. On the part of the therapist, similar experiences may result in overidentification. Supervisor patronisation can be in relation to the client and the supervisee, where cultural background differences may 'colour' the perception.

Supervision in this context is defined as the act of overseeing the development of therapeutic competence (Holloway 1992; Malchiodi and Riley 1996). As such, it fits the developmental model of supervision (van Ooijen 2000). The competence of the therapist has been researched. This is often defined and measured in terms of the years of experience post training. However, the role of supervision in the development of such competence has not been given equivalent attention (Roth and Fonagy 2005). Cultural competence of the (arts) therapist is considered an essential part of therapeutic competence (Calisch 1994; Sue and Sue 1999). As this literature tends to be American in origin, we would like to refer to the Health Professions Council (HPC) benchmark statement, which also stresses the importance of cultural competence for UK arts therapists (HPC 2005), but does not really define what cultural competence should consist of. The ability to engage with difference and to provide choices has been a cornerstone of intercultural therapy in the UK (Kareem and Littlewood 1992). Research into what constitues effective intercultural competence, though, has been hard to obtain (Lambert 2003).

'Cross-cultural supervision' refers to different cultural patterns of supervision and to supervision content, process and outcomes (Brown and Landrum-Brown 1995). Cross-cultural supervision here could refer to cross-discipline supervision. It can also refer to differences in expectations about the role of the supervisor as a 'teacher', provider of directive advice (Hanna 1990; Case 1998) or as a 'facilitator', a non-directive guide (Lahad 2000). Cross-cultural dynamics have been shown to affect therapeutic and educational relationships (Atkinson *et al.* 1993; Cattaneo 1994), again often in the levels of directiveness and reflexivity/initiative expected by and from both sides.

'Intercultural' (Kareem and Littlewood 1992) is a term more used in a UK therapy context. The term is chosen to indicate the interactive element in cultural dynamics between the different parties involved in therapy. At Nafsiyat, the London-based intercultural therapy centre, the emphasis is on client choice in the area of therapy, rather than client–therapist match (Moorhouse 1992); and on client and therapist learning from each other, rather than the therapist learning about different cultures (McGoldrick *et al.* 1996). The overriding issue in therapeutic cultural competence is the therapist's awareness of their own ethnocentric perspectives. This concerns both their personal perspective, and also the ethnocentricity inherent in their therapeutc modality and training. We will discuss this aspect of dramatherapy later in the chapter.

Culture in a UK context

Culture has been described as a system of social institutions, ideologies and values that characterises a particular social domain in its adaptation to the environment. It is often felt to be important that these traditions and beliefs are systematically transmitted to succeeding generations (Landau 1982). Kareem and Littlewood (1992) have argued that culture is not a bag of memories and survival techniques, but a dynamic recreation by each succeeding generation. It is a complex and shifting set of accommodations, resistances and reworkings.

Cultural differences refer to variations in attitudes, values and perceptual constructs that result from different cultural experiences (Zane *et al.* 2004). The study of cultural influences is the study of individual difference variables (Zane *et al.* 2004)). There can be confusion between the terms 'ethnicity' and 'culture'. Ethnic groups are those who conceive of themselves as alike by virtue of common ancestry, real or fictitious, and who are so recognised by others (McGoldrick 1996). They are sometimes grouped together under the term black and minority ethnic communities, and can include both visible and invisible differences. Language and religion, for example, can constitute invisible differences. It is interesting that the signs of visible difference have often received the greatest stigma. The ability to 'pass' for invisible minorities can be tempting but is often problematic in relation to identity orientation.

There are over two and a half million people in Great Britain who have origins in the new Commonwealth. Together with migrants from the Irish republic and mainland Europe, and their children, they comprise approximately 10 per cent of the UK population. The popular perception is that all immigrants are black. However, half of all black people are British born.

The majority of recent immigrants – partly due to immigration policies, the war in ex-Yugoslavia and the widening of the European Union to include former eastern bloc countries – have been white. Other factors involving migrant streams have been identified (Winder 2004).

For some time it has been known that to be black in Britain is to be exposed to a variety of adverse stimuli: the effects of migration on identity; the effects of discrimination and poverty, the loss of support networks and the effects of isolation. They can add up to a serious mental health hazard (Littlewood and Lipsedge 1997; Department of Health 1999). Resulting mental health problems are not simply a consequence of geographical and cultural dislocation, the adjustments and inevitable stresses of migration (Dokter 1998). The literature indicates that an important issue is the ongoing response of and to the white host society, its values and institutions (Kareem and Littlewood 1992).

Black researchers have critiqued ethnocentric assumptions about identity. Rattansi (1992) posits a continuum between *racism* and *ethnocentrism*. Racism defines groups of human populations into 'races' on the basis of some biological signifier, each race being regarded as having essential characteristics, or a certain essential character. Inferiorisation of 'races' may or may not be present within racism, where ethnic groups are primarily defined in cultural terms and are recognised as having essential traits. There is a tendency to view cultures from within the framework of one ethnic group (Rattansi 1992).

In the triadic relationship of supervisor, supervisee and client the experience of racism can influence the dynamic. It tends to arise early in the establishment of the therapeutic relationship, or resurface later to give expression to conflicts within that relationship. The issue of client choice of therapist, and therapist choice of client, can be ethically problematic if the choice is based on racism. The following case vignette described from the supervisee and supervisor perspectives illustrates this dynamic.

Case vignette: supervisee perspective

I was doing a six-week assessment of a 13-year-old girl, Annie, of white British ethnicity. She was a looked-after child, who had recently moved to a new foster family, where – due to various challenges in the relationships – the placement was in danger of breaking down. In Annie's first session she said that she hated her (white female) foster carer. She said that her carer was smelly, so smelly that she had to wind the window down every time they were in the car together. I enquired as to what smell she meant, to which she replied that it was like 'Indian people smell'. In that moment I felt quite frozen, unable to think creatively in the session and work with this material. Annie, seeing that I was clearly of Asian origin, then asked me where I came from, checked herself and said she knew I came from 'here', but where did my parents come from? I felt frozen, lacking in energy for most of the rest of that session.

Case vignette: supervisor perspective

This incident came to supervision, and as a supervisor I wondered how to work with it. As a first generation migrant I had been on the receiving end of similar remarks (Dokter 1998). The impulse was to purely point out the legal ramifications, the protection available to my supervisee not to have to tolerate this type of abuse. I could also side with my supervisee as belonging to a minority in relation to the abusive power of the majority, and so move in the supervision to look at how to empower ourselves. This strong countertransference alerted me to my responsibility towards the third party in the triad, the client. My professional experience had taught me that clients tended to react with offensive/defensive racism when they felt their identity was threatened. I chose to point out the legal protection available, but also pointed to the possibility that this would create a breakdown in the therapeutic relationship. Before deciding on any direction I thought it might be useful to try and understand what was happening in that relationship.

Case vignette: supervisee perspective (*continued*)

We broke down the meaning of the exchange for both me and for Annie. I knew that I had frozen because of the direct and offensive reference to my background, but how could I work with this? We thought through the element of smell, how a baby recognises its mum by its smell and how for this child the smell in the new home might smell different and new. Her reference to the smell of the carer could be her expression of feeling like a 'foreigner' in this home and perhaps her reference to my ethnicity could be a recognition of both our 'foreignness'. In the next session I brought this back to Annie and addressed the issue of the two of us feeling like a foreigner, an outsider in the home, and I helped her to identify this with people who came from foreign countries. In this way I was able to find a huge amount of empathy for her and work with her drawing on my own experience of being a foreigner.

Case vignette: supervisor perspective (*continued*)

The supervisor intervention helped to re-establish the therapeutic relationship and empowered the supervisee to empathise with the client. Later, both in the supervision and within the supervisee's therapy, we revisited this incident to think through the transference dynamic. We identified that Annie tried to break relationships before they could be established and she might become hurt by abandonment/rejection.

The ethics of whether to take a stance against racism by active invocation of legislation is complex. Policies impact on individual decisions and provide a legal framework of protection. My feeling is that it can be appropriate to invoke these if clients actively refuse to work with a member of staff on racist grounds, although the nature of personal responsibility can still be questionable in, for example, an acute psychiatric context. From a political perspective I wholeheartedly agree with immediately and directly challenging racism. From a therapeutic perspective I wish, in addition, to consider it by being aware of the interpersonal and intrapsychic perspectives within the therapeutic relationship. Blackwell (2004), in supervising therapeutic work with refugees, stresses working on four different levels for both supervisor, supervisee and client. These are political, cultural, interpersonal and intrapsychic levels. This model has proved very useful to me in the wider ramifications of working interculturally within supervision.

The personal and professional background of both supervisor and supervisee in this case example need to be taken into account in intercultural supervision. The supervisor describes herself as white Dutch, from a Calvinist Christian working-class background, and is a first generation migrant with English as a second language, who migrated alone aged 22. The supervisee describes herself as Indian Bengali/British Asian, Hindu Brahmin upper class and as a second generation migrant who migrated to the UK aged 11 with her family after an African/Singapore upbringing, with English as her first language. Both supervisor and supervisee are in mixed partnerships with white English partners. The implications of these mixed cultural backgrounds for identity are discussed elsewhere (Dokter 1998), but what both embody is the mixed cultural dynamics of being different from the general population, being different from others within the same cultural group, as well as from each other. The experiences of racism being brought into the supervision space by supervisor, supervisee and client contained factors that were both parallel and different. These included being from a visible and invisible minority, the experiences and values related to multiple migration versus single migration and class and religious differences. These themes, parallels and differences needed to be negotiated and thought through within the supervision. In the above case, the parallel experiences of alienation formed a useful connection to the client experience.

Both trained as therapists, the supervisor as dramatherapist and group analytic psychotherapist (whilst also being recognised by grandparenting clause as a dance movement therapist), the supervisee as integrative arts psychotherapist. The supervisee stated the following as criteria for selecting an appropriate supervisor: location, cross-cultural experience, core therapy practice experience within the arts, along with client experience in the NHS and with refugees.

For other discussions of cross-disciplinary supervision, see pp. 146–66

The differences in background between supervisee and supervisor need to be contextualised within the UK therapist population. There is limited data available about the cultural backgrounds of different therapists, whilst there is some evidence that client *choice* of therapist, not client–therapist cultural *match*, relates to the ability to establish a therapeutic alliance (Kareem and Littlewood 1992). The cultural complexity of the drama-therapy population in the UK was analysed as part of an equal oppor-tunities survey conducted by the British Association for Dramatherapists in 2007 and this will be discussed in the next section.

Cultural backgrounds of UK dramatherapists

An early establishment of a positive therapeutic alliance has been shown to be important in intercultural psychotherapy (Zane *et al.* 2004). A positive therapeutic alliance means an establishment of being able to work together between therapist and client. A positive alliance can be fostered by therapist empathy, warmth and understanding, perceived trustworthiness, experi-ence, confidence and an investment in the treatment relationship (Roth and Fonagy 2005). However, the impact of ethnicity is rarely examined as a mediating factor, as many researchers fail to capture the diversity of their resident population (Roth and Fonagy 2005).

At present there are no overall UK figures for dramatherapy clients. A small pilot project studied the cultural background of 58 newly referred clients for the year 2005–2006 in a dramatherapy department in an adult mental health trust in England (Dokter 2006). The 2001 UK National Census figures show that in the trust catchment area the black and minority ethnic (BME) population totals 11.2 per cent, of which 6.3 per cent is classified as non-white. Within the trust itself the ethnic breakdown of users is classified as 4 per cent ethnic minority and 91 per cent white British (Hertfordshire Partnership NHS Foundation Trust 2006). The background of the remaining 5 per cent is unclear. Even with that lack of clarity, the figures show an under use of trust services by BME clients. The dramatherapy department (three therapists) serves two cities where the percentage of non-white population is respectively 6.9 per cent and 4.6 per cent. However, if ethnic origin is to include Irish and 'White, other' categories (the latter often including recent refugees and migrants) the rates increase to 13.15 per cent and 8.3 per cent for the two cities. The more detailed demographic profile of the clients accessing the dramatherapy service in the two localities is:

- 'not known' (incomplete or not stated) for 12 out of 71 (16.9 per cent)
- 'white British' for 50 out of 71 (70.4 per cent)

- BME clients 9 out of 71 (12.7 per cent): 3 out of 71 'White, other' (4.2 per cent),
- 6 out of 71 (8.45 per cent) from Asian and Black African Caribbean backgrounds.

All therapists in the pilot study had female white majority identity; one white British, two white other. There are within the client and therapist group differences of nationality, religion, migration experience and language

The conclusion that could be drawn from this small pilot was that BME client rates are higher in dramatherapy than in the trust as a whole. Initial access to the service for BME clients is achieved, but the pilot indicated that the issue of attrition, whether they then stay, still needed to be addressed. Attrition rates tend to reflect the quality of cultural sensitivity and responsiveness of the service. The dramatherapy department's involvement of a higher percentage of BME clients than that of the trust population as a whole can be seen as a positive reflection on the department and the potential efficacy of dramatherapy. However, it was concluded that further research and comparison with the other trust departments who refer clients was needed. This would involve the consideration of whether cultural stereotyping in referral and assessment might play a role in referring clients to dramatherapy.

Potential threats to the validity of the findings of this pilot include the high non-appearance rates after referral: 19 out of 58 referrals never appeared for a first meeting. Out of the 19 clients who never came, 14 did not attend (DNA) any appointment and five declined assessment. How dramatherapy is perceived may influence whether a client accepts and attends an initial appointment. Unfamiliarity about dramatherapy, with the often expressed fantasy that they will be asked to 'get up and perform', may stop clients from attending. Once clients have made contact, the engagement improves. Of the four clients in the pilot study who dropped out after assessment, two moved out of the area and two initially declined, and then later accepted. More than half (10 out of 19) non-responding clients were young people (18–25 year olds). DNA rates in psychotherapy overall are a high 40 per cent, but this increases if the referrals are young people in comparison to adults. Initial refusal rates can be higher for certain therapies and client conditions (Roth and Fonagy 2005), especially for certain diagnoses.

The second threat to validity of the findings is the high non-completion rates for ethnic monitoring. NHS trusts are working on increasing ethnic monitoring in line with the National Services Framework and Race Relations (Amendment) Act (Department of Health 1999; Race Relations Amendment Act 2000), but the researchers found that in two trusts where research took place the figures for completion varied. An additional difficulty in analysing figures is the lack of clarity of terms and definitions used. Electronic record systems introduced in the NHS across the UK will make analysis of data more compatible, but still depend on the data being completed in the first place. Given that only 29.4 per cent of dramatherapists work in the NHS (Karkou and Sanderson 2006), the monitoring cannot rely on NHS systems alone. Karkou and Sanderson's research involved 40 per cent of arts therapists registered in the UK through their professional associations. Half of the sample were art therapists, only a fifth dramatherapists. The respondents' main working environments (many arts therapists work part time in a variety of settings) were the the health service (48.5 per cent), education (16.5 per cent), voluntary organisations (12.7 per cent), community settings (12 per cent), private practice (7.6 per cent) and 2.8 per cent in other settings. Given the mixture of employment settings and differences in recording systems, dramatherapists themselves need to take a more active role in ethnic monitoring, rather than depending on their employing context to do it for them.

In 2007 the Equal Opportunities Committee of the British Association of Dramatherapists (BADth) decided to survey all dramatherapists registered with BADth to analyse the diversity amongst dramatherapists (Dokter and Hughes 2007). The reasons for undertaking the survey were threefold:

- to test the hypothesis/stereotype that dramatherapists were mostly white, female, able-bodied, middle-class English, possibly with varied spiritual orientations and sexual orientations.
- to create a first step towards looking at dramatherapy training: is the background of dramatherapy trainees changing?
- to create a base for considering client/therapist match and access to dramatherapy for clients from varied backgrounds.

The response rate to the questionnaire was 60 per cent of a total of 450 dramatherapist registrants. The findings were that 75 per cent of dramatherapists describe themselves as white British, but 25 per cent of these were from first to third generation migrant origins. Half of these were from Irish backgrounds, while the other half was made up of a variety of European and mixed backgrounds. Only 5 per cent were from non-white backgrounds, with a variety of Asian, Latin American and Afro-Caribbean backgrounds. So, more dramatherapists have experience of migration than the general population, but a smaller percentage come from non-white backgrounds. The good news was that trainees are more ethnically diverse than qualified dramatherapists. The white British percentage here was 68 per cent, with 9 per cent coming from non-white backgrounds, of which 50 per cent were mixed. The white ethnic group of trainees showed similar within-group diversity to the qualified dramatherapists. However, the 7 per cent increase in mixed or non-white backgrounds shows the potential for a more diverse range of practitioners in the near future. Whether the greater range of dramatherapists who have experienced migration themselves within their family can create a greater empathy for others remains an area for research, as does the range of client backgrounds referred for dramatherapy.

Theoretical models used: cross-cultural adaptations

The different theoretical models we use as dramatherapists may blinker us. Karkou and Sanderson (2006) show that dramatherapists identify their theoretical orientations into humanistic, eclectic/integrative, artistic/creative, psychodynamic, developmental and active/directive. Some of the perspectives are derived from psychological theories, others from artistic ones. The ethnocentricity of dramatherapy perspectives are similar to those of other forms of psychotherapy and arts therapy.

The fields of psychology, counselling and art therapy increasingly recognise that members of various ethnic and cultural groups differ from each other in psychologically meaningful ways (Calisch 1998). These relate particularly to values and developmental or family experiences. The literature shows that three relationships in the supervisory process can be seriously affected by misperceptions and wrongly applied culturally specific knowledge and experience. Intercultural psychotherapy research shows that the following difference variables influence both within-group and between-group heterogeneity (Zane et al. 2004):

1   Country of origin.
2   Immigration history (voluntary/involuntary).
3   Place of residence (urban/rural).
4   Education level (both in UK and country of origin).
5   Motivation for leaving country of origin.
6   Acculturation level.
7   Socio-economic level.
8   English proficiency.
9   Ethnic identification.
10 Preferred language.

Calisch (1998) adds traditionality of interests and concerns, cultural values, mental ability, migration status, tribal identification and occupational and economic background both here and in the country of origin. She also stresses that to the extent that the supervisory triad members differ from each other on salient, between-group and within-group dimensions, they may encounter difficulties in identifying problems and goals for therapy and may encounter challenges to developing an effective working alliance. The dimensions mean that they can misunderstand each other's ways of understanding and interaction.

Given the ethnic (within-group) perspectives of psychotherapists/arts therapists, supervision is currently constructed to address characteristics most represented in the general population of therapists and supervisors (Brown and Landrum-Brown 1995). Quite a few models of supervision exist, but very few address cross-cultural issues (Loganbill *et al.* 1982). Models of supervision have paralleled the major schools of psychotherapy (Holloway 1992). As stated before, the main theoretical orientation cited by dramatherapists is humanistic and eclectic. Other less prevalent orientations are artistic/creative, psychodynamic, developmental and active/directive (Karkou and Sanderson 2006). The main orientations of the supervisors in the dramatherapy supervision survey (Jones and Dokter 2008) are psychodynamic, developmental and eclectic. Interculturally there are some difficulties to be considered within each of the theoretical models used.

Psychodynamic approaches see problems, in both content and process, as a function of intrapsychic rather than societal forces within the client (Atkinson *et al.* 1993; Brown and Landrum-Brown 1995). The goal of the supervision is to use the dynamics of the supervisor–supervisee relationship to 'work through' non-therapeutic patterns of relating to others (Russell *et al.* 1984). Too rigid a structure of interpretation and a lack of attention to societal influences can exclude the possibility of considering differing cultural perceptions. Humanistic orientations were identified by dramatherapists as their main therapeutic orientation (Karkou 2004; Karkou and Sanderson 2006), but not the main supervision orientation, which was psychodynamic (Jones and Dokter 2008). The use of confrontation or self-disclosure can provide difficulties cross-culturally (Sue 1990). There is also a lack of evidence that high levels of facilitative behaviour are linked to positive therapeutic outcomes (Russell *et al.* 1984).

Several dramatherapists describe both their own orientation (Karkou 2006) and that of their supervisors as eclectic (Jones and Dokter 2008). Eclectic, cross-theoretical models such as the social role model could be seen to be in line with Landy's (1997) dramatherapy approach to roles. They emphasise a set of roles for the supervisor that establish certain expectations and attitudes about what functions a supervisor will perform (Holloway 1992). The role model, however, does not consider the influence of between and within group cultural variables in shaping or mediating expectations or attitudes (Brown and Landrum-Brown 1995). The final theoretical orientation of dramatherapists and supervisors is the developmental model (Karkou and Sanderson 2006; Jones and Dokter 2008). This model presents clinical supervision as a process possessing sequential and qualitative distinct stages through which the supervisor and supervisee pass. Within dramatherapy there are also developmental practice models in use concerning expectations of developmental stages the client will pass through (Erikson 1963; Jennings 1994). A popular developmental supervision model within dramatherapy supervision training is that of Hawkins and Shohet (2000). Common to these notions is the assumption that novice therapists need more structure and instruction than experienced therapists.

The difficulty with this assumption cross-culturally is that cultural conflict and misunderstanding are most likely to occur in the earliest stages of the supervisory process. This can be exacerbated by the power differential between the supervior and supervisee as described by the models. Cultural oppression could be the result of a supervisor imposing their model/ assumptions on the supervision. Later stages of supervision are likely to include a more indoctrinated/acculturated supervisee, while the more collegial relationship between supervisor and supervisee tends to allow a more mutual growth experience (Brown and Landrum-Brown 1995).

An approach that allows for more mutuality and joint problem solving in the early supervisor–supervisee relationship can help overcome the ethnocentric assumptions of the theoretical psychotherapy and supervisory orientations. However, that still leaves the cultural differences of supervisor–supervisee–client to be addressed. One theoretical model used to provide a way of looking at these is the 'world view congruence model'.

The world view congruence model

A vessel to contain differences?

A useful way of construing the impact of differences is through the use of the 'world view congruence model'. World view is defined as the way an individual perceives his or her relationship to the world (Sue 1990). The concept of world view is used to explain how different individuals and cultural groups tend to experience the world in different ways. The concept of world view has been used by researchers (Myers 1991) to discuss how interpersonal conflicts are often a result of conflicts on eight world view dimensions:

- psychobehavioral modality
- aciology
- ontology
- ethos
- epistemology
- logic
- concept of time
- concept of self.

Brown and Landrum-Brown (1995) define this as world view incongruence.

World view conflicts within the supervisor–supervisee–client relationship may result in distrust, hostility and resistance (Calisch 1998). Their world views can be different, and this need not be problematic as long as the supervisor and supervisee are aware of the ways in which world view differences can disrupt the supervision and therapy process. Awareness and knowledge of such issues are a beginning in this way of working, and an assessment of world views is seen as a crucial part of the process. Calisch

(1998) recommends the use of art to explore the unconscious dynamic of one's own as well as the other's world view. Cohn (1997) advocates a body movement based approach. Most of these approaches have been applied in a training context: their use in a supervision context could be usefully explored.

In the following case vignettes the supervisor's style is predominantly verbal, with some inclusion of projective sculpting and embodiment. The intercultural aspects of the arts forms are not included in the context of this chapter, but are discussed elsewhere (Dokter 2000, 2007). The use of the arts form is however considered, as well as the triadic world view differences in the following two case vignettes.

Case vignette: supervisee perspective

Naila was referred to me in March 2003. I was told by her GP that she was a refugee from a north east African country. I later discovered she did not have refugee status and her period of leave to remain in the UK expired whilst we were working together. She was referred with depression and eating problems – she experienced pains in her stomach and ate very little. The first thing Naila said to me was that she did not know who I was and why she was coming. This became a metaphor for much of her migration experience.

Naila had fairly good spoken English – though at times in the sessions she struggled to express herself fully. Naila had been sent away from her home in Somalia in 2001, aged 21. Prior to her leaving, her father had been killed by intruders in their home. Naila told me that the intruders had wanted her – and her father was killed trying to protect her. It later transpired that this was her stepfather, her birth father lived in a country further south and was Asian/Indian by origin. Her mother had not been accepted by her father's family, and they had said that they did not want 'black' children in the family. They had separated and her mother had remarried. Naila told me that even in her community in the UK she was an outsider and people did not believe she was really 'one of them' until she spoke to them in their own language. Her skin tone was more Asian than African, and she said she felt that she looked different. The issues of race, colour, culture, community and identity were therefore a key part of working with this client.

Prior to her coming to the UK Naila had never been outside her immediate neighbourhood in a small village. When she was sent away, she had never seen the world outside this neighbourhood and had no idea what to expect. She said that a friend of the family had taken her by foot to a town a long way away – she did not know the name of the town. She had then got on a bus or coach. The rest of her journey is very hazy and I never made the connection between her leaving that town and ending up in a large city in the UK, nor how long that journey took. She said that there were some family friends who had met her here. When she arrived, she had no money and no English.

Naila had left behind her mother, her older sister and her younger brother. She told me that normally it was the boys who would get sent away to make a life for themselves, but that her brother was too young for this. She said that again normally the oldest child would be sent away, but her sister suffered from high blood pressure and diabetes so her family had not wanted to take that risk. Naila said she missed her family terribly and cried herself to sleep every night thinking of them. A big part of this was the guilt of being the one to have 'escaped', when in other circumstances it would not have been her.

Naila had attended college and very quickly picked up English. Her guilt motivated her to make the most of the opportunity she had been given. At the time I met her, she held down a college computer course, and two part-time jobs cleaning offices. In the time that I knew her, she was promoted from cleaner to being a cleaning supervisor, the youngest person in that company to have held a supervisory position.

In 2002, Naila's mother died under unknown circumstances. She heard the news from her older sister who still lived in her birth country. Naila had been very close to her mother, and became very depressed following her death. It seems that this was the trigger for her being referred to me. When I first began to work with Naila, I worked with the incorrect assumption (based on work with other clients from her country) that her issues and depression were a result of the traumatic events prior to her migration, and possible trauma around her journey. I was soon to realise that Naila's difficulties were around belonging and identity and that the traumatic experiences were secondary.

With reflection in supervision I was able to put Naila's plight into context. In particular, my supervisor and I thought about how Naila's original mixture of cultures was based on a group identity, and she struggled to come to terms with her now individual identity. This then also became my plight in the therapy, as I struggled to use a Eurocentric, and therefore individualistic psychotherapy, to address the group identity world view of my client. At first I offered Naila various contacts for community groups in the local and surrounding area, thinking that this would help with her feelings of belonging. However, Naila fed back to me that even within this community she was an outsider. In supervision I was challenged to think about my own countertransference with this client. I realised how much she reminded me of myself at that age – in particular the elements of loss of family, loss of identity, loss of language and loss of culture. I realised the potential to become very protective towards this client. There were similarities in our original cultures and we both recognised this about each other. I then had to be very careful with striking a balance between being empathic, but not colluding.

At the same time, I also was aware of the bereavement issue around her mother and the impact of her loss of culture on her mourning and grieving process. In supervision I began to think about rites of passage, and how Naila seemed to be quite stuck without these rituals. It was coming up to the first anniversary of her mother's death and I discussed with my client how she would have honoured this if she had been back with her family. Naila said that the one year anniversary was an important one and explained a ritual that involved the whole family, fasting, followed by feasting and prayers. She told me that she would not be able to do this alone, and I took this opportunity to ask her whether she would like me to do this with her. She seemed to brighten up at this idea, although it also made her giggle, which I later discovered was her imagining me kneeling on a prayer mat trying to repeat her prayers in a language I did not speak. We discussed the ritual thoroughly, and when I was clear that this would be felt to be permissable and appropriate for Naila, we made arrangements to have a session on that day and go through the ritual. We each agreed on who would bring what.

On the day of the anniversary, Naila came looking a little more worried than normal. I asked her how she was feeling, and she said that she did not want to do the ritual. When I explored this with her she explained that she was having her period, and that a woman is not supposed to take part in any sort of religious ceremony during her period. Interestingly, I recalled this 'rule' from my own cultural upbringing where I had been excluded from ceremonies for this reason. I felt very torn between wanting to honour her mother and wanting to remain sensitive to her cultural beliefs, a feeling very familiar to me from my own past. We began to explore how this felt for her, and in this exploration she suddenly said that she wanted to do the ritual, but without the prayers. She said she wanted to say some words instead of a prayer – it was a particular phrase that she recalled from her childhood. She taught this to me, and we both engaged in the ritual we had agreed. My pronunciation made her laugh. We looked at the one photo of her mum that she had managed to hold on to, and we thought about Naila's memories of her. We shared the painting of a picture together, and then shared some fruit and drink.

Naila had said to me that she did not cook for herself and hardly ate. She often survived on a bowl of rice a day, and had experienced stomach pains and nausea which seemed to have no clinical medical ground. As we shared the fruit that session, she told me that in her culture there is a saying: 'When you eat alone, you eat with the devil.' I reflected later in supervision about her eating problems, her group identity and her denied rites of passage, and thought about how these were so interlinked. Her fasting during the rite of passage ceremony could not be broken when there was nobody to share the feast with. She had become stuck in a very isolated, lonely place. She had adapted practically to life in the UK by learning the language and sorting out work and housing, but psychologically she struggled every day with the messages from her past and the reality of her present.

This session became quite a turning point for Naila. Although she continued to experience difficulties with her Home Office status, and although she continued to miss her siblings, she seemed somehow lighter in herself. She took some steps to travel further to places where she knew that some friends of her family lived. She began to go there frequently to attend a mosque.

Supervisee reflections on arts form and triadic world view (in)congruence

The use of arts with this client reflected the struggle with individual versus group identity. Using the art form as ritual became a key part of the therapy, where using arts in themselves was, at the beginning, problematic. The client seemed embarrassed or self-conscious making images, but responded well to the two of us making images together. So, being watched in the creative process was inhibiting to the client, whereas co-creation was acceptable and useful.

Therefore, by embracing this group identity and using the arts as a co-created ritual, the client and I were able to move through some key stages of life, working with rites of passage through bereavement, identity and womanhood. In Naila's final image, which showed her journey from home to the UK, she made a time line depicting herself as a child at one end, and a woman at the other. She put an aeroplane in the centre and told me she had grown up in nine hours (the length of her flight). This reflected for me the therapeutic journey in which we had worked together on 'growing up'.

Power dynamics and world view in triadic relationship

The interconnected themes of power and shame run strongly in intercultural work. My experience as an Asian supervisee going to a white supervisor is that in the beginning I perceived the supervisor as an 'expert' who would judge whether I was right or wrong. This was in large part based in my original family culture, where the experience of being foreign and non-white was linked with shame and inferiority in the context of the white majority. This message is activated strongly in a potentially power relationship such as supervisor and supervisee, and also that of therapist–client. In the case of Naila, this dynamic was played out in the sessions by the perception of myself as the 'expert'.

Case vignette: supervisor perspective

It was interesting to note that in her choice of a supervisor the supervisee had been quite persistent in identifying an 'expert' supervisor, in this case defined by having published on intercultural arts therapies work. I was a novice in supervising a client from this particular background. The supervisee worked in an area where this community was very prevalent, while my experience was conducted in a different location. This meant I had to ask my supervisee for 'expert' details, which in turn empowered her to realise that she was able to be her own expert. This seemed a mirror to the supervisee being inducted by her client into the ritual, values and language of her background. The differences in background were acknowledged and could thus be empowering, leading to mutual exchanges of the role of 'expert'.

Conclusion

The subtitle of this chapter was the issue of choice, because we feel that ideally a therapist, client and supervisor should be given choices in who they work with. We are very aware that choice tends to be restricted by resources. Those resources can be financial, but can also be location related. The issue of choice, or the lack of it, may still be an important issue to address in the early stages of a therapeutic and supervisory relationship, because it identifies some of the expectations influencing the power dynamic. Interculturally, we have some choices open to us as to how we identify ourselves. The difference in how others identify us tends to create tensions, both within the individual and in their relationships with others. If, as therapists and supervisors, those differences in perceptions and expectations can be addressed, we may have introduced the concept of choice, even if there are limitations in the actual choices we can provide.

References

Atkinson, D.R., Morten, G. and Sue, D.W. (1993) *Counselling American Minorities: A Cross Cultural Perspective*, Madison WI: Brown and Benchmark.

Blackwell, D. (2004) *Counselling and Psychotherapy with Refugees*, London: Jessica Kingsley Publishers.

Brown, M.T. and Landrum-Brown, J. (1995) Counselor supervision: cross-cultural perspectives, in J.G. Ponterotto, L. Suzuki, J. Casas and C. Alexander (eds) *Handbook of Multicultural Counseling*, London: Sage.

Calisch, A.C. (1994) The metatherapy of supervision using art with transference/countertransference phenomena, *The Clinical Supervisor* 12: 119–27.

Calisch, A.C. (1998) Multicultural perspectives in art therapy supervision, in A.R. Hiscox and A.C. Calisch (eds) *Tapestry of Cultural Issues in Art Therapy*, London: Jessica Kingsley Publishers.

Case, C. (1998) Reaching for the peak: art therapy in Hong Kong, in D. Dokter (ed.) *Arts Therapists, Refugees and Migrants*, London: Jessica Kingsley Publishers.

Cattaneo, M. (1994) Addressing culture and values in the training of art therapists, *Journal of Americal Art Therapy Association* 11: 184–87.

Cohn, K. (1997) Movement therapy as a bridge to the biculturalism of Ethiopians to Israel, *Arts in Psychotherapy* 24, 3: 281–89.

Department of Health (1999) *National Service Framework for Mental Health: Modern Standards and Service Models*. Online. Available HTTP: <http://www.dh.gov.uk> (accessed 15 July 2007).

Dokter, D. (1993) Dramatherapy across Europe – cultural contradictions, in H. Payne (ed.) *Handbook of Inquiry in the Arts Therapies*, London: Jessica Kingsley Publishers.

Dokter, D. (1998) Being a migrant, working with migrants, in D. Dokter (ed.) *Arts Therapists, Refugees and Migrants*, London: Jessica Kingsley Publishers.

Dokter, D. (2000) Intercultural arts therapies practice – the issue of language, in D. Dokter (ed.) *EXILE: Refugees and the Arts Therapies*, Hatfield: University of Hertfordshire Press.

Dokter, D. (2006) Samen over de drempel: BME access to dramatherapy, University of Nottingham, British Association for Dramatherapists National Conference keynote paper, unpublished.

Dokter, D. (2007) Cultural variables affecting client–therapist consonance in their perception of arts therapies group treatment, PhD thesis, University of Hertfordshire, Hatfield.

Dokter, D. and Hughes, P. (2007) *Analysis of Drama Therapy Equal Opportunities Survey*. Online. Available HTTP: <http://www.badth.org.uk> (accessed 15 July 2007).

Erikson E.H. (1963) *Childhood and Society*, New York: Norton.

Hanna, J. (1990) Anthropological perspectives for dance and movement therapy, *American Journal of Dance Therapy* 12, 2: 115–21.

Hawkins, P. and Shohet, R. (2000) *Supervision in the Helping Professions*, 2nd edn, Maidenhead: Open University Press.

Health Professions Council (HPC, 2005) Arts therapies benchmark statement. www.hpc.org.uk, accessed December 4 2007.

Hertfordshire Partnership NHS Foundation Trust (2006) Service Users Survey.

Holloway, E.L. (1992) Supervision: a way of teaching and learning, in S.D. Brown and R.W. Lent (eds) *Handbook of Counselling Psychology*, New York: Wiley.

Jennings, S. (1994) The theatre of healing, in S. Jennings, A. Cattanach, S. Mitchell, A. Chesner and B. Meldrum (eds) *Handbook of Dramatherapy*, London: Routledge.

Jones P. (2005) *The Arts Therapies: A Revolution in Health Care*, London: Routledge.

Jones, P. and Dokter, D. (BADth, 2008) *British Association of Dramatherapists Supervision Research Findings*, Cheltenham: British Association of Dramatherapists.

Kareem, J. and Littlewood, R. (eds) (1992) *Intercultural Psychotherapy: Themes and Interpretations*, Oxford: Blackwell.

Karkou, V. and Sanderson, P. (2006) *The Arts Therapies: A Research Based Map of the Field*, Amsterdam: Elsevier.

Lahad, M. (2000) *Creative Supervision*, London: Jessica Kingsley Publishers.

Lambert, M.J. (ed.) (2003) *Bergin and Garfield's Handbook of Psychotherapy and Behaviour Change*, 5th edn, New York: Wiley.

Landau, J. (1982) Therapy with families in cultural transition, in M. McGoldrick, J.

Giordano and J.K. Pearce, *Ethnicity and Family Therapy*, New York: Guilford Press.

Landy, R. (1997) Dramatherapy in Taiwan, *Arts in Psychotherapy* 24, 2: 159–72.

Littlewood, R. and Lipsedge, M. (1997) *Aliens and Alienists*, Harmondsworth: Penguin.

Loganbill, C., Hardy, E. and Delworth, U. (1982) Supervision: a conceptual model, *Counseling Psychologist* 10: 3–42.

McGoldrick, M., Giordano, J. and Pearce, J.K. (1996) *Ethnicity and Family Therapy*, 2nd edn, New York: Guilford Press.

Malchiodi, C. and Riley, S. (1996) *Supervision and Related Issues: A Handbook for Professionals*, Chicago: Magnolia Street Publishers.

Moorhouse, S. (1992) Quantitative research in intercultural therapy: some methodological considerations, in J. Kareen and R. Littlewood (eds) *Intercultural Therapy*, Oxford: Blackwell.

Myers, L.J. (1991) Expanding the psychology of knowledge optimally: the importance of cultural difference, in R.L. Jones (ed.) *Black Psychology*, Berkeley CA: Cobb and Henly.

Rattansi, A. (1992) Racism, culture and education, in J. Donald and R. Rattansi (eds) *Race, Culture and Difference*, London: Sage and Open University Press.

Roth, A. and Fonagy, P. (2005) *What Works for Whom? A Critical Review of Psychotherapy Research*, New York: Guilford Press.

Russell, R.K., Crimmings, A.M. and Lent, R.W. (1984) Counselor training and supervision: theory and research, in S.D. Brown and R.W. Lent (eds) *Handbook of Counseling Psychology*, New York: Wiley.

Sue, D.W. (1990) Culture specific strategies in counselling: a conceptual framework, *Professional Psychology: Research and Practice* 21: 423–33.

Sue, D.W. and Sue, D. (1999) *Counselling the Culturally Different: Theory and Practice*, 3rd edn, New York: Wiley.

van Ooijen, E. (2000) *Clinical Supervision: A Practical Guide*, London: Churchill.

Winder, R. (2004) *Bloody Foreigners: The Story of Immigration to Britiain*, London: Little, Brown.

Zane, N., Hall, G.C.N., Sue, S., Young, K. and Nunez, J. (2004) Research on psychotherapy with culturally diverse populations, in M.J. Lambert (ed.) *Bergin and Garfield's Handbook of Psychotherapy and Behaviour Change*, 5th edn, New York: Wiley.

Chapter 8

Using psychodrama and dramatherapy methods in supervising dramatherapy practicum students

Adam Blatner and Judith Glass Collins

Introduction

Methods derived from psychodrama and dramatherapy offer useful peda-gogical tools for experiential education, especially in the supervision of postgraduate students and interns in the fields of dramatherapy or expressive arts therapy in their practicum or training placement settings (VanderMay and Peak 1980; Williams 1995; Wooding 2003). The insights gained through such approaches involve personal as well as professional aspects of role development. This chapter presents a number of such techniques, the rationale for their use, and examples of their application.

The practicum, or placement, is the equivalent of some of the courses for senior medical students in which they are engaged in closely supervised clinical practice, somewhat similar to what used to be called the medical 'internship'. Practicum programmes are also part of the overall training of students in dramatherapy, creative arts therapies and the expressive arts therapies. It is an on-the-job experience, counting as a course, which offers opportunities to students to practically apply what they have learned. Practicum experiences may be in undergraduate or graduate programmes, or postgraduate internships. The process of supervision involves a review of clinical work being done by students during their practicum. Indeed, many types of helping professionals often make use of group supervision sessions for themselves during the first few years of their practice, and supervisors of such groups may find the techniques described here useful.

For other discussions of supervision in training placements, see pp. 68–82

Generally, the supervisor gets feedback from other staff members (i.e. social workers, psychologists, unit managers), or the dramatherapist or expressive or creative arts therapist on staff where the practicum student is placed. This is then integrated with the students' own reports of their experience and concerns. The focus of this chapter will be on how psycho-dramatic and dramatherapeutic methods can facilitate the process of supervision for practicum students specialising in counselling psychology using creative arts modalities, as well as for other students of psycho-therapy or counselling.

The first principle to note is that the creative and expressive arts therapies (i.e. drama therapy, art therapy, music therapy, poetry therapy, dance movement therapy), psychodrama, and/or any other approach should be understood as operating within a broader context of psychotherapy in general. That context in turn needs to be viewed within the even broader and continually developing understanding of psychology, psychopathology, and other approaches to healing, including the use of medications, for example (Blatner 2007b). Thus, the techniques of a particular modality (such as dramatherapy or psychodrama) alone should not be thought of as consti-tuting a comprehensive approach – nor can any other single school of thought suffice. What is really important is the cultivation of the good judgement and broad perspective of the therapist. There are many opera-tions in therapy that are basic skills in psychotherapy, such as certain interviewing and diagnostic skills, the art of encouragement, and so forth. Psychodrama too is a complex of concepts and techniques that are powerful, but these should be recognised as simply tools – tools that can be used well or misused, depending on the skill and judgement of the practitioner (Blatner 2000). The goal, therefore, is not merely acquiring knowledge of technique, but more, understanding of the deeper principles of therapy and supervision in general which guide their use.

For other discussions of the relationship between dramatherapy and other disciplines, see pp. 71 and 130–44

Differences and similarities between psychodrama and dramatherapy

Dramatherapy involves the use of theatre arts as a vehicle for healing. Its roots come from a variety of sources, including experimental theatre, hos-pital theatre (i.e. theatre used as recreation for the institutionalised), occupational therapy, which employed dramatic skits and scripted theatre, and of course traditional theatre. Another important source of ideas and methods has been the field of drama in education (Courtney 1974; Slade 1981; Landy 1983). Beginning in the 1960s, dramatherapy began to inter-mix increasing elements of improvisation and psychodrama, and Johnson (2000) notes that Moreno's approaches constitute a significant foundation for dramatherapy practice today.

Psychodrama was developed in the mid-1930s by J. L. Moreno, MD (1889–1974) as a method of psychotherapy – originally to be used mainly in group settings or as part of a milieu treatment in psychiatric hospitals, but later also adapted for use with families or even one-to-one therapy (Blatner 2007a). It became an approach used as an extension of psychotherapy, by professionals who were first psychotherapists, and then added psychodrama to their work as an approach, analogous to the way some psychotherapists subspecialise in psychoanalysis or Jung's analytical psychology. Interestingly, non-clinical applications emerged also, with books being written about psychodrama's application – in the form of role playing – in education or business, as well as other settings.

In the last two decades, psychodramatists have, in turn, used some techniques and ideas that originated in dramatherapy, such as the use of masks, rituals, involving more integrations with other creative arts therapies. Increasing numbers of professionals have had training in both dramatherapy and psychodrama approaches and members of the two professional organisations attend each other's conferences.

Other than the differences in the history of the two modalities, psychodrama, in practice, generally does not use 'distanced' role playing – i.e. people playing the role of characters who are not part of their own actual experience – while dramatherapy often uses this vehicle, especially for clients or patients who aren't prepared to fully own their issues in a group setting. Dramatherapists in general have had experience as theatre artists who then turn the potential of theatre toward the service of healing, while psychodramatists in general have a background in psychotherapy and secondarily learn to use dramatic contexts and techniques as aids in their work (Blatner 1994).

Drama as story in supervision

One pitfall in supervision with students is that they are trying to integrate what they have been learning about psychology, and that tends to involve the mastery of a large number of abstract terms, diagnostic categories and professional jargon. Alas, this mode of language is both necessary and yet of limited value, and at the stage of practical application, working with patients and clients, jargon can obscure rather than clarify the situation. Part of this is a product of the widespread acceptance of the official diagnoses, as if such terms really had implications for differential therapeutics – i.e. decisions as to how one might treat a person differently because of a shift in the nature of the disorder implied by the label. Admittedly, in a few conditions, such as making a differentiation between schizophrenia and bipolar disorder, the process of carefully noting the elements in the diagnostic manual is helpful. On the other hand, in the most common general categories of anxiety and depression, for example, it is more important to think about patients in terms of their actual psychological and socio-cultural dynamics – or, in a more concrete fashion, thinking and working with patients regarding the stories of their lives. Interestingly, both drama-therapy and psychodrama share a type of terminology – speaking in terms of the roles people play (i.e. applied role theory), and this approach further brings out the stories, the dramas of people's predicaments.

There are few generalisations that can be made about almost any diagnostic category – the individual variables involved in a person's life far outweigh the oversimplification of the official diagnoses (Blatner 2004). So the first job of a supervisor is to help students let go of thinking that there are certain ways to work with this or that diagnostic category. Instead, a supervisor can help the new clinician identify the problem more concretely and position that problem in terms of the unique story of the patient's life.

For other discussions of diagnosis, see pp. 40–1

Enacting projective techniques

Many of the dramatherapy techniques used in supervision with students not only lead to insight and development of their professional skills, but also become part of the repertoire of methods they may use with their clients (Haas and Moreno 1951). One type of technique that illuminates certain issues in supervision involves the integration of other materials as objects of imaginative projection. This is a significant principle in the use of many of the other arts therapies methods. For example, pictures, objects and other ambiguous figures can serve as the bases for a kind of projective test that are less abstract than the well-known Rorschach ink-blot test, but drawing on the psychological dynamic. Therapists have presented clients with cut-out pictures from magazines. People have used postcards, tarot cards, selection of miniature figures from a larger collection, toys, scarves or pieces of fabric. The individual chooses a few out of the larger number that seem to be of some significance. Such evocative items can be used to elicit in-depth material from students in a way that is non-threatening. Regarding supervision, these projective materials can offer images that represent both the supervisory process and feelings about work with the clients (Wooding 2003).

Vignette: notions of 'hospital'

As an example, in a first supervision session with psychology practicum students working on a medical unit, the notion of *hospital* was explored. The students were initially asked to draw (with pastels, watercolours, markers and/or crayons) an image that represented *hospital* to them. After the drawings were completed, the students were asked if there was an image (or even just an element of an image) in their own drawing with which they would be willing to embody, taking that role. Students were also asked to *double* the image (i.e. act as if the image, whether of a person, animal, or inanimate object, had feelings and thoughts that the student expressed out loud). After *role reversing with the image* by initially taking the role of the image, and then *doubling the image*, the student chose someone to *mirror the image*. The purpose of this exercise was to encourage the students to concretise their feelings and thoughts regarding the concept of hospital and explore what might be underneath their initial impressions of this particular hospital in which they found themselves. This was also a way of uncovering past experiences with hospitals or hospital personnel. The mirroring of the image by another gave the student insight into non-verbal communications elements that might not be conscious. By acknowledging, sharing and becoming their perceptions and biases, interns could begin expanding their perspectives – in a sense increase their role repertoire as new hospital employees. Here, techniques of concretisation through drawing, diagrams and art allow the externalised images to evoke other associations, and the process is used in terms of bringing transferences or shadow work into consciousness.

Vignette: feedback on supervision and practicum

In a later session (with this same group) a 'new' student was joining the group. The supervisor took this opportunity to gather feedback about supervision in a creative way. The supervisor brought three sets of cards to the sessions and laid them out on tables – a set of tarot cards, a set of cards depicting various animals, and a set of cards depicting figures from mythology. The students were asked two questions: (1) What card represents your *expectations* of supervision? (2) What card represents your *concerns* about supervision?

   The students chose cards that represented their general concerns as beginning therapists, their continued ambivalence about working in a medical facility, and their concerns about competition among themselves in the group. Some students spoke about the images; others chose to embody the images. The 'images' served as 'masks', revealing charged material, but in a contained, humourous and comfortably distanced way.

   Students in a case seminar kept referring to their practicum experience as 'being in the trenches' or 'being in the thick of it'. Using surplus reality, the instructor asked each student to stage and enact what 'being in the thick of it' looked like, felt like, sounded like and smelled like (taste could also be a used sense), using the other members of the group. Afterwards, participants shared what it felt like to be in the various roles, and also what came up for them personally.

Vignette: addressing self-expectation

Inexperienced practitioners often feel unduly vulnerable about their beginner role (Brightman 1984). It is as if their 'inner disciplinarian' uses the very common, but ultimately meaningless, reproach: 'You should have known this by now!' It is useful to bring this issue into explicit awareness as a problem for students. For example, in a group supervision session with the practicum students working at the same hospital mentioned in the above examples, roles were evoked regarding their newness on the hospital unit. The role of door-to-door salesman came up in reference to trying to coax hospitalised patients to come to group. The supervisor asked for a counter role to the image of salesman. The image of some kind of Wise One who allows for patients to come to his or her sacred space was explored. Mediator roles were then discussed as 'in-between' the salesman and the Wise One. Working with roles is, of course, a cornerstone for both psychodrama and dramatherapy. The concept of role, counter-role and guide (as a mediator between the first two roles) is a construct elaborated by Landy (1993, 2007) in his 'role method of drama therapy'.

In a third supervision session, practicum students on a medical unit referred to their experience on the unit as 'being on the moon'. The supervisor directed them to improvise on this theme, taking the role of aliens who had never seen people in wheelchairs or people in white coats or bedpans. The supervisor played as well, steering the play toward amplifying feelings toward the strangeness of the unit. In this way, surplus reality was employed to vent feelings of inadequacy and helplessness at being non-medical people on the unit. (Surplus reality is the term given by Moreno to describe the objectification of the imagined experience in drama.) The playing with the metaphor also helped to poke fun at the students' attitude that they had to immediately have the answers for their patients and also feel comfortable right away in a new situation.

Out of this role play or group psychodrama, evolved the role of the inner critic who judged the students' performance much more harshly than supervisors or other staff. Each student as well as the supervisor (role modelling both self-disclosure and continually remaining in the role of learner about the self) put out three empty chairs and role played in turn the following roles: the critic; the antidote to the critic; and a mediator between the two roles. What became apparent is that the opposite of the critic was often a role that is as detrimental in its passivity as the critic role is in its aggression. The mediator role served as a kind of couples counsellor between the other two roles, urging the driven role to make friends with the role that wanted to continually rest or vegetate. The passive role needed to thank the driven one for getting the student out of bed in the morning and helping structure activities that need to get done. Of course, this is reminiscent of the enduring psychoanalytic concept of id, ego and superego – but put into action.

In another supervision group, a theme was introduced around how peers and supervisor felt towards the complaining of students. The supervisor introduced an exercise in which each group member in the supervision group stood outside the circle of the group and did a soliloquy, describing that person's idea of how the group perceived the student. Afterwards, each peer and supervisor spoke about the accuracy of the students' perceptions. This action feedback made clear the students' fantasies about how they were being perceived, and helped them be more realistic and less harsh about their performance as beginning therapists. This exercise was less threatening to the participants than standing behind each person in the group and doubling (speaking the 'unspoken') what each member felt about each other.

For other discussions of the internal supervisor, see pp. 60–1 and 74–5

Role training and role playing

One of the components of the role of a dramatherapist (or any other creative arts therapist) is selling the method and oneself to other professionals, potential employers and clients. The image of therapy as primarily a process of verbal interchange – simply talking – is not as threatening as having to get up and involve the whole body in action. Both therapists and patients experience drama as threatening, so how can it be presented in a more engaging fashion? Training students to address this challenge can employ psychodramatic methods. For example, in a supervision group with dramatherapy students engaged in the practicum programmes at hospitals or mental health agencies, a role training session evolved in which the students were asked to image an individual (or individuals) whom they worked with in empty chairs, and explain to them what dramatherapy is and how it is therapeutic. This exercise was a result of a discussion about how dramatherapy interns felt intimidated by other staff who were not creative arts therapists and often did not understand the goals of dramatherapy. The supervisor then mirrored the explanations of the students, who were then able to role reverse with the staff who are not dramatherapists. The discussion after this role training session revolved around how in-services could be arranged and structured at the different sites to further illustrate the effectiveness of dramatherapy and other action methods.

Another problem that surfaced was how to warm up clients or patients to experiential work, particularly in groups. The supervisor took the role of a patient resistant to coming to group, and the students took turns role playing strategies to entice the patient to come to group. Just as students had previously practised (via role training) how to introduce action methods to staff, students rehearsed a 'rap' to explain to potential group members the potential and goals of a dramatherapy/psychodrama group.

Sometimes role playing is used to clarify the nature or underlying dynamics of the problem. Once a desired new behaviour or goal is identified, role training offers behavioural practice. Even for students in training, it is useful not only to learn these methods, which they can then apply in counselling their own clients, but also to experience the techniques in the service of clarifying and practising alternatives in their own developing role as a therapist.

Vignette: exploring 'resistance'

For example, in a group supervisory session, one of the student group members brought up the problem of having in her group a client who was 'resistant' to group work. This client did not want to attend or participate in groups – especially 'experiential' groups. How should we deal with that problem?

The supervisor began by having the student reverse roles, become the client and engage in a soliloquy. The scene being played was one in which the patient in the hospital was preparing to walk reluctantly toward the group room. With the aid of another student who played the client's unspoken inner voice, that is, the psychodramatic 'double' technique, the student in role of the patient said, 'I hate this bullshit about having to go to these damn groups in order to earn privileges.' A little later, with the help of the double, the protagonist (the student who originally brought up the issue) in role as the resistant client said, 'Not only do I resent being controlled by this residential programme, I'm afraid that if I start screaming and hitting I'll totally lose control!'

With this as a warming up, the next scene explored alternative strategies, a process that is closer to role training: how to coax this 'resistant' client to come to the group. The term 'resistant' has emerged from its analytic roots to become a bit of psychobabble, a blaming of the client for a lack of full co-operation. Interestingly, psychodramatists generally reframe the psychoanalytic concept of 'resistant' as a lack of sufficient warm-up. The other students role played strategies to 'coax' the client to group, including playing with the resistance by amplifying it (e.g. 'Isn't this the worst group and so-and-so the worst leader?'), at which point the client's 'resistor' role was stolen, and she started arguing back that it wasn't the worst group – there were much more boring groups, etc.

Another strategy dealt with having the client take on a kind of 'assistant' role in which she could 'coach' the leader/student on how 'scary' the group was getting and when to 'pull' back or distance from the action. Other strategies focused on finding out what the client wanted or needed most, and how this group she was avoiding could help her directly or indirectly get her what she wanted from treatment. The role training helped the student discover other roles or strategies to take with this client, as well as helping to build empathy by role reversing with the client.

Another technique in role training is to try the 'worst possible' approach, which often loosens up the group and makes the search for probably more effective tactics more playful. Different students showed how they might do it really, really clumsily. In one supervision session we all took turns being the 'really mean therapist'. Through this exercise, one student realised that he was confusing 'assertive' or 'directive' with 'mean.'

Having students enact these dynamics rather than just talk about them cuts through the psychological defence mechanism of intellectualisation and abstraction and thus makes the 'action insight' learning more experiential and more effective (Siegel and Scipio-Skinner 1983; Siegel and Driscoll 1995; Tomasulo 2000).

For other discussions of role play in dramatherapy supervision, see pp. 99–110 and 212–13

Using role reversal

The theme in the following supervision session concerned the issue of working with staff. However, the theme deepened into one of problems with authority figures and the issue of developing one's personal therapeutic style within the confines of the rules and norms of an institution. As a student revealed personal difficulties with a particular supervisor, the group supervisor had the student image her 'boss' at the agency in the Empty Chair. This technique involves the placing of a chair in front of the student, and inviting her to name a role which will be held by the Empty Chair. The student then spoke to this image with the support and help of a double, chosen from among her peers. The student also role reversed with her supervisor by sitting in the Empty Chair and playing the role of the supervisor. Just as a theme in a psychodrama therapy group evolves and deepens, so this continued theme of working with varied staff deepened into the theme of intrapsychic difficulties which might get in the way of clinical practice. The student becomes aware, through action, of formerly unconscious needs and biases.

Transference

Although psychoanalysts first described transference, the dynamic being referred to is ubiquitous in human relations, being nothing more than the tendency to overgeneralisation of experience (Kellerman 1983). If one has had an unpleasant experience with a teacher with a moustache, there may be a slight tendency to expect a repetition of that experience when one encounters another teacher with a similar moustache years later. The earlier the experience, the deeper and often more unconscious is the reaction. Students and experienced practitioners have transferences as much as patients. It is hoped that they can learn to become more aware of their own dynamics and tendencies, so as to update the reality in the present. Sometimes this activity can be difficult, and part of the task of supervision is to use the evidence of transferences evoked in the course of working with clients as an opportunity to help students to address them more consciously and constructively.

Many transferences are positive. Patients who find the therapist helpful are inclined to believe that their working together might lead to further gains – a belief that galvanises hope and furthers tendencies towards healing. Overdone, it can lead to idealisation and the development of unrealistic expectations on the parts of either or both therapist and patient. The challenge is not to avoid any positive expectation, but rather to detect events that might become problematical.

The relationship between the supervisor and the students is also fraught with transference, and occasionally needs to be worked with. The term 'countertransference' actually refers to the transferential reaction to a client's or student's transferences, but some people use it to refer to the transference from the therapist to the patient, even if it has nothing to do with the patient's transference. For example, if a therapist has an aversion to tall people, this needs to be addressed so that encounters with such patients are not contaminated with unfair attributions. In other words, therapists can have transferences to patients just as much as vice versa, and teachers can have transferences with students.

For other discussions of transference and countertransference, see pp. 99–110 and 209–12

The most common transference arises from a mixture of identification with the aggressor and other dynamics, leading teachers or supervisors to slip into behaviours that are subtly sadistic. It is easy to become tactless, impatient, crude, or insensitive in doing supervision, but such behaviours need to be watched for and addressed – perhaps in the supervisor's or teacher's own therapy or psychodramatic enactment with a colleague. A psychodramatic technique that sometimes helps here is the assignment of a specific role of critic to one or several of the group members. The director – or, here, in the role of supervisor – might say something like: 'As group leader, I am likely to slip, lapse into errors of bias, transference behaviour, ways of working that are annoying, unfair, or unhelpful. This is part of the challenge of being a helper, a therapist, a teacher, a group leader. We mess up. Let's make it explicit. The code phrase for you to use is "I want to challenge you in the role of leader." By naming it as a role, I then can stand back and work on it. With the help of the group and trust in the process, I'll try to clarify and work out the issues raised.'

Vignette: dealing with 'countertransference'

An intern was having great difficulty with one of his older male patients. The patient was ambivalent about being seen in treatment and would repeatedly call the intern 'son'. I took the role of the male patient, while the intern tried to present a strategy of working with the patient that day. (This patient has a habit of derailing the 'offers' of the intern.) This role-play began as more of a role training session for the intern to practise directive, assertive behaviour. However, as the 'drama' continued and one of the other supervisees doubled, the action evolved into the intern working through some of his own issues, and then coming back into the scene and doing a 'psychodrama' (again I was portraying the patient) with the patient regarding the patient's biological son. It was quite an intense drama. Much sharing and deroling had to occur afterwards.

The social atom

This is a technique in which the client is helped to portray his or her most relevant social network. Designating a small figure to represent oneself in the network – usually in the centre, but not always, the person also draws little figures (circles for females, triangles for males) to indicate the key others in a social network (Blatner 2000: 181–83). It can be done with pencil and paper, small objects, or even through 'action sociometry' – the actual predecessor of family sculpture.

For example, a student wanted some ideas about how to deal therapeutically in an individual session with a patient who was experiencing family problems. The technique of the social atom was suggested as an assessment tool to begin talking about relationships in this patient's family. Drawing a social atom could be a launching pad to enact relationships using sandtray figures or speak to family members using the empty chair. The social atom technique can also be used with students to work through countertransferential feeling toward clients or patients. An interesting variation is to have the student draw a traditional social atom, and then a 'work' atom – clients and staff that are relevant and influential. Comparing the two 'atoms' can reveal information to the student that can clarify transferences.

Vignette: mirroring

Mirroring involves the depiction of one person by another. This needs to be done straight, as close to it being like a videotape feedback as possible, because in a sense that is all this technique is, a rapid feedback system without the actual technology. No mocking or editorial elaboration is allowed, as just feedback itself can be threatening to the person being depicted.

In a supervisory group session, a student who led groups in her clinical setting complained that in one of those sessions, a co-leader had co-opted the leadership role. To understand how this might have happened, the group interaction was staged and role played. At one point, the student started behaving very tentatively – not speaking up so patients could hear her and not being directive enough (i.e. saying: 'If it's okay with you, let's do this exercise' instead of just modelling the exercise and inviting the group – 'Let's do it!') To bring this into focus, the psychodramatic 'mirror' technique was used. The student came out of her role in the interaction and stood at the side of the director, a bit back from the stage area. Another student took the role of the first student in the scene and 'mirrored' the problematic non-verbal behavior. The student, looking at her 'mirrored' self, could recognise that her non-verbal communications were less than effective, and was able to imagine how else she could sit and gesture, use her facial expression and eye contact, so that her own leadership role would be maintained. She then re-entered the scene and replayed the interaction just before the loss of leadership experience occurred, feeling re-empowered through this brief role training experience.

During the sharing after this interaction, another student who role played one of the 'patients' realised that the patient's issues were reflected in the conflict between the two leaders – 'mirroring' in a different sense, reflecting a parallel process between issues in the clinical group and issues between the two co-leaders. She could almost hear the two stances as different roles and voices within her own mind. This sharing deepened the students' understanding of the way conflicts between leaders can evoke and reflect the conflicts among group members and within the minds of any of the individual clients.

Vignette: sociodrama

The protagonist in a sociodrama is an *issue*, not a person. One sociodramatic technique which has been useful in supervision is that of the composite character who reflects an issue or issues in a group. I went on the unit with my supervisees and we ran a group together on the skilled nursing unit. I had one of the students take the role of a 'new patient' who came into the group with all sorts of questions that the other patients tried to answer. I wanted the patients to feel empowered as 'experts'. Also, when the 'patient' left the group talking about how 'depressed' she felt, that she should 'relax' and ways that she could do that, the exercise became a projective device for the patients to speak about concerns they had about anxiety and depression. The patients could talk about these issues without having to refer to themselves. The composite character was a reflection of all of them, but not one person in particular. No one was in the spotlight.

This technique is particularly useful to warm up participants to psychodramatic action, as well as useful in groups that are constantly changing (i.e. inpatient psychiatric admissions). There may not be enough group cohesion yet to work on issues that are particular to a person, but there are common themes in the group which are coming up and need to be addressed. Composite characters are also effective in educational groups in which the participants are not in the group for therapy, but are dealing with difficult issues that are common to the group (i.e. a parenting skills group).

Vignette: termination

In a supervisory group, we were discussing termination, because one of the students in the group was leaving the site. The group needed to say goodbye to her and vice versa, but also we were talking about action techniques to use with clients who are leaving treatment. The following vignette shows how a variety of techniques helped engage with this issue in the supervision.

I placed three chairs in the centre of the room. The chairs were labelled thus: (1) What you brought with you to this practicum; (2) What you received from this practicum; (3) A future projection – i.e. an imagined scene of event in the future. The student sat in each chair and took each role. I then had her choose someone to be the mirror for each of these three roles, and then had her double each role. We shared and spoke about how this exercise could be adapted to clients, particularly around the issue of encouraging the client to understand that he or she can take the work from the therapist and the treatment, that the work is not dependent on the person of the therapist or the context of the therapy session. We talked about another exercise, in which three chairs are placed in the centre of the room. The three chairs would be labelled: (1) What I got out of treatment; (2) What I would have liked more of in treatment; (3) What I didn't get from treatment. The client could speak from each chair, or use objects or scarves and put them on the chairs to represent the different things gained and not gained, along with the 'things' the client wanted in greater numbers. Of course, with the student we substituted 'supervision' for 'treatment'.

Conclusion

Summary of key points

1   Integrate dramatherapy with other modalities being used in the therapeutic context.
2   Using the metaphor of life as drama and the predicament of a role within a situation, focus less on diagnostic categories and more on the clients' stories.
3   Drama may be used in conjunction with other arts therapies techniques as they all bring forth the clients' projections about their attitudes to life. Some of these techniques may also be used to help the practicum students identify and correct their own attitudes that may be interfering with their optimal performance.
4   Address practicum students' feelings of inadequacy and unrealistic expectations through concretising their metaphors, portraying their inner critics, and other techniques as needed.
5   Use role playing and role training to rehearse therapeutic tactics in the fail-safe context of group supervision. This offers support, feedback and opportunities to 'do-over'.
6   Dramatherapy and psychodramatic techniques allow for a playful atmosphere that decreases anxiety among new therapists and increases self-disclosure in a 'non-spotlighting' way.
7   Because psychodrama accentuates that the director is 'part of the group', psychodramatic techniques illustrate to students the model of therapist as lifelong 'learner'.

Supervision is ideally a container, in which the supervisee can feel safe to be expressive and risk to 'fail.' Ideally, the issue of 'failure' or 'mistakes' is transformed into 'Let's play with this' or 'Let's experiment in this safe laboratory of supervision.' One of the cornerstones of psychodrama theory is a reverence for 'spontaneity'. The psychodramatic definition of spontaneity is *the novel, effective, and appropriate approach to a new or an old situation.* Dramatherapy values creativity and play. The use of psychodrama and dramatherapy techniques with practicum students in supervision enables the practising of different behaviours with an emphasis on creativity, play and spontaneity. Through the use of the psychodramatic techniques of mirroring, role reversal, doubling and the social atom, students in supervision can garner more information about themselves as clinicians (and even as humans, which can enhance their humanity as clinicians!). Participants in supervision can increase empathy toward their clients and patients. Transference and countertransference can be explored in a non-judgemental atmosphere.

Psychodrama and improvisational dramatherapy techniques enhance the efficacy of role playing and role training as well as the related use of sociodrama and projective techniques. Trainees can become aware of unconscious material that may be affecting their clinical work, as well as roles that support their development as therapists, and those roles that sabotage that development.

Finally, the supervisor, using dramatic methods, can also embrace the role of colleague, playful peer, and other myriad numbers of roles in the supervision process, modelling flexibility and spontaneity. The supervisor can continue to broaden his or her role repertoire while helping the supervisees to develop their clinical roles.

References

Blatner, A. (1994) Foreword, in R. Emunah, *Acting for Real: Drama Therapy Process and Technique*, New York: Brunner/Mazel.

Blatner, A. (2000) *Foundations of Psychodrama: History, Theory and Practice*, New York: Springer.

Blatner, A. (2004) The real diagnostic variables. Online. Available HTTP: http://www.blatner.com/adam/level2/dxvariables.htm (accessed July 5 2005). *Note*: this and a number of other papers on this website offer practical guidance for students of counseling or therapy, on the art of case presentation, case formulation, various pitfalls and techniques, etc.

Blatner, A. (2007a) Psychodrama, sociodrama and role playing, in A. Blatner (ed.) *Interactive and Improvisational Drama: Varieties of Applied Theatre and Performance*, Lincoln NE: iUniverse.

Blatner, A. (2007b) Perspectives on metatheory, in C. Baim, J. Burmeister and M. Maciel (eds) *Psychodrama: Advances in Theory and Practice*, London: Routledge.

Brightman, B. K. (1984) Narcissistic issues in the training experience of the psychotherapist. *International Journal of Psychoanalytic Psychotherapy* 10: 293–317.

Courtney, R. (1974) *Play, Drama and Thought*, New York: Drama Book Specialists.

Haas, R. B. and Moreno, J. L. (1951) Psychodrama as a projective technique, in H. H. Anderson and G. L. Anderson (eds) *An Introduction to Projective Techniques*, Englewood Cliffs NJ: Prentice-Hall.

Johnson, D. R. (2000) The history and development of the field of drama therapy in the United States and Canada, in P. Lewis and D. R. Johnson (eds) *Current Approaches in Drama Therapy*, Springfield IL: Charles C. Thomas.

Kellerman, P. F. (1983) Transference, countertransference and tele, *Journal of Group Psychotherapy, Psychodrama and Sociometry* 32: 38–55.

Landy, R. J. (1993) *Persona and Performance: The Meaning of Role in Drama, Therapy, and Everyday Life*, New York: Guilford Press.

Landy, R. J. (2007) *The Couch and the Stage: Integrating Words and Action in Psychotherapy*, Lanham MD: Jason Aronson.

Siegel, J. and Driscoll, S. (1995) Law enforcement critical incident teams: using psychodramatic methods for debriefing training, *Journal of Group Psychotherapy, Psychodrama and Sociometry* 48, 2: 77–9.

Siegel, J. and Scipio-Skinner, K. V. (1983) Psychodrama: an experiential model for nursing students, *Journal of Group Psychotherapy, Psychodrama and Sociometry* 36, 3: 97–101.

Slade, P. (1981) Dramatherapy, in G. Schattner and R. Courtney (eds) *Drama in Therapy*, Vol. 1, New York: Drama Book Specialists.

Tomasulo, D. (2000) Culture in action: diversity training with a cultural double, *International Journal of Action Methods* 53, 2: 24.

VanderMay, J. H. and Peak, T. (1980) Psychodrama as a supervision technique, *Group Psychotherapy, Psychodrama and Sociometry* 33: 25–32.

Williams, A. (1995) *Visual and Active Supervision: Roles, Focus, Technique*, New York: Norton.

Wooding, S. (2003) The use of creative techniques in supervision, *British Journal of Psychodrama and Sociodrama* 18, 2: 21–31.

Chapter 9

Applying generic clinical supervision training to arts therapy supervision

Clare Hubbard

Introduction

This chapter explores the author's experience of multidisciplinary clinical supervision training and asks how it can be applicable to arts therapists. I begin by looking at the content of this generic training and how it compares to specialised arts therapy or psychotherapy supervision trainings. I then focus on how I was able to use the training to explore models for application to supervision of someone from a different profession. Finally I give some consideration to the importance of the art form in clinical supervision.

Literature to date on dramatherapy supervision has often focused on the use of drama in supervision. The approaches have been based around the different dramatherapy models, such as theatre, role and story making. Jennings (1999) uses her embodiment, projection, role model (EPR), the mandala and text. For Couroucli-Robertson (1999) the art form is both the container and catalyst in the supervision. She describes the use of story in supervision to draw parallels with the supervisee's client. Couroucli-Robertson (1999), Jennings (1999) and Landy (1999) all refer to our internal client and internal supervisor. Couroucli-Robertson and Landy include the internal therapist, who allows the supervisor and supervisee to see the triangular relationship from the three different perspectives. The internal client is our empathy with the client from our own experiences; the internal therapist 'possesses the structure, the aim and the methods' (Couroucli-Robertson 1999: 97); and the internal supervisor is the guide and observer, seeing the therapy from a distance. The dramatherapist can use these psychotherapeutic concepts dramatically in supervision Landy (1999) illustrates his role model as a way of addressing role ambivalence to create a bridge between the three roles. Lahad (2000) uses his BASIC Ph model (the six underlying coping modes: beliefs, affect, social support, imagination, cognition, and physical activity) to help the supervisee understand their own style of meeting the world, as well as their client's.

Tselikas-Portmann in her introduction to *Supervision and Dramatherapy* (1999: 26) describes the qualities she believes the dramatherapy supervisor needs. They include 'artistic/expressive capacity . . . capacity to play . . . the sense for bodily and non-bodily communication . . . sensory awareness . . . imagination and sense for the metaphysical'. She says these 'connect to the very nature of dramatherapy'. These are qualities we might expect a dramatherapist to have already. So what is it then that they need to learn in order to transfer these skills and abilities from clinical practice to clinical supervision? Tselikas-Portmann (1999) draws on literature outside drama-therapy with Holloway (1995) for her definition of the tasks of supervision. She sees them as 'promoting the reflection on professional practice, the building up of professional skills, developing or preserving the ability to conceptualize the situation (case), reflecting on the professional role, pre-serving emotional awareness and enabling self-evaluation (thus promoting autonomy)'. She defines the functions as: 'advising; eventually instructing; modelling; consulting; supporting and sharing; monitoring' (pp. 25–6).

Jenkyns (1999) writes about her psychodynamic approach to arts therapy clinical supervisor training and draws on models from psychotherapy, nursing and social work. In fact most of the literature and theory on supervision come from these three areas. If then the literature and theory come from disciplines outside dramatherapy, can a generic clinical super-vision training teach the knowledge and skills relevant to the specific discipline of dramatherapy?

Multidisciplinary supervision training

I was surprised to learn that supervision was recommended for psychiatric nursing by the Horder committee as early as 1943, and brought into nursing training in 1982. This was before clinical supervision was introduced into dramatherapy training in the mid-1980s, and the first dramatherapy clinical supervision training began in the late 1980s. Yet, there has been a distinct lack of appreciation for the importance of clinical supervision in health and social care organisations in the UK. Where there has been an understanding of the need for supervision of the clinical work, it has often been addressed from a management perspective. In recent years health and social care organisations have begun to recognise the value of a separate space to reflect on clinical work. Supervision policies are being developed in NHS trusts, generic for all clinical staff, which differentiate between management and clinical supervision and recognise the need of both for professional staff:

> All staff must have regular management supervision and, in addition, all direct care staff must have some form of regular professional/clinical supervision . . . For some areas of practice, the importance of the separation of the two types of supervision (to enable practitioners to have a supportive reflective space) is acknowledged.
>
> (Local NHS trust supervision policy, 2005)

Training in clinical supervision is being provided or funded by employers. In 2006 I completed one of these multidisciplinary courses. The training was for mental health professionals such as nurses, occupational therapists, social workers and psychological therapists. It was taught half a day a week over one semester. The teaching hours totalled 36, the learning hours 120. As an NHS-based dramatherapist working with adults with severe and enduring mental health problems, I clinically supervise within my role. I was looking for a way to develop my current practice and be accepted on BADth's register of supervisors. I applied for this training to supplement the experience I had gained so far of supervising both a dramatherapist and a non-dramatherapist and to increase my theoretical knowledge of supervision models and processes. The choice of a generic over specialist arts therapies/psychotherapy supervision training was influenced by time and money. This reflects the move within the NHS to keep costs down by providing in-house training. The trust had a relationship with the university running the course and funded a number of places each year. I was apprehensive about undertaking training aimed at a multiprofessional group, wondering what understanding of clinical supervision, if any, the other students might have, and how this would correspond to my own. Would I learn anything new? I rang the course tutor, who is a nurse, to ask if this course was appropriate for me. My fear that I would be the only psychological therapist was confirmed. However, she was keen for the student mix to be multidisciplinary. She felt that the course content would be relevant to me and that the students could learn from each other's approaches and experience.

The structure of the nine three hour study sessions was a theory lecture on a different topic, followed by a practical session consisting of discussion and role play. The course covered the key areas for consideration in clinical supervision. In the first two sessions we looked at the historical context and the different models and approaches. They included models that describe the elements of the main functions or role of supervision and the roles of the supervisor and supervisee. Structural models give a step-by-step guide of what to do, the developmental approach emphasises the educational function, often focus on the supervisory relationship. Some models are bound by a theoretical approach or discipline specific, while reflective models emphasise 'a seeing rather than a knowing attitude to practice' (Fish and Twinn 1997: 69). They focus on increasing understanding by guided reflection on clinical practice, such as Driscoll's What Model which asks 'What? So what? Now what?' (Driscoll 2000). In the remaining sessions we considered the contract, including five key areas: practicalities, boundaries, working alliance, session format and organisational and professional context (Hawkins and Shohet 2000: 54). We covered legal and ethical decisions, approaching examples of supervision issues and how we would tackle them, and record keeping. We looked at the types and dynamics of group supervision: authoritative, participative, co-operative and peer. We touched on different therapeutic approaches, first with a session on the application of psychodynamic concepts and person centred theory to the supervisory relationship. This involves applying the core conditions: genuineness, unconditional positive regard and empathy, to help the supervisee confront their defences and reflect on the relationship between the dynamics in the supervision and patterns in the client–therapist relationship. Then we looked at applying Socratic questioning, a cognitive behaviour therapy tool, which involves repeatedly questioning 'What then?' in order to follow a train of thought and uncover the core belief behind the response to a situation. We had the opportunity to practise and discuss the application of these different tools to our supervisory practice. We also looked at areas that might not be covered in a more specialised training, but which were very relevant to my work setting. These were multiprofessional/across-discipline supervision within health and social care, distinguishing between management and clinical supervision, establishing clinical supervision in the workplace and monitoring effectiveness in response to value for money, clinical governance and evidence based practice. We discussed confidentiality and fitness to practise, responsibility to the employer, and our own professional codes of practice and conduct.

Before commencing the course I had assumed that nurses, social workers and occupational therapists would not be familiar with the psychodynamic concepts, which were a big part of my own supervisory practice. I was surprised therefore to hear, in the first session, statements from these different professions about the relationship between therapist and client, suggesting that supervision on this is seen as an important part of safe and effective clinical practice:

> All registered nurses, midwives and health visitors should develop an understanding of the relationship issues and the processes whereby a client transfers experiences and expectations from the past onto the practitioner and vice versa. All practitioners should have access to appropriate supervision and support.
>
> (UK Central Council for Nursing, Midwifery and Health Visiting 1999: 8)

My preconception was further challenged as the course progressed; both by the use of psychodynamic concepts, such as transference and projection by some of my fellow students, and through their demonstration of counselling skills in role play scenarios.

There were frustrations, however. It was apparent that most people on the course did not have direct experience of clinical, as separate from managerial, supervision. There was much focus on clarifying this distinction in the first two sessions. The managers on this training found it hard to put on a different hat. This difficulty in separating the two was mirrored in some of the literature from social work and nursing. Hawkins and Shohet (2000) note in their review of different literature on supervision that the main roles of the supervisor appear to be: teacher, monitor evaluator, counsellor, colleague, boss, expert technician, manager of administrative relationships. I was confident that I was clear in my own practice and at times I felt impatient waiting for others to catch up. I particularly remember one role play where I played the supervisee. When bringing a particular client issue to the 'supervision', wondering about the way I was feeling about them and what might be happening in the therapeutic relationship, I found my 'supervisor' concentrated on risk: who to tell and what the care co-coordinator should be doing. However, another 'supervisor' helped me to think about the transference.

I found my confidence challenged when I began to write my supervision journal. For the past year my manager, a dramatherapist, had been my clinical supervisor. This was my choice, as I wanted to learn from her experience and knowledge. Although this was not what BADth recommends as good practice, I felt that we were able to separate the two roles, meeting on different days and times, and to use the clinical supervision productively. Once I began to pay closer attention to the supervision through reflection in my supervision diary I began to notice that sometimes the roles overlapped and the boundary blurred. My first entry in my supervision diary began:

I am starting to notice the overlap of boundaries between the two types of supervision. When does she put her manager's hat on? Do I want an answer to the issue from my manager or my clinical supervisor?

In my diary I recalled a situation where I wanted to check out with my clinical supervisor whether my involvement in a staff performance was appropriate before discussing it with my manager, but this was not possible within the supervision arrangements. My apprehension was acted out by me bringing the issue into the clinical supervision right at the end of a session. I suppose that I hoped, but not confidently believed, that my supervisor would be able to respond with only that hat on, perhaps in reality an impossibility. I experienced her first response as my manager's. I wrote in my diary: 'She said she had big concerns about this, particularly as it is not what therapists in the trust do.' But then she suggested we take it into the next supervision and think further about my role at the unit and why I was feeling the need to blur it. I wrote in my diary: 'I felt upset after supervision, as if I had been told off by a teacher, but once this immediate response had gone I felt I could bring it back to the next session. I wonder what else I am reluctant to share with my supervisor, what I hide and whether this is because she is my manager?' In contrast, earlier in the same session I had discussed a situation that I was being self-critical because of the way I had handled it, and I received reassurance from my supervisor.

The role approach to supervision suggests the supervisor has a range of different roles. It is important to identify which you are playing and it requires skill to switch supportively from one to another. The roles I identified in my diary for my supervisor in that supervision session were guide, human being, consultant, teacher and disciplinarian. In a small profession like dramatherapy it can be difficult to separate the different roles we may have with each other at different times. My clinical supervisor and manager was also once my teacher and I wonder how this role impacted on our relationship. There were also organisational dynamics in play as my manager was not the manager of the unit for which I was providing this particular work and the expectations of both differed.

Despite this important insight into my clinical supervision and a strong awareness of how much I had learnt from the course, at the end I remained ambivalent about generic training in supervision for dramatherapists. Reflecting two years on, I can see that I developed significantly from the training, benefiting from a space to think and discuss, to share perspectives and to practise with others. It helped me to expand my theoretical knowledge and consider in detail the professional and the workplace guidance. The inclusion of an exam in order to pass the course really motivated my research into different models and I was able to take it into areas particularly relevant to my practice. Keeping a supervision diary helped me reflect on my process as supervisor and supervisee. The encouragement to keep distinguishing between management and clinical supervision, and an awareness of how this has overlapped in my own supervision, has continued to be very helpful.

A comparison of generic to specialised clinical supervision training

So were there any disadvantages or advantages in choosing a generic over a specialised arts therapy or psychotherapy training? What did I miss out on? (See Table 9.1.)

Commonalities

Hours and timescales

The four months duration from beginning to final exam did not allow for many supervision sessions to take place before submitting our formative assignment after 12 weeks. Looking into the various specialised clinical supervision trainings for counsellors, psychotherapist and arts therapies by

Table 9.1 Comparison of generic and specialised clinical supervision training

Commonalities	Not covered in generic training	Specific to generic training
Teaching hours	Specific client material	Multidisciplinary experience/
Areas covered	supervisee might bring	discussion
Contracts	Use of the art form	Across discipline supervision
Boundaries	Orientation specific	Organisational context and
Ethical issues	Experience of being in a	policy
Transference	supervision group	

the British Association for Psychotherapy (BAP), Westminster Pastoral Foundation (WPF), Institute for Arts in Therapy and Education, and Creative Arts Therapies Supervision (CAST) among others, I found that length ranged from one day (seminars) to 18 months for a qualification. The average was ten monthly half-day sessions, 36 hours, the same teaching time as my training, but over a longer timescale. Most arts therapies trainings had more contact hours. The longer time period might perhaps allow for more development during training, and time to put learning into practice.

Many topics were covered in the generic training and the specialised trainings, for example, contracts and boundaries and ethical issues. Others, such as transference, were touched upon in the generic training but may have been more of a focus in the psychodynamic orientated supervision trainings.

Differences

Not covered in the generic training

A few areas were not covered in the generic training. One training looked at the specific issue of supervision of work with a suicidal client. Some psychotherapy supervision trainings were specifically psychodynamic in orientation, focusing on transference and countertransference and the triangle of the supervisor, therapist and client. As I do not have a recognised psychotherapy or counselling qualification, some of these were not open to me. The creative arts therapies trainings included sessions focused on the use of the arts and the creative process in supervision, and this was something that I missed. Being part of a supervision group for supervision practice was an important part of some trainings, increasing opportunity for reflection.

Specific to the generic training

There were things I gained from the generic training that could only be covered in a multiprofessional group: reflecting and sharing experiences with others in the multidisciplinary team and gaining an awareness of how other professions approach clinical supervision. Importantly for my current practice, I was encouraged to think about supervision of other disciplines. When I looked at the components of one of the psychotherapy supervision trainings, I noticed the module 'Supervision in NHS Settings' and realised this was the background to my training. All of us worked in the NHS, mostly in the same organisation, as this course was targeted at the local NHS mental health trusts. We looked at local policy and clinical supervision in the context of the workplace, thinking about the difficulties of implementation and the organisational influences, and how we could help change some of the resistance/apathy. I was able to apply this to my developing private practice, but this was a training that was particularly relevant to clinical supervision in an organisation.

I conclude that a generic training is not a substitute for a specialist training if you know how you want to work as a supervisor, for example, psychodynamically or with an emphasis on the use of the art form. A generic training looks at core issues and supports the development of a process of reflection and a theoretical knowledge base. The length of training may be a factor in developing supervision skills and the opportunity for reflection and discussion with peers. I would not advocate a one- or two-day in-house training as a substitute.

Supervision across professions

As I mentioned earlier, one of the elements covered on the generic training that I found particularly relevant to my work in the NHS, and rarely included in the specialist trainings, was multiprofessional or across-discipline supervision. This is an area that is not well researched or written about. As such it has not been recognised as effective as same discipline supervision, but it is a growing area, particularly in the health service. On the course we wondered whether a supervisor who might approach client work and their client relationships in one way can successfully supervise someone of another profession, who might approach the same client issues in a different way. For example, an occupational therapist might look at relaxation techniques to help a client sleep, a nurse might do a physical examination and be considering their medication, and a psychotherapist might want to explore what could be troubling them or any associations they have with sleeping or night time.

We were encouraged to consider a number of questions when contemplating the supervision of someone from a different discipline. How much do you need to know about the supervisee's profession? What is shared across the professions? What are some of the possible barriers and can these be overcome or worked with? Does there need to be the same ideology, approach and aims to the work brought to supervision? Which is more important – being from the same profession or having the same approach to the client work? Are there occasions when supervision from someone trained in a different discipline is preferable?

Bringing it back to basics, the core objective is the same for all practice – client care – so perhaps this is the place to begin. We agreed in our course discussions that sharing values and aims would be important for effective clinical supervision; also an awareness of possible barriers such as ideological differences, power relationships and terminology, which might need to be checked out in the first few meetings. This could be the same for two people of the same profession as theories and approaches can be different within the same profession. This is certainly true in dramatherapy, as summarised in the introduction to this chapter. The skills and knowledge of the supervisor are not, necessarily, profession bound. Whether clinical supervision from another discipline is appropriate and safe might depend on how experienced the supervisee is. It seems important that the trainee or newly qualified professional has clinical supervision from someone of the same discipline. More mentoring, teaching and role modelling is needed for their particular professional role at this stage. BADth stipulates this for the first 40 hours of supervision on qualifying as a dramatherapist. At the other end of the spectrum, there may be times when an experienced professional is undertaking a new piece of work. They may need to seek supervision outside their own profession in order to receive the most helpful support and that might be in addition to other clinical supervision for the remainder of their work. My recent undertaking of supervision from a cognitive analytic therapy (CAT) practitioner for my CAT-orientated work is an example of this. An advantage of clinical supervision from a different discipline could be an opportunity to learn from that discipline's approach, enhancing the supervisee's own practice and skills.

In our discussions on the training we felt that, alongside supervision from another discipline, there would be a need for some form of supplementary profession-specific supervision or forum, be it peer or occasional supervision from outside the organisation if it is not available inside. The frequency might depend on whether the supervisee is working with others of the same profession, who they can exchange ideas with, or a lone practitioner. What came across from other students in a minority profession was a picture of not being given an option of same discipline clinical supervision, where this was not available in the immediate team. The reality seemed to be that in multidisciplinary teams the experienced practitioner is likely to be called upon to supervise other professions than their own.

Having considered different models and approaches to supervision, I wonder if one of the most important things in clinical supervision of same, or across disciplines, is that the supervisor uses a supervision model that the supervisee finds helpful. If the model is a reflective one rather than a discipline bound or a structural model, then perhaps the supervisor can use their skills to facilitate the supervisee's reflection without having to have an in-depth understanding of their profession. Giving space to talk about the situation or client, brainstorming, exploring options, enabling the supervisee to find a way forward and take action should be the case for all good clinical supervision. Butterworth and Faugier (1998) reflect that when a psychodynamic approach has been transferred in its pure form to nursing supervision, without considering the nurse's role, it has not been successful, and suggest a model that facilitates both educational and personal growth. Research from Weaks (2002) suggests that the supervisory relationship is paramount to good supervision and the core conditions for this are safety, equality and challenge.

Practice vignette

When starting the course I had, for 18 months, been clinically supervising Mick, a senior support worker, with his drama group at a day centre for people with mental health issues. The aim of the group was to increase confidence. For his other work Mick was supervised by an assistant team leader within day services. The effect on the supervision of us being from different disciplines had, for me, been a conscious consideration for some time. The training helped me explore this further, as I investigated different models and how they might apply to this supervision.

Was a dramatherapist the best person to clinically supervise Mick for his group? The work for which I supervised Mick was closely related to my discipline of dramatherapy, and the group was linked to the dramatherapy department. Some of the same approaches to the client work would therefore be applicable, and there was common aim and understanding, but I needed to be aware of where these differed, and when my therapeutic perspective on issues the clients presented would not be helpful to apply. The relationship and boundaries with clients were different for Mick than for the therapist. Mick had more than one role with the drama group members, as facilitator of other creative or recreational groups and as a supportive figure at the drop-in centre. As a dramatherapist, I saw my task as helping Mick think about both the application of drama in the sessions and the therapeutic benefit for the clients. The latter included reflecting on group dynamics, Mick's interventions, and his feelings about the group. I found this was helpful for Mick in increasing his awareness of why things might be happening in the group, his relationship with the clients, and how to work with the dynamics, not to explicitly explore these with clients but rather using his understanding to inform his practice.

In the first few months of supervision Mick confided that he was fearful of stepping over the boundary between a drama group with a therapeutic benefit and dramatherapy. He worried that he would not be aware whether he was encroaching on the role of a therapist and he might inadvertently have a detrimental effect on the clients. Two years later he told me that he was feeling much more confident about the way he was working, and our supervision had been instrumental in this: 'The supervision made the division of roles clearer to me and I felt able to develop the group and identify its strength in its informality.'

The journey to an appropriate model of supervision

Part of the work for the clinical supervision training was to explore different models and relate them to our supervisory practice. I used this as an opportunity to find one that I could usefully apply to supervision of Mick. The developmental approach described by Hawkins and Shohet (2000) and van Ooijen (2000) refers to three stages that the supervisee may be at, dependent on experience, and suggests the corresponding role of the supervisor. For the dramatherapist there is a clear progression from trainee, to newly qualified and more experienced therapist, but I found this approach limited for Mick's supervision. With regards to his own profession, Mick fitted into level three: an experienced independent craftsman, increasingly able to trust his own judgement. In the drama group however, he was only beginning to focus on the process. He was not used to thinking psychotherapeutically about the clients, and although our supervision was comfortable, it did not feel collegial. I felt that Mick saw me as the expert. Overall, he probably fitted in level two: the client-centred adolescent and journeyman, sometimes dependent and self-doubting, sometimes confident, but still learning to think holistically. For level two, van Ooijen (2000) says that the supervisor needs to know when to support and when to let go. This made me wonder how I should be expecting Mick to develop in respect to the group he was facilitating.

Another question was where my role sat as supervisor for only one aspect of Mick's job. Kadushin (1976) talks about three main functions of supervision: educative, management, and supportive. For Proctor (1988) these are formative, normative and restorative. Proctor's model gives a basic outline of supervision from which different approaches have been developed (Hawkins and Shohet 2000: 52; van Ooijen 2000: 70), but he does not suggest how to balance the three functions, or how to carry them out. Hawkins and Shohet (2000) elaborate on what the functions involve. Formative/education is about increasing one's understanding of the client and the dynamics through facilitated reflection. The restorative/supportive function is to help the supervisee become aware of the effect of the client's material on them and deal with their reactions. The normative/managerial function is quality control: ensuring professional standards are upheld. Jenkyns (1999: 187) relates the functions to the developmental stages: the newly qualified therapist may need more educative supervision. She adds that the supervision can move between the functions according to the supervisee's individual needs. Bishop and Butterworth (1995: 39–44) add a fourth function: protective, which Chesner (1999: 43) sees as a 'proactive device to help with difficulties, which is preferable to reactive solutions to damage already done'. This adds an element that many of the nursing models leave out. John's Reflective Cycle (1997, in van Ooijen 2000), for example, asks 'What is the issue?'; assuming that the supervision is reflecting on a particular issue or incident, rather than helping the supervisee to explore and find ways of approaching different client material.

It was helpful to identify the different functions in Mick's supervision. The formative was often the main focus, usually initiated by me. This type of group was new for Mick and, particularly in the first year, one of my roles was teacher, both of drama and of a therapeutic approach to group facilitation:

Mick talked about low attendance following a three-week break. I encouraged him to think why this might have happened and what the clients' responses to the therapist's absence might be. I reassured him that this was a common response to breaks in therapy.

Under the restorative function Mick could express his feelings about the group:

I asked Mick how this low attendance had made him feel. He said he felt frustrated and it had lowered his own motivation with the group.

The protective function was present throughout in planning the sessions, but more specifically when preparing for a break or anticipated low attendance:

Mick told me he would be cancelling the group for a week. As the last time attendance had decreased following the break I encouraged him to think about the effect of breaks on the group and how he can prepare them. If it was a therapy group I would have encouraged Mick to explore this with the group, but as they resist reflection, I felt it was at least important for Mick to hold this for them.

The normative function was where I struggled. Mick did not have the same codes of conduct as dramatherapists and I was not his manager, nor did I report back to his manager. However, it would be remiss not to acknowledge any management role in my supervision with Mick. The drama group is linked to the dramatherapy department and we make referrals to it, so I had a responsibility for the quality and safety of the group.

In Proctor's model there does not seem to be a place to reflect and identify the external issues in the supervisee's life which affect his feelings towards the clients and his facilitation of the work:

> Mick talked about things in his life which were affecting his functioning at work. I listened, allowing the space. From my empathic responses, e.g. 'It must be hard to concentrate on the group when you have this going on', Mick began to explore how these external forces were magnifying his negative feelings about clients, for example, feeling angry that people didn't turn up when he had made the effort.

The developmental model, and Proctor's model, helped me target the supervision to the supervisee's developmental stage, and identify the different functions of the supervision. But these models did not provide me with ideas about how to approach and prepare for clinical supervision, and lacked the more psychodynamic elements that I was looking for. So I continued my search.

Carroll's seven tasks of supervision in the Generic Integrated Model (1996) suggest a range of generic tasks that underlie all supervision approaches:

- monitoring administrative aspects
- consulting
- counselling
- monitoring professional ethical issues
- setting up a learning relationship (relating)
- teaching
- evaluating.

He emphasises the need to move between tasks so as not to restrict the supervision. He acknowledges that professionals from different therapeutic orientations stress different tasks. Carroll (1994) interviewed 23 counsellor supervisors on how they saw and implemented these tasks. There was little agreement on the definition of relationship, variation on how teaching is implemented, the counselling task was only used if arising from client work, and not more than necessary, and consultation was seen as a major part of the supervision. There was apprehension from some about formal evaluation and a lack of clarity on how evaluation is carried out, but a consensus of opinion that that this task does involve a power relationship. In further research, reviewing tapes of six supervisory relationships over 12 months, Carroll (1994) found that supervisors and supervisees take responsibility for different tasks, with supervisors typically initiating relating, teaching and evaluation, and supervisees initiating consultation and counselling. His research found that consultation was the most frequently used task, initiated by the supervisor 27.25 per cent of the time and the supervisee 54.3 per cent, more so with the more experienced supervisees. This would make sense under Carroll's definition of consultancy as '[describing] the whole area of process in supervision' (p. 75). For supervisors, teaching was the second most frequent at 26.9 per cent, and for supervisees it was counselling at 18.6 per cent. In contrast, exploring supervision with Mick I discovered that when he introduced personal reactions to the client work I initiated reflection (counselling), and any thinking about the psychodynamics (consultation), where Mick would ask for answers (teaching) and evaluation from me. This is not typical of the trend Carroll identified in his research, and likely relates back to the developmental level and the difference in our orientation. Mick being used to supervision with a more management than reflective focus.

Although I identified which tasks Mick and I tended to emphasise and the importance of monitoring them, I was still not content that I had found the right model and was perhaps looking for one that focused primarily on the reflective component of clinical supervision, and could provide a framework for me to follow.

Carroll cites a process model, which concentrates on the consultancy role of supervision, 'aimed at understanding all the processes of the system, examining them and looking at ways of influencing them, i.e. uncovering what is happening, understanding it and looking at other ways of intervening' (Carroll 1996: 75). This is the Double-Matrix or Seven Eyed Model (Hawkins and Shohet 2000). With it I felt I had found the model that allows for a more psychodynamic orientation, whilst being flexible enough for supervision of a non-psychodynamically practising supervisee. The model focuses on the supervisory relationship, which the other more general models do not. It involves looking at the therapy matrix by both reflecting on the therapy session and the here and now of the supervision session. This was a familiar concept to me as supervisee, and as therapist. Jenkyns (1999) taught the model on her arts therapies supervision training course. The model is divided into seven modes:

1   Reflection on the content of the therapy session.
2   Exploration of the strategies and interventions used by the therapist.
3   Exploration of the therapy process and relationships.
4   Focus on the therapist's countertransference.
5   Focus on the here-and-now process as a mirror or parallel of the there-and-then process.
6   Focus on the supervisor's countertransference.
7   The wider context – the outside influences.

Hawkins and Shohet (2000) see one of the advantages of the model as thinking about which processes you are using and which you are avoiding.

In Mick's supervision we reflected on the therapy session, but not so much on the here and now. Hawkins and Shohet make reference to the developmental model, stressing that new therapists may need the focus to be on modes one and two, then working down as they become more confident. My feeling had been that Mick was not yet able to really think about the parallel process in mode five (not yet process centred), and was just beginning to acknowledge his countertransference (mode four), but perhaps it was my role to guide him into this? Without thinking of it as an approach, I had been using my countertransference in the supervision to understand and sometimes reflected back to Mick processes that might be happening for him with his group, as well as trying to get him to think about his countertransference from/towards the clients, e.g. wanting to make the group more interesting and feeling irritated by members.

Both Hawkins and Shohet's (2000) and Carroll's (1996) models had been helpful in exploring how Mick's supervision was and could be used. In the extract below of a supervision session with Mick I will illustrate the different tasks (Carroll) and modes (Hawkins and Shohet) used.

Mick had written a script for his group and wanted me to read it and give my opinion.
Evaluation. Mick was asking me to evaluate his script, both as a piece of literature and its appropriateness for the group.

I was interested in why Mick had written the script as this was a new way of working for the group and involved extra work for Mick. I invited Mick to tell me how this had come about.
Modes 1 and 2: reflection on the content of the session and exploration of the strategies and interventions used. Rather than evaluating the merit of Mick's script at this stage, I wanted to think with him more about the process that led to up to it and its meaning for the group.

Mick explained how the group had expressed feeling bored with the content of the sessions, which followed a familiar structure. He suggested writing some dialogue as a group, which they initially responded to positively, but at the next session they were very reluctant and asked Mick to do it. He agreed to write the first one and they would write the next. It emerged that the attendance had been low recently and it was two consistent members who were pushing for change. I felt there were some important issues here about how Mick is feeling about the group, his role, and what the purpose of the group is. Mick seemed relieved to share with me his frustration with the group that they wanted to do something but then passed the task to him. Rather than telling him what I thought he should do, I facilitated further reflection with questions, e.g. 'Why do you think the group were reluctant to write their own script? I wonder what the members who are frustrated are saying. Where do you want the group to go?'

Consultation: as consultant I had the experience and knowledge of similar situations to what Mick was describing but rather than teaching him by telling him my answers I was asking Mick questions, which I felt would help him explore what was happening in the group and find his own answers to what he should do about the situation.

I made observations about the clients from what he has told me. 'Joan has been in the group for some time now, and you have found her to often be quite dominant and critical.' Mick agreed and was able to think a little about her effect on him, perhaps feeling a need to impress her.

Mode 3: exploration of the therapy process and relationships. Here we began thinking about Mick's relationship with the client and how he was responding to her.

I made observations about the here and now, trying to draw Mick's attention to possible countertransference: 'It's interesting that you have brought your script to me to give my opinion. You seem anxious about the group reading it?'

Mode 4: focus on the therapist's countertransference. I wanted to encourage Mick to identify what he was feeling in response to the group's feelings about writing the script, and how that may have caused him to respond. I had a view on what was happening but it was important for Mick to develop his own understanding rather than just accepting my interpretation.

When Mick responded by saying he was worried it might reveal something about himself, or not be seen as good enough, I wondered with him about parallels to how the group felt when asked to write something.

Mode 5: focus on the here-and-now process as a mirror or parallel of the there-and-then process, counselling. In the counselling task I was acknowledging and being supportive of Mick's feelings whilst helping him get in touch with the clients' feelings through identifying his own in the here-and-now space of the supervision, in order that he could use that understanding in his facilitation of the group.

We thought about the low attendance and how this fed into Mick's own fear that the group wasn't interesting and that people might drop out. Although Mick was able to think about some of the dynamics he was still keen to use the script. I did read it and gave some feedback, but I felt a little uncomfortable as it felt quite personal and I was worried about appearing critical in my feedback. This was an interesting countertransference for me, but one I didn't share with Mick. The need to relieve his anxiety was more prominent (I was caught up in the transference).

Mode 6: focus on the supervisor's countertransference. I used this mode in my own reflection, but did not share this with Mick as a parallel of what might be happening in the group. Partly, I think, I was caught up in the transference and drawn into evaluating, but also I felt this would be too much to expect Mick, as a non-therapist, to process.

The Double Matrix model has helped develop my awareness of what level we are working at in the supervision at different times, and when it might, or might not, be right to change this in supervising a non-therapist of a non-therapy group. I have been able to see how the supervision has progressed so far and can plan and reflect on future sessions with this framework in mind. It is a model that can be applied to supervision of different supervisees as it allows for different levels of exploration, whilst sitting well with my own psychodynamic orientation.

The role of the art form in generic clinical supervision practice and training

In the introduction to the chapter I said that much of the writing so far on dramatherapy supervision has focused on the drama. It is important to acknowledge this aspect of the supervision as a unique way of working. One of my original goals from supervision training was learning ways to bring the drama into the supervision. When choosing a generic training it was important for me to supplement this with two workshops on the art form in supervision facilitated by a dramatherapist and supervisor. Although I have focused so far on the aspects of clinical supervision and clinical supervision training that can be shared across professions, I do believe that creative tools can enhance supervision, and that as arts therapists we have something important to offer supervisees from other professions. What I find special about arts therapy supervision is how the art form can be used to aid reflection:

> Through staying with a dramatic framework, the artistic skills of the supervisee will be enhanced thus enabling her internal guide to emerge, nourishing her and activating her internal supervisor.
>
> (Tselikas-Portmann 1999: 204–5)

Tselikas-Portmann (1999) sees the aesthetic distancing of drama as enabling 'letting-go' (p. 27) in order to 'expand perception' (p. 28) of the material brought to supervision.

In Mick's supervision we explored the symbolic content of the clients' dramatic material and the relationship to the group dynamics, two of Chesner's three areas for attention in dramatherapy supervision (Chesner

1999: 43), and perhaps another dimension the drama brings to Hawkins and Shohet's matrix. Mick relayed the drama from the session and we thought how the clients found the exercise, the roles they chose to play and what this might be saying. In one session he talked about the need of some members to make a story violent and tragic but with comedy, while another member found this uncomfortable and always added a happy ending. I facilitated thinking on what this might be about, and whether this was a pattern. I wondered how this could be acknowledged in the group without being therapy, and how it might relate to the issue of confidence, the focus of the group.

As a dramatherapist it seems natural to use the art form in the supervision when this can add something helpful. I think that our dramatherapy skills/tools can actually enhance supervision with any professional who is open to them. One way of using drama is to represent the therapy material, or relationship, brought to the supervision with projective objects/figures or through role play. Lahad (2000) uses this in supervision groups with non-dramatherapists, sometimes asking the group members to take on the roles and reflect back what they felt, etc. About a year into Mick's supervision I initiated this approach. I could see that the dynamic of the group was changing, along with Mick's role, but he was struggling to see this clearly. He also had frustrations about some members which might be helpful to express. I suggested he represent the group with animals and figures to help us think about the dynamic and conflict of the different roles.

Mick chose a dragon, a cat, a 'fluffy bunny' and an action man to represent the group members, and a magician to play himself. He arranged the characters on the table. He had the dragon at the front and the magician slightly behind the others, but close to them. I encouraged Mick to stay with the characters, to describe them, and prompted exploration with questions. He described the dragon as strong and dominating, but thought this was a defence. The bunny wanted everything to be happy. The cat was amenable but could defend itself (get its claws out) when it needed to. The action man was very powerful when present, but sometimes retreated; his absence was even more powerful. Mick had initially chosen an old man for himself, a father figure who takes care of the group, but rejected that in favour of the magician. The magician held the creativity and could magic up scripts for the others.

Mick was able to explore the different roles the group members played, how they interacted, and the effect on the group dynamic. His ambivalence about whether he was an old man or a magician, and where he was positioned, was a good indicator of Mick's role in the group. It highlighted an area that was difficult for him, i.e. being facilitator rather than one of the group, and something we would consider again.

We returned to this way of working in a later session, when Mick was co-facilitating the group with a dramatherapy trainee. We compared how they saw the group and their role within it, exploring the differences and similarities. Thinking back to the developmental model, bringing together a trainee and a non dramatherapist allows an interesting comparison of how the same work is viewed, and supervising them together (albeit briefly) highlighted the differences in their approach and perspectives and the need for me to be flexible in bringing these together.

Conclusion

The different supervision trainings developed to date vary in length and orientation but many have similar teaching hours. Some training courses include a supervision group, some are orientation specific. All seem to include boundaries, ethical issues, transference and contracts in their content. The generic training included these areas, but did not include the use of the art form. There was, however, opportunity for individuals to explore areas relevant to their own orientation.

I conclude that a generic supervision training can address some of the learning needs of the arts therapist supervisor. It provides them with a structure to find which model of supervision they want to use, and to develop their own approach. It also provides a forum to think about across discipline supervision, and a distinction between management and clinical supervision. The arts therapist may feel some frustration during such a training, as they may be ahead of the other students in their understanding of clinical supervision and important boundaries. The training is an introduction and needs to go alongside development of supervisory practice, giving and receiving, and sufficient clinical experience. Personally, it significantly raised my confidence by increasing my knowledge. It facilitated my reflection on the supervision I give, and taught me structures and models to refer to. I believe it has enhanced my supervision practice. The training lacked ideas to facilitate creative exploration, so I supplemented it with two workshops on the use of the art form in supervision. This satisfied my craving for exploration with people who shared my understanding of the processes in the creative work.

Can training alongside other professions substitute for training with other arts therapists? Having supplemented with the two workshops, I would say both experiences are valid and useful. Arts therapists training together will not all have the same orientation and approach to supervision. In the generic training I felt confident in asking questions that I might not have asked in a profession-specific training for fear of showing my ignorance. I was surprised that these other professional groups do have models of clinical supervision that I can apply, or adapt, and that most of the models come from nursing and social work. Most of the students worked in the same organisation, which meant we could compare experiences and look together at the policy. There was also something useful about sharing with other professional groups, learning from and about each other. I noticed that the work of the psychological therapist is often of a different nature – working inside the boundaries of time and space and developing a relationship – to nurses who are managing a large group of clients on a busy ward. Perhaps it is easier for us as a profession to separate clinical from managerial supervision for this reason. Putting it in context though, I work in a dramatherapy team, and am part of other forums where I can think creatively and psychodynamically. I have regular clinical supervision with a dramatherapist where I can bring my supervision practice. I may have needed different things from a training if I had been an isolated, psychological therapist.

After graduating from the training I was invited to give a seminar to the next intake of students on the use of creative tools in clinical supervision. This was an opportunity to share my skills as a dramatherapy supervisor with other professionals and enable them to start bringing creativity into the supervisions they give and receive. Watching the group working in pairs with small figures and animals to represent a client relationship or team dynamic, finding new perspectives, generating ideas and enjoying playing in this way, I was reminded what dramatherapy adds to clinical supervision. In this chapter I have described what I learnt from other professions' approaches, perhaps we should teach them about ours.

References

Bishop, V. and Butterworth, T. (eds) (1995) *Proceedings of Clinical Supervision Conference*, London: Department of Health.

Butterworth, T. and Faugier, J. (1998) *Clinical Supervision and Mentorship in Nursing*, 2nd edn, Cheltenham: Nelson Thornes.

Carroll, M. (1994) The generic tasks of supervision: analysis of supervisee expectations, supervisor interviews and supervisory audio taped sessions, Phd thesis, University of Surrey, Guildford.

Carroll, M. (1996) *Counselling Supervision: Theory, Skills and Practice*, London: Sage.

Chesner, A. (1999) Dramatherapy supervision: historical issues and supervisory settings, in E. Tselikas-Portmann (ed.) *Supervision and Dramatherapy*, London: Jessica Kingsley Publishers.

Couroucli-Robertson, K. (1999) Supervisory triangles and the helicopter ability, in E. Tselikas-Portmann (ed.) *Supervision and Dramatherapy*, London: Jessica Kingsley Publishers.

Driscoll, J. (2000) *Practising Clinical Supervision: A Reflective Approach*, Edinburgh: Baillière Tindall.

Fish, D. and Twinn, S. (1997) *Quality Clinical Supervision in the Health Care Professions: Principled Approaches to Practice*, Oxford: Butterworth-Heinemann.

Hawkins, P. and Shohet, R. (2000) *Supervision in the Helping Professions*, 2nd edn, Maidenhead: Open University Press.

Holloway, E. (1995) *Clinical Supervision: A Systems Approach*, London: Sage.
Jenkyns, M. (1999) Training the supervisor-dramatherapist 1: a psychodynamic approach, in E. Tselikas-Portmann (ed.) *Supervision and Dramatherapy*, London: Jessica Kingsley Publishers.
Jennings, S. (1999) Theatre-based supervision: a supervisory model for multi-disciplinary supervisees, in E. Tselikas-Portmann (ed.) *Supervision and Dramatherapy*, London: Jessica Kingsley Publishers.
Kadushin, A. (1976) *Supervision in Social Work*, New York: Columbia University Press.
Lahad, M. (2000) *Creative Supervision: The Use of Expressive Arts Methods in Supervision and Self-supervision*, London: Jessica Kingsley Publishers
Landy, R. (1999) Role model of dramatherapy supervision, in E. Tselikas-Portmann (ed.) *Supervision and Dramatherapy*, London: Jessica Kingsley Publishers.
Proctor, B. (1988) Supervision: a co-operative exercise in accountability, in P. Hawkins and R. Shohet (2000) *Supervision in the Helping Professions*, 2nd edn, Maidenhead: Open University Press.
Tselikas-Portmann, E. (ed.) (1999) *Supervision and Dramatherapy*, London: Jessica Kingsley Publishers
Tselikas-Portmann, E., Jennings, S., Couroucli-Robertson, K. and Kyriacou, D. (1999) Training the supervisor-dramatherapist 2: the theatre-based approach, in E. Tselikas-Portmann (ed.) *Supervision and Dramatherapy*, London: Jessica Kingsley Publishers.
UK Central Council for Nursing, Midwifery and Health Visiting (1999) *Practitioner–Client Relationships and the Prevention of Abuse*, London: UK Central Council for Nursing, Midwifery and Health Visiting.
van Ooijen, E.V. (2000) *Clinical Supervision a Practical Guide*, London: Churchill Livingstone.
Weaks, D. (2002) Unlocking the secrets of 'good supervision': a phenomenological exploration of experienced counsellors' perceptions of good supervision, *Counselling and Psychotherapy Research* 2, 1: 35–9.

Chapter 10

An exploration of supervision in education

Mandy Carr and Emma Ramsden

Introduction

How does supervision of dramatherapy operate in a non-clinical context? To what extent are schools exploring the supervision process with their staff, or ignoring it, making its presence invisible? Does supervision have a role at all in educational settings? Can teachers be supervised using a dramatherapy supervision model? Within the stressful culture of education in the UK, how might underlying anxieties of schools, staff and young people be reflected within supervision? This chapter aims to explore these issues within the context of education. We hope that it will further the debate about the importance of supervision in education, and provide ideas for plotting this process more firmly on the educational map. Key ideas are illustrated by vignettes drawn from dramatherapists' experiences, as well as supervision sessions with staff teams, all based in inner city primary or secondary schools.

Contexts: dramatherapy, education and supervision

Sometimes dramatherapists work as part of multidisciplinary teams, for example, so-called 'behaviour support' services. However, many will be the only clinically qualified practitioner in a school, and may feel isolated. Dramatherapists in schools work with young people with a wide variety of needs, ranging from young children with a range of emotional and behavioural needs, to teenage girls who are self-harming and adolescent boys who may have experienced violence in war-torn home countries. The vignettes in this chapter illustrate the need for specialist supervision: in one session a self-harming 15-year-old girl disclosed to the dramatherapist, 'Don't worry, I'll be dead by lunchtime.' In another, an Eritrean girl spoke of witnessing soldiers arresting and beating up her father because of his Christian beliefs. In both cases the therapist responded by arranging extra supervision sessions to explore whether she had supported the young people in the best way possible, and to look at a range of alternatives and perspectives. In the first instance, for example, the therapist, as supervisee, needed to check that she had followed the school's child protection procedures to the letter. Second, she needed to examine her own emotional, spiritual and cultural reactions for a number of important reasons: to ensure that her own emotions did not blind her to the needs of the client; to see if her intuitions could give her more information about the client; and, most importantly, to look at her cultural conditioning, so that unconscious bias did not obfuscate the issues.

Registered professionals who offer psychological or medical services in every configuration of client settings in this country enter into an ethical contract to be accountable for their working practice and to engage in regular clinical supervision. The British Association of Dramatherapists states in its *Code of Practice*:

> Dramatherapists have moral and ethical responsibilities towards clients and must ensure that they practise with integrity. Dramatherapists should monitor their practice to ensure that they are not making discriminatory decisions based upon a client's race, class, culture, nationality, gender, age, marital status, physical or mental ability, physical appearance, religion, political opinions or sexual orientation.
>
> (BADth 2007)

Further, when consulting the *Code of Conduct* of the British Psychological Society (BPS 2007), detailed in the section 'Ethical Principles – Standards of General Respect', guidance given for practising psychologists states that registrants must '(ii) Respect the knowledge, insight, experience and expertise of clients, relevant third parties, and members of the general public. (iii) Avoid practices that are unfair or prejudiced . . . and (iv) Be willing to explain the bases for their ethical decision making' (BPS 2007: 10).

The supervisor enters into a balanced alliance with the supervisee in order to provide a mutually safe, secure and confidential environment in which the latter feels professionally supported. This support consists of regular sessions with a clinical supervisor (as opposed to a managerial supervisor) where the supervisee explores all aspects of their practice in order to gain insight (the process by which understanding of an issue, person or thing is gained through reflection and focus) into their client's internal landscape. The aim is to facilitate healthy intrapsychic changes for their client(s), by complying with safe and ethical service delivery, and through the furthering of their own professional process. In order to practise within this ethical framework, practitioners must enter into 'a process of ethical decision making that includes . . . reflecting upon established principles, values, and standards' and 'seek consultation and supervision when indicated, particularly as circumstances begin to challenge their . . . professional expertise'. Further, they should 'Engage in additional areas of professional activity only after obtaining the knowledge, skill, training, education, and experience necessary for competent functioning' (BPS 2007: 15). This directive regarding continuing professional development (CPD) is written into the code of practice for professional modalities, both medical and psychological, albeit with different wording and some differences of clinical language. The Health Professions Council (HPC), the body which stipulates registration by the state for a variety of practitioners including arts therapists, defines CPD as 'a range of learning activities through which health professionals maintain and develop throughout their career to ensure that they retain their capacity to practice safely, effectively and legally within their evolving scope of practice' (HPC 2007).

Clinical supervision is also offered to a variety of workers in other settings who are not registered therapeutic practitioners. The material discussed in this chapter focuses on providing supervision in educational contexts, both primary and secondary. It explores supervision for both dramatherapists and teachers working in inner city schools in England, in recognised areas of social and economic deprivation.

There are many different methods of supervisory practice. In this chapter we place focus on working within a psychodynamic framework. However, we acknowledge that this is only one of many ways of approaching client material in the supervisory space. For example, supervision can focus on developing the supervisee's knowledge of strategies and interventions by engaging in exercises from a learning perspective. Issues may also be worked with placing emphasis on the expression through various aspects of a creative medium. It might be suggested that the supervisee draws, or paints, an image to represent their client(s) as if they were an animal or object, then embodies that image using movement to explore creative connections with the material, free of verbal input or interpretation. This process may be witnessed by the supervisor, or witnessed and reflected back to the client, using, for example, mirroring and sculpting techniques.

In this chapter we draw on aspects of the Double Matrix approach to supervision, especially mode five, as detailed by Hawkins and Shohet (2000), where focus is placed on the concept of the 'parallel process' (2000: 80). Parallel process is a concept that has developed from psychoanalytic theory. It reflects the idea that clients' issues are unconsciously mirrored within the supervisory relationship, or within an institution in which the therapy is taking place. Hawkins and Shohet comment:

The job of the supervisor is tentatively to name the process and thereby make it available to conscious exploration and learning. If it remains unconscious the supervisor is likely to be submerged in the enactment of the process.

(Hawkins and Shohet 2000: 81)

We suggest that parallel process should be understood in relation to mode six, which focuses on the supervisor's own process, that is, an exploration of how 'the therapeutic relationship enters into the internal experience of the supervisor' (2000: 82). There are many ways in which this might occur, including the supervisor noting a sudden mood or energy change (such as becoming tired). This might also be indicated by the unexpected intrusion of thoughts, images or material not pertaining to those brought to the session by the supervisee. By consistently rechecking and relearning about their own process, the supervisor can help identify what is his, or her, own material (countertransference, see below) and what material might be unconsciously brought by the therapist which the 'supervisor is tentatively bringing . . . into consciousness for the therapist to explore' (2000: 83).

The exploration of the notion of transference is a key aim in supervision, which grew from Freud's realisation that often clients developed feelings in particular ways within the analytic relationship. These feelings, although sincere, were really about other people in their lives, transferred on to the analyst. Barnes *et al.* (1999) summarise this as follows:

> [Freud] came to recognise that it was the way in which the relationship between the analyst and the patient developed which allowed this unconscious material to come to consciousness through the patient's feelings and fantasies about the analyst. The analyst tried to be as neutral as possible to allow the patient to transfer his feelings (of which he had previously been unconscious) onto the analyst. These feelings turned out to originate in past relationships with people who were highly significant for the patient, often family members. This process was termed transference.
>
> (Barnes *et al.* 1999: 17)

Approaching supervision from this perspective recognises that transference is unconscious and occurs in every therapeutic and supervisory exchange (and indeed every human exchange). The supervisor, as well as the supervisee, will be re-enacting historical relationships on an unconscious level and exploring them throughout their professional alliance.

Countertransference could be described as the feelings that the therapist may be unconsciously projecting on to the client involving, as Hawkins and Shohet suggest, 'some sort of predominantly unaware reaction to the client by the therapist' (2000: 78). They comment that 'it is essential for the therapist to explore all forms of counter-transference in order to have greater space to respond rather than react to the client' (2000: 78). Learning to understand instinctual feelings evoked by the supervisory exchange is learning to acknowledge countertransference and to separate this out from the parallel process that may be present. It is essential for the supervisor to have a good level of awareness of their own process, and to engage in therapy and supervision themselves, as the case vignette explains.

After talking about a dramatherapy session which featured sword play with a boy who made regular attempts to scale the school walls and escape (leading to the therapist being involved in risk managing escape attempts in the playground on a variety of occasions), the supervisor fed back the feelings of heaviness in her body that she had been experiencing whilst the supervisee was speaking. The supervisor explained that this was an unfamiliar feeling for her and wondered how it might relate to the clinical problem being discussed. The supervisee was not able to make any conscious links, but was keen to think about the difficulties of escaping whilst feeling heavy.

The supervisor (as supervisee) in her own supervision on her supervisory practice later in the week, found herself talking with her supervisor about her own schooling and the conflicting behaviour she communicated by being disruptive in class, ensuring over time her continued exclusion from the classroom, set against her desire at the age of 14 to be included, but not knowing how to ask or how to access the curriculum. The supervisor explored the feelings of hopelessness and despair that might belong both to her supervisee in her professional role, and also to the child.

Back in the supervision space the following week, the supervisor informed her supervisee that she had experienced a significant countertransference regarding their previous session, which led to her wondering about feelings of despair and hopelessness with regards to this work. She did not name her wondering whether they were situated within the supervisee. However, the supervisee explored, using sculpting techniques, her feelings of being exposed, by proxy of the boy, in the eyes of the school's CCTV camera, situated and monitored in the large and busy general office, which monitored the playground from various angles and captured the boy's attempted escapes.

The supervisee noted feeling stuck whenever hearing colleagues' accounts of the boy's recent escape attempts. She further noted her own feelings of wanting to escape from what she perceived to be the judgemental eyes of her colleagues. The child, she suggested, also felt the virtual eyes and did not know how to ask for support.

In this vignette we see how the supervisor's own history of behavioural difficulties in childhood, and their associated emotions, were evoked within the supervision session. These remained unconscious until she had an opportunity to explore, using creative expressive methods, this work with her supervisee in her own supervision. This working through of the heavy feeling was identified as a countertransference. This led to an empathic offering in the following session with her supervisee, which enabled the supervisee, in turn, to explore her own countertransference during her involvement in the exchange with the child in the playground. The supervisory spaces of both the supervisee and the supervisor, in this case, provided the containers to allow unconscious connections to come to the fore and to be reflected into the clinical exchange with the client. This vignette focused upon the ways in which psychodynamic processes are present within dramatherapy supervision. Another powerful presence, which can also been seen within the vignette, is that of the context of policy and practice within which the dramatherapy occurs.

For the past ten years, it could be argued that education in the UK, particularly in the inner cities, has attempted to shift from an academic/results orientated perspective to a realisation that young people may be facing complex psychological issues that impede their access to the curriculum, incorporating such notions as 'emotional intelligence' (Goleman 1996). There has been a gradual move from the idea that schools exist to promote academic achievement, to a more holistic 'whole child' approach. Schools develop in-house behaviour management policies in an attempt to adhere to inclusive practice by containing problematic children and young people within the school environment, when instances of antisocial and problematic behaviour occur.

The publication of the green paper *Every Child Matters* (ECM) (DfES 2004), which incorporated five rights for children, was a key development in that it included 'staying safe' and being 'healthy', with specific reference to mental as well as physical health. It emphasised the need for education, health and social services to work together with the child and her, or his, family. This potentially groundbreaking document shifted the focus from dealing with the consequences of difficulties in children's lives, to preventing things from going wrong in the first place. Many educationalists and therapists now see this shift as sporadic, and largely dependent on the commitment of particular individuals within local education authorities (LEAs) and schools, rather than the intended national initiative. Proposed in the Every Child Matters legislation was the Common Assessment Framework (CAF). This is a strategy which uses a standardised approach to assessing the needs of children and young people. CAF training by local authorities for all staff who work with children and young people in statutory environments began implementation in April 2006 and is due to be completed by March 2008. This standardised approach for the commitment to working together in the interest of the child by all involved, from social services to education to the health service, is timely. It was partly a response to cases like Victoria Climbié, a child who died as the victim of neglect and cruelty, despite regular involvement by a variety of agencies. In 2003 the enquiry emphasised the importance of effective inter-agency collaboration (Victoria Climbié Inquiry 2007). The Children's Society (2007) has asserted in its research-based document *Just Justice Report* that its findings can be seen as showing how ECM does not adequately address racism in relation to its definition of 'staying safe':

> Failing to identify, challenge and redress children's racist experiences is a failure to promote the welfare of young people who suffer the indignity and physical and emotional impact of racism. Joint action to protect children from racist abuse, harassment and discrimination should be planned and addressed under the 'staying safe' outcome in the Children Act 2004.
>
> (Children's Society 2007)

Gary Walker (2007) maintains:

> The government's use of antisocial behaviour orders (ASBOs), is in direct contravention to the aims of Every Child Matters. The rhetoric may be very appealing, and yet fundamental questions and issues arise . . . the proposals appear to view children and young people as malleable. It seems to suggest that if they can be coaxed, supported, tweaked or pushed, then they will do what the state wishes. Individual agency of children appears to be absent, as if what will be rewarded is behaviour that reflects, or fits in with the prevailing values and norms of adults . . . the area of youth justice is riddled with inconsistencies. Ten young people a week are jailed as a result of ASBOs, a far cry from the aim stated in . . . the Every Child Matters publication on the Criminal Justice System to 'minimise the use of custody' (DfES, 2004, p3) . . . [this] seems to oppose the apparently child-centred vision contained in Every Child Matters. The legislation on ASBOs makes no distinction between a 10-year-old child and an adult in terms of issuing an order.
>
> (Walker 2007: 147–49)

Many arts therapists share the view that if therapeutic interventions are not offered within school, then many young people will be denied access to them altogether. Parents/carers, particularly, if they perceive the need for therapy as a source of shame, simply will not allow their children to attend a 'clinic' outside school hours. It might also be that due to the practicalities of other childcare needs, distance and/or finance, families are unable to make or keep appointments at child and adolescent mental health services (CAMHS) or other such agencies. The provision of such help within school can depathologise it, render it part of normal development and reduce any associated stigma. However, where work in schools exists it is mostly in inner city schools, the majority within primary and special education and fewer in secondary schools.

Parents and teachers are often more willing to consider behaviour management support rather than therapy in school. In behaviour management, focus is placed on equipping teachers with the knowledge and skills to 'manage' behaviour in their classrooms, by developing a positive attitude towards 'emotionally and behaviourally disturbed pupils . . . to support their pupils in their attempts to change their behaviour' (McNamara and Moreton 1999: 17). Therapy, practised either with individuals or small groups of children and young people away from the classroom environment, in a confidential room, aims to enable the client(s) to explore and transform their difficulties and concerns at their own pace. The therapist creates 'a sense of safety, of being "held", opening up the possibility for play' (Pearson 1996: 12). The report of the Practitioners' Group on School Behaviour and Discipline aimed to promote and disseminate good practice in all schools regarding the management of behaviour (DfES 2005). One of the group's beliefs suggested that 'consistent experience of good teaching engages pupils in their learning and this reduces instances of poor behaviour'. Further, 'the consistent application of good behaviour management strategies helps pupils understand the school's expectations and allows staff to be mutually supportive' (DfES 2005: 12).

Behaviour management can be explored as part of the delivery of ECM outcomes via an extended schools service. The responsibility for working with the individual needs of each child is therefore owned by the community of the school, the multi-agencies who offer interventions and links in schools (including therapists), along with families, parents and caregivers. Behaviour management looks at ways of exploring many aspects of behaviour, including 'how parents can be more effectively engaged in supporting schools in promoting good behaviour and respect' (DfES 2005: 6).

The term 'behaviour management' does not engender fear in the way that therapy often can. However, there will always be a small percentage of parents who are results-focused themselves and view it as a disadvantage if their child/young person misses curriculum time for emotional support. Parents look to teachers to provide this management. Teachers frequently feel unable to offer the individual attention often required by troubled children and young people. They feel under pressure to perform and provide a service that is outside of their specialised training of educating groups of children. Whilst many teachers are insightful as to the factors affecting performance, they do not have the environment or skills to engage in this way with children who experience significant difficulties. Even experienced teachers can feel deskilled when faced with persistent behavioural difficulties: 'This can give rise to a sense of failure and then a tendency to "re-act to" rather than "reflect upon" a pupil or situation . . . Few teachers are equipped with the . . . skills needed to address emotional and behavioural problems affecting learning' (Jackson 2002: 142–43).

We suggest that a parallel process is occurring, in that the teachers are experiencing the lostness of the parents with regard to behaviour management. Aspects of the phenomena experienced at home are being brought into the classroom, rejecting both the teacher and parent as if they were one autonomous representation of negative power. This in turn mirrors the negative power being projected by the client and 'caught' in dynamic terms by both parent/caregiver and teacher. As we shall see in our writing about primary education, behaviour management is an accepted term in the school system and there are many courses and resources which attempt to equip teachers with the skills adequately to contain these difficulties.

Supervising groups of teachers in primary education

There are several innovative projects in the UK which provide supervision to teachers in schools. The Hackney Learning Trust, and other local education authorities, have run pilot projects in giving an entire staff of a primary school access to group supervision (Bruck et al. 2004). Other initiatives include Jackson's (2002) work at the Brent Centre for Young People that involved developing ideas for staff groups in 1998 in secondary schools in the borough.

The project described below was provided by a BADth approved supervisor and consisted of two supervision groups which ran over an academic year. The delivery of the project was funded, managed and administrated by an educational trust with a positive and long standing reputation with schools in the borough for their quality service delivery of their programmes, which included behaviour management for nursery, Key Stage 1 and Key Stage 2. The trust, a registered charity funded from various statutory and non-statutory sources, provides behavioural and educational support to primary schools within the inner city borough where it is geographically based.

Six sessions were offered to each group. With the exception of the initial session, each session lasted for three hours. Sessions were held every half-term during school time, at a local off-site venue. Supply cover was provided by the educational trust for each member of staff. This arrangement enabled the project's accessibility and ensured attendance. With the supply cover, supervisor fee and venue hire, one three-hour session cost approximately £3000.

The project was pitched by the educational trust to the schools' headteachers (the gatekeepers for any training offered to teachers) as behaviour management groups. The schools in this area operated in collaboratives of six schools. Behaviour management was a concept that headteachers and other personnel in the education system were keen to engage with for staff members. Various training days (INSETs) were programmed during the academic year, to look at strategies and models relating to this area of enquiry. Many schools scheduled a whole staff meeting each term to review the behaviour management policy. Headteachers had various forums throughout the academic year to meet together and discuss and plan future resources with regard to behavioural input.

The ethics of setting up a supervision group under an assumed title may be questioned, as it could be seen as misleading to participants due to its 'false' advertising. However, the thinking behind this was the belief that if the groups were set up simply as supervision groups the project would have received little or no uptake by headteachers. The language of the project would probably not have made any direct connections with the needs of the school or the local authority's directives. In education, behaviour management is part of the correct language in the current climate, whereas the term supervision, in a non-managerial context, is rarely used.

Having previously managed an arts therapies department in the UK National Health Service (NHS), the supervisor had experience of playing a role not dissimilar to the weavers in Hans Christian Andersen's story, 'The Emperor's New Clothes' (Andersen 1982), as described by Dearnley (1985: 60). The Emperor, who cared for nothing but showing off his clothes, was duped by the two cheating weavers who undertook the difficult task of miming the making of clothes on large looms, whilst subversively eliciting more power than the Emperor himself. The weavers, by their confidence trickery, which could be seen as toxicity disguised as hard work and expertise, could be said to have changed the culture of the kingdom into something 'psychotic', where invisible clothes were believed real. This in some way parallels the setting up of the supervision groups. Unlike the weavers, who were great cheats, stealing the gold and finest silk of the kingdom for their own malevolent greed, this supervisor's motivation was to set up a healthy and supportive provision of supervision for teachers in schools.

To make this successful, the supervisor needed to find the right language that would be heard, just as the weavers found a language in their invisible clothes, making the statement that the clothes would 'become invisible to anyone who was unfit for the office he held, or was incorrigibly stupid' (Dearnley 1985: 60). There is perhaps a need to name a 'stupidity' within the educational system that does not recognise the efficacy of supporting teachers and other staff members, in order to provide better quality teaching, as well as the impact on staff retention and well-being for all in the workplace. The actions of one impact greatly on the actions of the other. This process can be seen clearly in the Emperor's story.

The ethics of the project were restored at the start of the initial session, when the supervisor became like the 'innocent' child in the story (Dearnley 1985: 63) declaring that the Emperor was naked. The supervision group was first introduced to the theoretical 'supervisory' model underpinning the group, as well as hearing a definition of behaviour management. This framework sought to balance supervisory and behaviour management ideas, suggesting that no one model of behaviour management would be favoured or didactically explored during the group's life.

In therapy it is hoped that the dramatherapist will negotiate a healthy therapeutic language within which the work can take place, and the client can begin to move forward with their issues and difficulties. This thera-peutic language is different and unique for each individual or each group worked with. Similarly, in supervision in education, the skills, interventions and strategies are offered at a collective developmental level appropriate to the group. This is created through experiential and action-based explora-tions and group discussion. By assessing the collective developmental level, the facilitator responds to the needs of the group as a whole, by aiming the intervention at a level which is inclusive and accessible to all. Delivering the correct level of development is achieved by continually assessing the group's ongoing presentation and engagement, whilst being mindful of individual and group process. This delivery has a two-fold function: to explore the emergent themes creatively; to illustrate some of the techniques available in the supervision space. The supervisor is aware that for many the internal fabric of psychodynamic supervision will be a new framework in which to work and experience. There can, therefore, be a danger of being flooded or swamped by previously unknown theoretical and experi-ential processes.

Some advantages of group supervision include having more opportunity to explore working with diversity and difference. Kareem argues that 'a psychotherapeutic process that does not take into account the person's whole life experiences, or that denies consideration of their race, culture, gender or social values, can only fragment that person' (2000: 16). In inner city areas, the majority of educational professionals are working with people from cultures other than their own for the majority of the time. Yet very little opportunity is given to explore cultural identity and any assump-tions one might be bringing into a situation which may be unhelpful or even damaging. Group supervision also provides an opportunity to experience professional group cohesion and reciprocal support. Disadvantages of group supervision can include: less time to explore individual cases, the presence of phenomena such as scapegoating, and a limited opportunity for quieter group members to feel supported and for their material to be heard. However, dramatherapy supervision can accommodate these dynamics by using exercises which enable pair and small group work, as well as whole group exploration, discussion and reflection.

Inevitably, as mentioned before, the historical relationships that make up unconscious transference will be present in the sessions, with elements remaining unconscious. Other aspects surface over time, dependent on the individual process and the overall trust and belief in the group. The trans-ference brought by the supervisees is explored in relation to the concept of parallel process to look at possible re-enactments, collusions and conflicts that relate to the supervisees' experiences within their school staff teams. The presence of unconscious processes is seen in the following case vignette which looks at the opening session of a supervision group, and the re-enacted and familiar actions of group members faced with a new process.

The vignette then moves to the end of the process to document the development of trusting exchanges between group members.

It was the first session. The group consisted of teachers with varying degrees of professional experience. Everyone arrived on time and the session began promptly. The teachers sat in the pre-prepared circle, many took out a notebook and pen. One person asked the supervisor if a space was needed to include the flipchart, which was lying flat against the wall.

The supervision model was outlined, making it clear that the group members' (supervisees') input was at the centre of the process. Throughout the session the group explored their responses to their work using a mixture of directive exercises and non-directive spaces for reflection (which included time for self-reflection). The group was equipped with skills for communicating non-verbally as well as directed in exercises which demanded reflective ways of working, focusing on looking, listening and introducing themes of the unconscious, interrelating and intrarelating.

The group began to form. Increases in confidence were experienced, along with a physical freeing of movement. The supervisees were introduced to an exercise using beanbags, which focused on co-ordination and spatial awareness, listening and group development skills via a silent collaboration of passing beanbags to others in the group without dropping them.

Reflections of the session were asked for both during an ending discussion and on feedback forms. Positive comments were given which included statements such as 'It isn't what I was expecting, it's better', 'I'm looking forward to the next session', 'I've never thought about my behaviour and what I bring in such detail'.

This beanbag exercise became the group's ending ritual at each session. Initially group members appeared too shy and reserved to engage in game playing and action-based work away from the safety of the circle of chairs where each session began. With each new session their confidence grew, along with their obvious relaxation and enjoyment of the action-based working, particularly the beanbag exercise. This activity is an example of how action methods can be used to track the development of a supervision group.

The final session at the end of the academic year was closed with the beanbag exercise. Already in a circle in the 'designated action area' of the room, the feeling in the group was one of knowing enthusiasm. It felt as if each group member was checking in with themselves in terms of their responsibility, both to self and other.

The concentration from the outset was notable. This was the last time the group were to work together using this exercise. The group, now closely formed, but in the mourning phase of the work, clapped enthusiastically as the task ended and gasped with surprise when the amount of beanbags were revealed (one less than there were group members).

The exercise had been carried out in a culture of both work and laughter, pleasure and education. It seemed like a metaphor for the appreciation of group members towards each other. A true creative process. The supervisor also experienced a strong sense of appreciation being silently shown towards her.

It was an incredibly moving experience for the supervisor who, at the start of the year, had not known what to expect. She had been nervous in the first session, and feared failure and rejection by the group. This could be seen in terms of both countertransference and parallel process. The themes of being good enough, of teaching and learning with mounting pressures of SATS results, administration and recording, paralleled the journeys of many of the children brought to the sessions. Another parallel concerned the ways the teachers' fear of failure and judgement reflected that of the supervisor. The children with persistent behavioural difficulties communicated in various, often attention-seeking ways the same questions that the teachers themselves brought: 'Am I good enough?' As Winnicott suggests, that is all we can hope to be (1999: 139).

Supervising dramatherapists in secondary schools

In secondary schools, dramatherapists can experience a struggle in finding and maintaining an appropriate, consistent space for their work. They can struggle to make their work 'visible' to parents and staff. In the following vignette, the questions 'Is there enough space for me? What can I reveal about myself and what do I need to hide?' will be explored. The way these issues might resonate for staff, therapists and young people in inner city schools will be examined. These questions, often unconscious, can be made manifest through the supervision process.

C had been working as a dramatherapist for three years in an on-site emotional and behavioural unit in an inner city comprehensive school of 2000 students. The most recent Ofsted report describes a context in which the socio-economic backgrounds of students are well below the national average.

An innovative headteacher had engaged counsellors, a music therapist and a dramatherapist to work alongside learning mentors. The dramatherapist had been working with M, a 12-year-old boy, who was withdrawn, anxious and who had not spoken at all in his term at the school.

She came to supervision in a distressed state. She was about to start her seventh session with M, having spent 20 minutes at lunchtime setting up the space with fabrics, art materials and musical instruments, when a tall male learning mentor had come in and said, 'I'm sorry you have to get out. This room is booked.' She felt quite shaken, but asserted that she had been using the room for six weeks, that consistency was important and that the client was due in five minutes. The learning mentor returned several minutes later, saying that the head of unit had said she had to get out. C said she couldn't let down a client in that way and would be happy to discuss the situation after the session.

She felt guilty that she had found it hard to focus on the client during the session, but happy that he had seemed to develop his impulse to communicate using the musical instruments and a dialogue drawing activity. She had been so upset that she was unable to remember much about the detail of the session. Straight afterwards, the head of the unit, in the presence of a trainee dramatherapist had shouted, 'There isn't space for two dramatherapists here.'

In the supervision session, C explained how she had felt belittled, bullied and humiliated, and all of this in front of a student dramatherapist. She also felt furious with the head of unit, but unable to express her anger in a safe way. She felt confused and unable to address the needs of the client as well as her own. She was ashamed that her client had almost 'disappeared from her view' in the midst of this furore. Her supervisor was a drama-therapist with ten years' experience of supervision. She encouraged C to use objects to portray the situation. She used string to mark out the space, creating an enormous complexity of 'rooms' with the dramatherapy space shown as tiny and right at the side of the building. She used shells for the characters, the client 'shell' being submerged by the therapist 'shell', who was submerged by the learning mentor and the head of centre and the head teacher. C observed that all the voices seemed to be suppressed, and that the voice of her 'selective mute' client was the most suppressed of all. She reflected that in, some ways, the unit was being used by the school to exclude as many challenging young people as possible, and that the pressure on the head of the unit and its staff was almost intolerable. The use of such creative methods within supervision can enable a therapist to see a situation from a wider variety of perspectives. In this case, the process of having recounted her story and expressed her feelings about it could be said to have freed her to be able to imagine the situation from the head of unit's point of view. Hawkins and Shohet point out that 'teachers . . . will often complain that they are constantly drained by supporting so many clients and receiving so little support themselves' (2002: 17).

The therapist was then encouraged to role play the conversation with the head of the unit, alternating roles. Having embodied the head of unit, she reflected how disempowered she felt. She was also able to express her anger towards her. She noted that the situation had triggered some of her anger with her mother from childhood. She had felt 'infantilised'. She remem-bered that the learning mentor has apologised for interrupting the session, saying that he felt forced to do it. The young client himself had experienced 'bullying', one suggested reason for his selective mutism. The skill and experience of the supervisor as well as the therapist's willingness to engage with the process had resulted in a greater clarity. She was subsequently able to explore the needs of the client and look at ways of negotiating future use of the space, as well as exploring issues of the client being seen and his voice being heard.

In Moylan's chapter 'The Dangers of Contagion: Projective Identification Processes in Institutions', she emphasises the challenging nature of exploring intense feelings in a creative, constructive manner. She describes staff as 'constantly barraged by clients' projections' (1994: 55). The supervisor in this vignette could be said to have been 'barraged' by unconscious projections of 'being silenced', bullied and infantilised, from her client, her manager, the learning mentor and others in the workplace, resulting in a kind of ricochet sense of disempowerment, and the ensuing difficulties with communication. Moylan pinpoints 'the helpful nature of projective identification, if it can be understood as a communication' (1994: 55). Supervision helped this dramatherapist to stand back from her experiences and use her own feelings 'to understand what is going on' (1994: 58).

It can be seen that a parallel process reflecting the client's issues, in this case expressed through selective mutism, were unconsciously mirrored within the relationship between the dramatherapist and the head of unit. Supervision had enabled the therapist to bring these ideas into conscious awareness, with the intention, as a consequence, both of improving the relationship with the head of unit and working with greater understanding of the client's needs.

Conclusion

Using the overarching concept of parallel process, we have attempted to locate, identify and explore this phenomenon at various levels of service provision, both within the work with clients and the institution as a wider context which Hawkins and Shohet refer to as 'Mode 7' (2000: 84). For example, in the vignettes, where themes of heaviness and being silenced were noted, we have looked at the ways in which supervision helped to bring the parallel processes to conscious awareness with dramatherapists. We have also explored how using action-based method within group supervision for staff groups can explore group dynamics and patterns of change. We have aimed to demonstrate that supervision can play a crucial role in education. However, it is not widely seen as part of a mechanism for support in this sector. Supervision by creative arts therapists is, in our view, of particular relevance in a school setting, as it mirrors the creative and action-based educational styles adopted by many schools through the delivery of a creative and inclusive curriculum. The acceptance of supervision requires a whole school approach in order to give it credence. Furthermore, the idea for supervision should ideally be discussed and offered at teacher training level.

Some of the ideas in the chapter might challenge the system in ways for which the process is not easy to document, for example, exposing work pressures. Schools are required to provide teaching methods which match different learning styles. This is clearly not the case in the majority of schools for the children who fall into the emotional and behavioural difficulties remit. Raising the profile of supervision practice in education is one of the key tasks and hopes for this chapter. The profile being raised in the institution will also be felt within the supervisory relationship for 'the low value placed on supervision from outside can produce internal doubts, even when the supervision has gone well' (Dearnley 1985: 55). Again, parallel process is seen here. The supervisee, who on reflection, thinks they didn't do 'as well' as they might have parallels the experience of the child in class who feels that they are constantly failing. This sense of failure is often explored in individual dramatherapy sessions. It is also seen in the transference of the institution that is acting the role of 'teacher' to the teacher, who is 'infantilised' and plays the role of 'child'. Raising the status of supervision could be a major factor in raising the awareness of the need for support in the school. In this way the past could be truly remembered, re-enacted and revisioned, so that condemnation and repetition are avoided.

Given that the quality of leadership in schools varies on a wide continuum including conscious or unconscious styles of autocracy, bureaucracy and democracy amongst others, how then does the practitioner educate and advocate supervision in different settings? Indeed, the NCSL's report on successful leadership of schools identified the following leadership styles: 'shared leadership, distributed leadership, instructional leadership, transformational or transactional leadership, and charismatic leadership' (2003: 3). It went on to suggest that 'to be effective, a headteacher's leadership style needs to be attuned to the specific context experienced by a particular school' (p. 3). We have already identified learning the correct language for the education authority, but this can be further broken down into a learning for each school, an understanding of the individual culture of each school. Ironically, the supervision of dramatherapists, which normally takes place outside the workplace, is as 'invisible' as the dramatherapy work which takes place in a confidential setting.

The more that the emotional needs of young people, school staff, therapists and supervisors can be 'made visible' in education, the more likely are local authorities and schools to engage with the process of supervision itself. Tonnesmann (1979) is cited by Hawkins and Shohet (2000: 195) as observing that 'the human encounter in the helping professions is inherently stressful. The stress aroused can be accommodated and used for the understanding of our patients and clients. But our emotional responsiveness will wither if the human encounter cannot be contained within the institutions in which we work'. In supervision, such stress can be expressed, explored and contained. She goes on to conclude that 'if we can maintain contact with the emotional reality of our clients and ourselves, then the human encounter can facilitate not only a healing experience, but also an enriching experience for them and for us' (Hawkins and Shohet 2000: 105). The demands of educational institutions can result in staff losing touch with their own feelings as they rush from task to task, from target to target, at worst leading to stress-related illness and often to a sense of numbness and alienation. Personnel Today's online poll of 823 teachers 'showed that two-thirds felt that their jobs were "very stressful", with inadequate support from the headteacher or senior management cited as the biggest cause of stress' (Personnel Today 2007). Furthermore, 'seven out of ten respondents to the survey by *Teachers' TV* also cited pupils' behaviour among the most stressful aspects of the job'. Perhaps dramatherapy style supervision could support staff in processing their feelings and in using creative methods to view things from a broader perspective.

Applying psychoanalytic (and therefore unconscious) principles when working with staff support groups in educational settings, Jackson suggests it can be 'a very powerful resource and intervention' (2002: 144). Supervisory practice in general, and a greater understanding of the processes of transference and countertransference in particular, as we have demonstrated in this chapter, have the potential to transform the working lives of educational staff, and ultimately the educational opportunities and life chances of children and young people.

References

Andersen, H. C. (1982) *The Complete Illustrated Stories of Hans Christian Andersen*, London: Chancellor Press.

Barnes, B., Ernst, S. and Hyde, K. (1999) *An Introduction to Groupwork: A Group Analytic Perspective*, Basingstoke: Palgrave Macmillan.

Brent Centre for Young People (2007) http:www.brent-centre.org, accessed November 30 2007.

British Association of Dramatherapists (BADth, 2007) *Code of Practice*. Online. Available HTTP: <http://www.badth.org.uk/code/index.html#intro> (accessed 25 November 2007).

British Psychological Society (BPS, 2007) *Code of Conduct*. Online. Available HTTP: <http://www.bps.org.uk/document-download-area/document-download$. cfm?file_uuid=5084A882-1143-DFD0-7E6C-F1938A65C242&ext=pdf> (accessed 3 December 2007).

Bruck, T., Herschberg, E. and Kelly, C. (2004) Hackney Learning Trust, unpublished report by behaviour educational specialist team.

Childrens Society (2007) *Just Justice Report, The Children's Report*. Online. Available <http://www.childrenssociety/org.uk/NR/rdonlyres> (accessed 30 November 2007).

Dearnley, B. (1985) A plain man's guide to supervision or new clothes for the emperor, *Journal of Social Work Practice* 2, 1: 52–65.

DfES (2004) *Every Child Matters*, London: DfES.

DfES (2005) *Learning Behaviour – The Report of the Practitioners' Group on School Behaviour and Discipline*, London: DfES.

Dix, A. (2001) All our children, *Dramatherapy, the Journal of the British Association of Dramatherapists*, Spring: 22–4.

Goleman, D. (1996) *Emotional Intelligence*, London: Bloomsbury.

Hawkins, P. and Shohet, R. (2000) *Supervision in the Helping Professions*, 2nd edn, Maidenhead: Open University Press.

Health Professions Council (HPC, 2007) *Continuing Professional Development*. Online. Available HTTP: <http://www.hpcuk.org/aboutregistration/education andtraining/continuingprofessionaldevelopment/> (accessed 1 December 2007).

Jackson, E. (2002) Mental health in schools: what about the staff?, *Journal of Child Psychotherapy* 20, 2: 129–46.

Kareem, J. (2000) The Nafsiyat Intercultural Therapy Centre: ideas and experience in intercultural therapy, in J. Kareem and R. Littlewood (eds) *Intercultural Therapy*, Oxford: Blackwell.

McNamara, S. and Moreton, G. (1999) *Changing Behaviour – Teaching Children with Emotional and Behavioural Difficulties in Primary and Secondary Classrooms*, London: David Fulton.

Moylan, D. (1994) The dangers of contagion: projective identification processes in institutions, in A. Obholzer and V. Zagier Roberts (eds) *The Unconscious at Work*, London: Routledge.

NCSL (2003) Successful leadership of schools in urban and challenging contexts. Online. Available HTTP: <http://www.ncsl.org.uk/> (accessed 30 November 2007).

Pearson, J. (1996) Discovering the self, in J. Pearson (ed.) *Discovering the Self through Drama and Movement – The Sesame Approach*, London: Jessica Kingsley Publishers.

Personnel Today (2007) Stress causes half of UK teachers to think about quitting. Online. Available HTTP: <http://www.personneltoday.com/articles/2007/02/19/ 39342/stress-causes-half-of-uk-teachers-to-think-about-quitting.html> (accessed 30 November 2007).

Tonnesmann, M. (1979) The human encounter in the helping professions, paper presented at Fouth Winnicott Conference, London, March.

Victoria Climbié Inquiry (2007) Online. Available HTTP: <http://www.victoria-climbie-inquiry.org.uk/fineport/6recommend.htm> (accessed 1 December 2007).

Walker, G. (2007) Safeguarding children: visions and values, in P. Jones, D. Moss, P. Tomlinson and S. Welch (eds) *Childhood: Services and Provision for Children*, Harlow: Pearson.

Winnicott, D.W. (1999) *Playing and Reality*, London: Routledge.

Chapter 11

Making space for thought

Supervision in a learning disability context

Noelle Blackman

Introduction

As my title suggests, I am concerned with the issue of thinking in its broadest sense and the connection of this with learning disability. This chapter is concerned with the clinical supervision of dramatherapists working with people with learning disabilities. This is a broad term covering a spectrum of people with a wide range of abilities. I have therefore chosen to limit my focus to the supervision of dramatherapists who are working with people with mild to moderate learning disabilities. Also, because there are complex considerations to be made when using dramatherapy with groups of people with learning disabilities, I am concerned in this chapter with the supervision of one-to-one work. I write from my perspective as a dramatherapist having provided just such supervision over the last decade. Most of this supervision has been delivered as a clinical supervisor from outside of the organisation where the dramatherapy is being practised, which provides a very specific view. From this experience I will pose the following three questions. How can clinical supervision support a dramatherapist to:

- go about developing reflective thinking within her client with learning disabilities?
- recognise when lack of thinking gets into the system and affects the therapeutic relationship?
- ensure that she does not collude with not recognising invisible losses?

The term used to describe what we currently refer to in England as 'people with learning disabilities' has changed regularly throughout history. Sinason (1992) states that no human group has been forced to change its name so frequently. Many of the names once used medically, have ended up being used as terms of insult. It is as though it is unbearable for society to name what it is that differentiates people who may have difficulty with thinking. Sinason defines the word 'stupid' as having the original meaning numbed with grief, this would seem to emphasise the painfulness.

The society in which we live places a high value on beauty, intelligence, independence, youth and wealth, all elements important in our drive towards perfection. In the western world we have begun to shift from a medical model view of disability, where the person's disability is what is most focused on and is seen as a 'problem' with emphasis put on diagnosis; and all the difficulties being located within the person, to the social model of disability. The social model was formulated by activists and scholars in the UK, and locates disability not in an 'impaired' or 'malfunctioning' body, but in an excluding and oppressive social environment (Marks 1999).

However, although there is some shift towards the social model in the provision of learning disability services, society as a whole is still a long way behind. The message given to parents of a child born with a disability is that the birth is a tragedy or a personal burden. If it can be avoided, then there is an unspoken moral duty to do this (Loach 2003). This leads us to consider a more sinister collective view, which Sinason has highlighted (1992) as a death wish that society harbours towards people with disabilities. For example, no doctor was ever prosecuted for war crimes against disabled people (Gallagher 1990). Yet we know that alongside the genocide of the Jewish people, thousands of disabled people were systematically murdered in the holocaust (Proctor 1988; Lifton 1986). As Marks (1999) writes: 'The implicit and pervasive nature of eugenic philosophy in Western society helps to explain some of the extreme violations carried out against disabled people in the twentieth century.' Even in our so-called humane society today, we can still see ripples of this sad heritage in the second-rate health care that is offered to people with learning disabilities (Mencap 2004, 2007; Disability Rights Commission 2006).

In the context of this chapter we can now turn towards considering the mental health of this client group. Non-behavioural psychological services such as counselling, psychotherapy and psychoanalysis have historically rarely been available to people with learning disabilities, who have experienced trauma or who have psychological difficulties, e.g. depression (Sinason 1992; O'Driscoll 2000). There were occasional exceptions to this such as Pierce Clark (1933). Historically, there has been a lack of clarity over what constitutes a person's learning disability (which would be untreatable) and symptoms of psychological disturbance, which may have been masked by the disability and which are often treatable. A number of researchers have claimed that people with learning disabilities manifest the full range of mental health conditions seen in the general population. However, it has been highlighted that there are enormous problems regarding diagnosis in this population which can also impede any chance of treatment.

The landscape is changing, particularly with pioneering individuals such as Sinason (formerly from the Tavistock, 1992) and Hollins (current chair of the Royal College of Psychiatrists, 2002), who both until recently jointly ran psychotherapy groups at St George's teaching hospital in London. Beail

(Barnsley LD service, 1998) and Frankish (originally from Rampton Hospital, 1992) in the North of England are also widely published and well known in their own right. All have also been instrumental in setting up the Institute of Psychotherapy and Disability (IPD). The IPD is currently seeking status within UKCP and has started to set up specific training courses. Organisations such as Respond (a London-based charity) and a few specialist services within the National Health Service such as the Tavistock Clinic and the Specialist Loss and Bereavement Service (formerly roc) have taken the lead in developing psychotherapy with people with learning disabilities over the last decade or more. The rise in arts therapists, particularly within the National Health Service, has also meant that many people with learning disabilities are being referred specifically to creative therapists, as these forms of therapy have proved themselves often to be far more accessible to people with learning disabilities, who may not always find it easy to express themselves through words alone.

Before moving into exploring the three questions that I highlighted earlier I would like to define clinical supervision, its role in practising dramatherapy, and to examine the supervisory relationship. Tselikas-Portmann (1999: 13) states: 'The supervisor senses, understands, yet stands at the edge, looks with the "eye of the stranger", does not subscribe to the self-evidences of the supervised system.' This is particularly true when the supervisor is independent of the organisation where the dramatherapy is taking place; this position has advantages and disadvantages. One advantage is that it is sometimes easier for the supervisor to pick up on issues that are specific to the 'system' or organisation by being slightly outside and in a more objective role. A disadvantage is that it can also be easy to be pulled into a persecutory role 'alongside the therapist' of blaming the organisation and seeing it as a bad object, rather than trying to understand some of the deeper forces at play. Another disadvantage is that from such a removed position it can be difficult to gain a good sense of the session, the client and the setting. However, a positive point from the perspective of being 'an outsider' is that the supervisor has to become more curious and ask more questions than perhaps they might if they were from the setting, when they may have specific knowledge and familiarity, including perhaps first-hand knowledge of the client, which can lead to assumptions being made.

The point a dramatherapist has reached in their professional journey will also have an impact on the supervision. For example, a newly qualified and inexperienced dramatherapist will need the supervision to be primarily a place for ongoing professional development. The task of the supervisor at this point can best be summed up by Holloway's description: 'the primary goal of supervision is the establishment of an ongoing relationship in which the supervisor designs specific learning tasks and teaching strategies related to the supervisee's development as a professional' (Holloway 1995: 7). This sounds perhaps more structured than I would make a supervision session, but nonetheless these tasks and strategies would be at the back of my mind and would guide the way I worked with the fledgling dramatherapist.

Hawkins and Shohet (1996: 3) state that: 'supervision offers a framework where professional experiences can be survived, reflected upon and learnt from'. This is perhaps closer to my own view of the function of supervision. I met recently with a supervisee I had worked with for many years. We reminisced about the beginning of our supervisory relationship. I reminded her of how she needed to challenge my credentials and knowledge in the very early days of our work together. At this time she was fresh from her training and had just landed her first paid dramatherapy post. She remembered feeling a lack of confidence and anxiety about being 'good enough', or being 'found out' as a fraud. She said she needed to know that she would be 'held'. She remembered exploring the boundaries of supervision and working out what belonged in our sessions, what might need to be taken to a different kind of space such as personal therapy. All of these issues can be difficult and confusing in the journey towards establishing one's professional identity as a dramatherapist.

Holloway goes on to state that: 'Supervision provides an opportunity for the recognition of a professional's own resources, in combination with the information and skills available. If the learner remains dependent solely on the supervisor, then successful supervision has not taken place' (Holloway 1995: 7). This highlights the overall aim of supervision, which is to develop an internal supervisor within the dramatherapist, in order that they become more confident in their own practice. This is not to say that regular sessions with a supervisor would become redundant. It is my view that this external sounding board is a necessary process for safe practice for all therapists throughout their working life.

To return to the three points that are important when working therapeutically with this client group; the first is one that we see reflected by society generally: we often have too low an expectation of people with learning disabilities. There is a danger that this can be mirrored in the therapeutic relationship. One of the central aims of therapy with all clients is to develop the capacity to think and to reflect and yet this opportunity can get lost for many clients with learning disabilities. There will be a small number of people where this may not be possible and the relationship will then be the main tool for change. In my experience the challenge to the supervisor will be to ensure that the client is offered the opportunity to develop reflective thought, and when this does not appear to be happening, to explore why that is. In my experience dramatherapy, as well as being a useful and freeing therapeutic modality for people with learning disabilities, also has inherent within it the tendency not to be reflective, to be more reactive or responsive, or to work only in the metaphor, without bringing to conscious thought what might be lying dormant. There can be a danger to mirror the client group and function in a non-thinking manner. There is a danger that the therapist does not allow herself to theorise, as a defence against being intelligent, when faced with the learning disabled client. The supervisory space can be the place where it is safe to examine whether this may be happening. Although there may be good reason at some points early on within the therapy to work only on a symbolic level, it is important to establish whether there may also be an unconscious countertransference happening.

Stokes and Sinason (1992) distinguish between emotional and cognitive intelligence, stating that people with learning disabilities often have emotional intelligence. They describe what they see as the 'handicapped' and 'non-handicapped' parts of the personality. This suggests that there are parts within the person with a learning disability that could use psychotherapy, which implicitly means that they may also have the ability to develop thought and reflection. Bicknell (1983) suggests that insight into having a disability is far more present in people with learning disabilities than has often been believed. However, it is well documented that people often develop defensive reactions to the insight into their own disability (Bicknell 1983; Sinason 1992; Marks 1999). This is not surprising, when there is rarely the opportunity for people with learning disabilities to think or talk about this with others in a supportive environment. These defences can then further disable the person. In people with learning disabilities we often see this defence manifest in a phenomenon Sinason names 'the handicapped smile'. For 'adults who know they are not wanted, smiling is a way of paying to stay alive' (p. 143). A second defence is the opportunistic handicap, where every destructive aspect of the self finds a home in the disability. It can take a long time to move beyond what can be presented as either unthinking complacency or aggressive destructiveness, in order to establish a deeper therapeutic alliance. It is, therefore, imperative that if someone with a learning disability is given the opportunity of being in therapy, space is made to explore thoughts and feelings about living with a disability.

Research has shown that defensive behaviour will often stop within the first year of therapy (Carlsson et al. 2002). This has important implications in the debate over long-term therapy as a necessary treatment model for people with learning disabilities. The fact is that it can take some time for long-term defences to come down in order that deeper work can take place. In supervision, the therapist and supervisor can consider the original reason for referral and what foundation work needs to happen before it may be possible to work with the referring issue. This kind of reflection may support the therapist in considering realistically the length of the task at hand. In the climate of finance-driven health services and commissioning it can be difficult to contemplate the possibility of long-term therapeutic work. Yet with this client group there are important and legitimate arguments to be made for it. Ending therapy too early can leave a client with learning disabilities in the vulnerable position of having recognised their defensive coping mechanisms, and perhaps a feeling of having been 'found out'; but without any chance of further work on ego strengthening or developing the ability to think.

The second concern I would like to turn to is how processes that are associated with learning disability can get into 'the system' surrounding the client, in particular issues of dependency and difficulty with thinking. This can enter the therapeutic relationship or affect the environment in which the therapy is taking place. It is often the case that organisations offering services to learning disabled clients mirror the client group's experience in the way they function. Dependency, lack of autonomy, inappropriate infantalisation, anger, frustration, neglect or even abuse are all experiences which may be acted out by a service which is not given the opportunity to pay attention to unconscious processes (Obholzer and Zagier Roberts 1994). The emotional pain of disability already referred to, and the difficulty with thinking and processing thought that many people with learning disabilities experience, can affect the thinking of the supporting environment surrounding them. This can sometimes take the form of dissociation, where care givers seem to distance themselves emotionally so much from the people they care for that they can act in abusive ways. The worst examples of this are two recent reports of abusive behaviour by staff in two different NHS long-stay services in Cornwall and Surrey (HCC 2006, 2007).

Smaller examples of a similar process are the many complaints that I hear from therapists over difficulties in establishing even the most basic therapeutic requirements or being managed in a very infantilising paternalistic manner. Sometimes these complaints are about organisations that have chosen to employ a dramatherapist, yet continually sabotage the work by not engaging thoughtfully over what is really needed in order to provide the dramatherapy.

One supervisee called Jane experienced contradictory attitudes by the organisation that employed her. On one level they embraced the idea of having a dramatherapist and saw it as the answer to many difficult issues amongst the clients. On another level they sabotaged sessions and made passive aggressive attacks. This could be seen through the therapist's continual battle to secure a room she could use on a regular basis for her sessions. She would often arrive to find the room she had been assigned suddenly being used for something else, or being overhauled by builders without having been given any warning. Staff regularly 'forgot' to bring people for their sessions, or booked other appointments or outings that clashed with session times. Jane reported in supervision that she sometimes felt overt hostility from the care staff towards her. She said that they appeared jealous of what they saw as her 'special' relationships with clients. There was often a sense of blame that sessions with her would sometimes appear to provoke epileptic seizures. Strong emotions can make people with epilepsy more prone to seizures.

I listened to these reports and would facilitate Jane to consider why the staff might behave in such an angry and jealous way towards her. She could recognise that the clients were often very challenging, could be violent and that staff were dealing with this day in and day out. As we talked more about the people with learning disabilities who lived in this setting, Jane thought about how many reasons they had to feel jealous and angry towards the staff. For example, many of them rarely saw their families, but would have been very aware that the staff had partners, perhaps even children and/or parents, and that staff clearly had much more freedom and choice in their lives. It seemed that perhaps there was a cycle happening here, with the people with learning disabilities acting out their frustration on the staff and in turn, the staff acting out against the therapist. But it also seemed as though the staff placed themselves in competition with the dramatherapist. By splitting of their own feelings of hopelessness and inadequacy they could blame Jane for not being useful and ensure that this was the case by sabotaging her work.

The above situation is not an uncommon one in this kind of setting and highlights the importance of consultation or supervision for all staff involved in 'caring' work. Without a space in which to understand what might be happening, the unbearable feelings will continue to be acted out. Obholzer (1994: 91) describes how an ideal position for staff in this sort of setting to reach would be: 'an acknowledgement of the difficulties involved in working with the handicapped, and an acceptance of the fact that nobody knew the answers or had a simple solution. Recognising this led to greater sharing of difficulties and uncertainties, moving towards teamwork rather than competition and blame'.

I sometimes consider with my supervisees the possibility of them holding some training or consultancy sessions with the staff teams in order that these kind of issues can be addressed. Sometimes the mirroring process first becomes apparent within the supervisory dyad. The supervisor may find herself unable to reflect and process in her usual manner, or behave in an uncharacteristically parental role. She may have difficulty following the material the therapist presents. The therapist may appear very stuck or limited in her work with a particular client. There may be a real sense of chaotic thinking in the sessions. All these signs may indicate that a parallel process is occurring in the supervision or that unrecognised transference or countertransference processes are going on.

Maureen discussed a session with one of her learning disabled clients whom I will call Susan. The session took place after Maureen's two-week holiday break. She described how Susan had arrived in a distressed state clutching a broken tape recorder. Apparently she had fallen over on her way to the session and broken the tape recorder (she had decided to bring her own one with her as she hadn't liked the one Maureen used). Maureen described how she had begun to feel angry towards Susan, as she became so focused on the broken machine she couldn't settle in the session and had insisted on leaving the session to find her key worker who she felt would be able to mend it. Maureen said she resented the relationship that Susan had with her key worker, as it was 'overdependent'. I suggested that perhaps there were other reasons why she felt angry. She began to explore these uncomfortable feelings a little more and recognised that she felt jealous of the way that Susan had made her feel so inadequate by wanting to bring her key worker in to the session to make things better.

Voorehoeve and Van Putte (1994: 400) describe how 'defence mechanisms from (pre)oedipal and pre-verbal development phases play a role, while an appeal is made to dyadic relationship formation with staff, which can be further reinforced by the dependency-increasing character of the setting'.

I wondered if perhaps Susan wanted to reinforce her need for a dyadic relationship with Maureen, which had been interrupted by the break, by creating an envious dynamic. Maureen recognised this and we continued to explore the content of the session in more detail, eventually focusing less on Maureen's anger transference and more on her feelings of inadequacy. What was clear was that something was being expressed about disability, but it had almost got lost as we focused on the jealous and angry feelings. With the clarity of distance it is easy to see that there were many issues being expressed, including perhaps Maureen's fear that she was becoming too dependent on me. Within the supervision session our thinking was laboured. It would seem that we had been affected by the 'attack on thinking' that learning disability can so easily generate. Just before the end of the session Maureen said that Susan's desperation to find someone who could mend the machine was a clear expression of how Susan wanted not to be disabled. The tape recorder had become a metaphor for Susan's feeling of being, as Maureen put it, 'all broken and no one can fix her'. Again from outside the session this can seem very obvious. However, it was not possible for Maureen to process this within the therapy session, as the hopeless feelings that it brought up in her of not being able to 'mend' Susan were unbearable. This is a good example of the importance of clinical supervision as a place to examine and process uncomfortable or painful issues raised in therapy sessions which otherwise may remain invisible and be able to place this insight back into the therapeutic work.

The final concern I would like to turn to is the often invisible nature of loss, as it can feature in the lives of people with a learning disability. This is loss in its widest context and is best summed up by the three secrets to which Hollins (2002) refers – disability, sexuality and mortality. These subjects are painful and can be associated with complicated loss for this client group. It is important for the therapist and supervisor to be conscious of and to keep these issues in mind. There may be reference to these three subjects implicit in the material from the therapy, but without vigilance the connected losses can continue to remain invisible and overlooked.

One of the most difficult of these three taboos is the meaning of disability for the individual. It can be difficult to acknowledge disability which can become the unspoken 'elephant' in the room. I have touched on this point already at several stages earlier in the chapter. The therapist needs to be able to keep in mind the loss or pain that a client may feel in connection to having a disability; a client may or may not be able to verbally acknowledge this. It is all too easy for the therapist to collude with the defensive behaviour of the client. It can often be apparent within the creative clinical material that difference and disability is being explored (see example of Maureen presenting Susan above). Yet, the therapist may not reflect on this and the supervisor needs to ensure that they do not also become complicit in this. A gentle challenge of the therapist's interpretation of the session may uncover unrecognised countertransference. It is a fine balance between being gently supportive of the client and making demands on the learning disabled client to think. Sinason (1992: 74) warns us that in order 'to reach and explore this emotional intelligence a great deal of guilt must be dealt with, guilt of the patient for his 'handicap' and guilt of the worker for being 'normal'. One of the most common defences that a person with a learning disability will employ against the knowledge of disability is to not think (Simpson 2002). When a therapist enables the client with mild to moderate learning disabilities to think, alongside the pain of the insight of the disability there is room for personal growth. It is therefore imperative for the clinical supervisor to provide a space where the weight of this possible guilt can be shared and countertransference issues understood.

Bicknell (1983: 173) states that insight into the implications of a person's disability can often be linked not only to their cognitive ability but also to their life experience. She adds:

> Insight is also linked with failure to reach self-imposed standards. The mentally handicapped [sic] child in a large sibship often imposes standards that are just above the younger sibling. Somebody must be less capable than him. Families can be warned that there may be problems when the younger sibling of normal intelligence overtakes the handicapped older sibling.
>
> (Bicknell 1983: 173)

She goes on to suggest that if we are really to understand the meaning of disability beyond simply the organic meaning, we need to ask: What does it mean? For this person? To have this disability? At this time in his life? With this caretaker? In this environment? And in this peer group? If we can find answers to these questions for the people with whom we are working, we will have far greater understanding of the insight that they have into disability and what it means for them.

Sarah brought her concerns regarding how much she was struggling with a new client called Ann. She described how Ann would say 'yes' to everything but that there was also a sense that she didn't really want to 'do' anything. Ann was in her late twenties but would present herself as quite a young child and would often be quite clingy with Sarah, not wanting to leave at the end of the sessions. Sarah was feeling rather guilty because she often felt bored in these sessions. We explored this and thought a little more about Ann. Sarah knew that she had lived in institutions from an early age and felt that this had left her with a feeling of having been abandoned. She also knew that Ann still had contact with her sister who was married with children. We considered how hopeless Ann may feel about her own life as she watched her sister's life develop in parallel with her own life stagnating. We also thought about her clinginess and considered that it was likely that she had not had a very strong attachment to her own parents and that perhaps she was searching for an attachment figure in Sarah. This could explain why she wanted to please by saying 'yes', but she was perhaps too anxious or even depressed at this point to engage in anything more than seeking a relationship with Sarah. This seemed to resonate for Sarah and in future sessions she was able to be available and present in the sessions for Ann without any expectation for anything else. This freed them both up to use the sessions more fully, once the therapeutic relationship had been more securely formed.

Sexuality is another area which we can so easily suppress. I have seen situations where young female therapists who may just have got married or may recently have become pregnant seem to be in denial of the effect that this may have on their male or female client. It can be uncomfortable and painful to be the object of envy, which makes it all too easy for the sexuality of the person with a learning disability to be denied. There is a strong opportunity for an erotic transference to develop, especially when the client has little opportunity to develop romantic relationships on an equal basis outside of the therapy. But as Schaverien (1997: 11) states: 'All human relations are in some way bound by eros and the early mother/infant bond is the first erotic relationship. Sexual relationships are developed out of this early erotic bond.' She argues that it may be more acceptable for a female therapist to attribute the transference to its infantile origins, rather than give attention to the sexual reality of the dynamic in the present context.

At another time Sarah presented a situation that had come up for her. She had been working for some time with Emily, a woman in her late twenties (about the same age as Sarah), who had been brain damaged when she was very young after a serious fall. Emily had some insight into the life she might have led. From time to time little glimpses of regret and sadness had emerged in the therapy, but they were so painful they were often very difficult to work with and the insight often seemed to disappear as quickly as it had appeared. Sarah was in the early stages of pregnancy and felt worried over having to break the news to her clients, in particular to Emily. Sarah worried how it would be for Emily to see her growing more and more pregnant week by week. A few sessions later, Sarah reported how a new poignancy had entered the sessions since she had declared her pregnancy. Emily became very interested in the pregnancy and the baby, but was also more able to be in touch with the regret and grief that she felt about how her own life had turned out. This began to enter the creative work in the sessions, allowing her some safe form of expression, which enabled her then to reflect and talk about these feelings more openly than she had been able to before the pregnancy.

There is now more awareness of the affect of bereavement on people with learning disabilities. There is a growing body of literature (e.g. Blackman 2003; Read 2007) to this effect, and many referrals for dramatherapy may be made in connection with this issue. However, there may be many hidden losses connected to a bereavement, such as loss of familiar routine, loss of identity as someone's daughter/sibling, loss of home and all that goes with that, but also fears about the person's own mortality which may need to be uncovered and made sense of.

Julia worked in a residential setting for people with learning disabilities who also had severe and life-threatening epilepsy. There was a very real fear that each time someone had a seizure they could die. One week Julia arrived for supervision and told me that one of the young women that she had been working with had died from a massive seizure during one weekend. She was very shocked when she had learned this and said that it had suddenly made the reality of the danger so much more real. She then went on to describe how difficult it was in the setting to register feelings, or to talk about the death with any of the staff there and how she wasn't sure that the other residents had been told what had happened. Shortly after this a second death occurred. Julia discussed how this time she wanted to support the residents. She wanted to ensure they were given the news clearly, were able to mourn the two people who had died and take an active part in any rituals surrounding the deaths. Along with a couple of staff she arranged to meet with a group of residents who had lived closely with the women who had died. After briefly introducing why they were there, they allowed the clients to talk about what had happened and ask questions or say what they needed to say. Julia said she had been amazed at the amount of insight and the strength of feeling that there had been. After this experience her therapy sessions seemed to provide more of a possibility for clients to discuss their fears or thoughts about death, whether it was their own, their peers or their parents. It was as though she was herself now more open to this need and that in itself created the space.

We discussed how difficult it was in a setting where fear of death was a constant shadow; this was rarely acknowledged. We considered the impact that this must have on the residents. Most of the residents would be aware of their own possible sudden death, and yet there was not an atmosphere where fears or concerns about this could be discussed. I suggested that perhaps the staff did not feel well enough supported themselves to emotionally support residents. Julia supported the organisation to organise some loss and bereavement training for the staff. This went some way towards creating a better climate and at least opened up a dialogue where before there had been a complete denial.

Conclusion

Dramatherapy with people with learning disabilities can provide a rich context in which a client can develop insight into the challenges and trauma of their own life experience. This, in turn, can enable clients to become more autonomous in their thinking and therefore to be engaged in making more choices within their lives. However, there are many challenges within this therapeutic work. It is, therefore, important that the dramatherapist receives supervision, which provides a safe containing environment in which to deconstruct and reflect on their work. The supervisory space should be one in which the dramatherapist can develop and become more confident in their own knowledge. The role of the supervisor is to be vigilant to the issues raised in this chapter; attacks on thinking, the disabling of the 'system' and hidden losses. In the early years of a dramatherapist's career there is more responsibility on the supervisor to take the role of mentor or teacher. Later on this may change to be more a relationship of equals working together to fully understand the material and hold the best interests of the client at heart. The chaos that disability can bring to the individual and everyone around them can in some small but significant way be contained and untangled within clinical supervision in order that this too can happen within the dramatherapy work.

Note

Throughout this chapter I have used the female gender but it could just as easily be interchanged in most places with a male dramatherapist. The erotic transference issue would have many of the same issues in therapeutic dyads across gender or even within same sex dyads.

References

Beail, N. (1998) Psychoanalytic psychotherapy with men with intellectual disabilities: a preliminary outcome study, *British Journal of Medical Psychology* 71: 1–11.

Bicknell, J. (1983) The psychopathology of handicap, *British Journal of Medical Psychology* 56: 167–78.

Blackman, N. (2003) *Loss and Learning Disability*, London: Worth.

Carlsson, B., Hollins, S., Nilsson, A. and Sinason, V. (2002) Preliminary findings: an Anglo-Swedish psychoanalytic psychotherapy outcome study using PORT and DMT, *Tizard Learning Disabiity Review* 7, 4: 39–48.

Disability Rights Commission (DRC, 2006) *Mind the Gap*, Stratford upon Avon: DRC.

Frankish, P. (1992) A psychodynamic approach to emotional difficulties within a social framework, *Journal of Intellectual Disability Research* 36: 295–305.

Gallagher, H. G. (1990) *By Trust Betrayed: Patients and Physicians in the Third Reich*, London: Henry Holt.

Hawkins, P. and Shohet, R. (1996) *Supervision in the Helping Professions*, Maidenhead: Open University Press.

Health Care Commission (HCC, 2006) *Investigation into Services for People with Learning Disabilities at Cornwall Partnership NHS Trust*, London: HCC.

Health Care Commission (HCC, 2007) *Investigation into Services for People with Learning Disabilities at Sutton & Merton Primary Care Trust*, London: HCC.

Hollins, H. (2002) Developmental psychiatry – insights from learning disability, *British Journal of Psychiatry* 177: 201–6.

Holloway, E. (1995) *Clinical Supervision: A Systems Approach*, London: Sage.

Lifton, R. J. (1986) *The Nazi Doctors: Medical Killing and the Psychology of Genocide*, London: Papermac.

Loach, E. (2003) The hardest thing, *Guardian*, weekend supplement, 31 May: 35–7.

Marks, D. (1999) *Disability: Controversial Debates and Psychosocial Perspectives*, London: Routledge.

Mencap (2004) *Treat Me Right*, London: Mencap.

Mencap (2007) *Death By Indifference*, London: Mencap.

Obholzer, A. (1994) Fragmentation and integration in a school for physically handicapped children, in A. Obholzer and V. Zagier Roberts (eds) *The Unconscious at Work: Individual and Organizational Stress in the Human Services*, London: Routledge.

Obholzer, A. and Zagier Roberts, V. (eds) (1994) *Stress in the Human Services*, London: Routledge.

O'Driscoll, D. (2000) Do the feebleminded have an emotional life? A history of psychotherapy and people with learning disabilities, unpublished MA dissertation, Regents College/City University, London.

Pierce Clark, L. (1933) *The Nature and Treatment of Amentia*, London: Ballière Tindall.

Proctor, R. (1988) *Racial Hygiene: Medicine and the Nazis*, Cambridge MA: Harvard University Press.

Read, S. (2007) *Bereavement Counselling for People with Learning Disabilities*, London: Quay Books.

Schaverien, J. (1997) Desire and the female therapist, *British Journal of Psychotherapy* 14, 1: 3–16.

Simpson, D. (2002) Learning disability as a refuge from knowledge, *Psychoanalytic Psychotherapy* 16, 3: 215–26.

Sinason, V. (1992) *Mental Handicap and the Human Condition. New Approaches from the Tavistock*, London: Free Association Books.

Stokes, J. and Sinason, V. (1992) Secondary mental handicap as a defence, in A. Waitman and S. Conboy-Hill (eds) *Psychotherapy and Mental Handicap*, London: Sage.

Tselikas-Portmann, E. (ed.) (1999) *Supervision and Dramatherapy*, London: Jessica Kingsley Publishers.

Voorehoeve, J. N. and Van Putte, F. C. A. (1994) Parallel process in supervision when working with psychotic patients, *Group Analysis* 27, 44: 459–66.

Chapter 12

A place of containment

Supervising dramatherapists in a secure setting

Sally Stamp

Introduction

The idea of working in a forensic setting can appeal and repel in equal measure: people can be excited at the idea of working with criminals or be appalled by their offences. It can be easy to see the criminal solely in terms of their crime, rather than considering the context of the crime. The person is seen as a drug dealer and thief, for example, and not as someone from a background of poverty whose parents were drug addicts. I do not excuse the actions of criminals, but point out a frequent response to working with offenders. It is one example of the extreme responses one finds in relation to forensic work, and is one example of the splitting which occurs in order for professionals to be able to do this work. This chapter looks at issues arising from supervising dramatherapists working in forensic settings. I describe some of the settings and the issues that are particular to prison or hospital setting. I discuss the patient group and give a brief outline of the issues in providing dramatherapy in these settings. I examine the role of the supervisor who works in the organisation and the role of the one who is external to the organisation, but paid on a freelance basis to undertake the clinical supervision of an employee.

I refer to patients and not prisoners as they are in treatment. I discuss generic issues which could apply to men, women, adolescents or children in forensic settings rather than concerns specific to particular patient populations. It is important to say again and again, and then to repeat once more that there are many and complex difficulties facing the patients. These have a powerful impact on the dramatherapist, the supervisor and the organisation, making it hard to think. What I mean by the inability to think is that the processes of finding meaning and linking words to feelings and actions become severely impaired. An indication would be that the dramatherapist suddenly finds that they cannot remember what has happened in the session or cannot follow what is being said. It is vital to point out that dramatherapists working in any setting are likely to have patients who have committed a crime. It can happen that someone offends but this is not detected, or that the crime is dealt with outside the criminal justice system, or that the offence is minimised because of the type of person they are, for example, someone with learning difficulties, or a child. So, although I am focusing on supervising dramatherapists in secure settings, this chapter will be useful for all supervisors.

I begin with a review of relevant literature and then look at the contexts of the work in three sections: the organisation, the patient and dramatherapy. I discuss the different contexts and then describe issues relating to each of the contexts. These are in subsections which are titled with possible countertransference reactions from the supervisor. They aim to give a sense of immediacy, as direct clinical material was excluded for confidentiality issues.

Literature review

I take a psychodynamic perspective. The key theoretical concepts underpinning this chapter are the Kleinian concept of splitting (1975) and Bion's theories about containment and thinking (Bion 1967). To inform an understanding of the organisations, Menzies Lyth (1981) discusses how staff in an organisation unconsciously develop structures to manage difficult feelings about their patients. Hinshelwood (1993) illustrates the problems facing staff working in forensic settings, particularly prisons. Welldon's view that the offence is a re-enactment of early trauma is crucial to understanding the forensic patient because this is re-enacted in therapy (1997).

There are different treatment models in dramatherapy. Pearson (1996), Mitchell (1996) and Jennings (1987, 1992) discuss different schools of thought, while Jones (1996) gives a historical overview of dramatherapy as an intervention. Dramatherapists discussing treatment of forensic patients outline practice and theoretical issues are King (2000), Stamp (2000), McAlister (2000, 2002) and Winn (1996). Holloway (1995) writes about dramatherapy in an acute intervention setting rather than a specific forensic placement, but the point he makes about multidisciplinary working and working as a therapist in a predominantly medical framework is useful in thinking about dramatherapy in hospital settings.

Contexts

The organisational setting

The *Concise Oxford English Dictionary* defines forensic as 'of, used in, courts of law'. Forensic settings are institutions dealing with those who have been placed there by the criminal justice system. However, there will be people who have committed a crime but, for various reasons, have not been charged with the crime. There are many places where dramatherapists might be doing forensic work. These are broadly prisons, hospitals, or community settings, while adolescent forensic services could also include units run by social services.

I concentrate on a psychodynamic understanding of crime, but this is also influenced by the social context. A dysfunctional family background, lack of education, limited employment opportunities, poor housing and inner city deprivation all contribute to the likelihood of someone committing a crime. This led to the initiative: tough on crime, tough on the causes of crime. Different settings and different treatment approaches take up these strands or not in a variety of ways.

There are adult men's and women's prisons, young offenders institutes which are prisons for 15 to 21 year olds and secure training centres for adolescents between 15 and 17 years old. Prisons are categorised by their level of security, with category A being the most secure and Open being the least secure. The higher the security, the more restrictions there are on the patients, with more focus on containment, so with fewer activities available. The lower the security, the more the focus is on rehabilitation; consequently there are wider education and rehabilitation programmes. Hospitals cover special hospitals, medium secure units and adolescent secure units. Special hospitals are for the treatment of people with a mental illness who need the highest security. Medium secure units were developed in the 1980s for patients who needed less security, and for patients moving from special hospitals back into the community. Community settings are linked to probation services and focus on working with offenders who are not in custody.

These settings vary in levels of security, with different authorities running the institution, and this will affect the professionals working there and the treatment philosophy of each. Prisons come under the Home Office and their focus is primarily custodial: keeping offenders out of society for the safety and protection of the public. Secure hospitals and secure units are run by the Department of Health. They are concerned with the treatment of people who have a mental health diagnosis and have committed an offence. However, in prisons, prison officers and other staff can care for the prisoners and want to help them, while in hospital settings, nurses and therapists may want to punish patients. The patient/prisoner can be seen as a victim in need of treatment or a perpetrator who needs to be punished: they are both a prisoner and a patient. It can be difficult to manage these, usually contradictory, feelings about the patient/prisoner at the same time, and one can swing between the two attitudes to the inmate in one meeting. The same feelings are aroused in the supervisor, and it is important to keep this in mind.

It can be very difficult for the professional to cope with wanting both to care for and punish the inmate. This is especially so when they find their professional feelings for the inmate not fitting with their role. Menzies Lyth's (1981) paper about the institutional defences against anxiety is well known. She writes about how nurses organise themselves to manage their feelings of disgust and sexual excitement for their patients. When the patient has committed a crime the nurse or professional will have to manage complex responses to the offence. Another issue is that the prisoners/patients are predominantly men, while the therapists are predominantly women. Because of this I will refer to the patient/prisoner as he, and the therapist as she. The relationship between staff and inmate will also be affected by the setting, as has been described by Hinshelwood (1993). He describes how staff groups are used to manage the difficulty of both locking up and caring for prisoners. In a prison the dramatherapist may be one of a few people offering care or treatment among staff whose role is locking up and maintaining discipline and security. This can lead to the dramatherapist being seen in a maternal, positive transference while the rest of the staff are seen as hard and uncaring. This in turn can create a fantasy of the dramatherapist having a symbiotic, perfect understanding of the patient. The patient and the dramatherapist can get caught in a cycle of feeling that there is an understanding between them that does not need words. The patient may believe that the dramatherapist has the same views as him and that she is his ally against the other professionals who do not understand or give him what he needs. This, of course, is an illusion and when this fantasy is punctured it can be very dangerous for the dramatherapist and the patient. The dramatherapist may then be seen not just the same as the 'awful' prison officers and others, but as worse. She is felt to have betrayed the patient, his sense of safety has been attacked, repeating a pattern from early childhood. It is at this point that the patient may become angry with the dramatherapist and is likely to be verbally and physically violent.

Obviously other members of staff may be caring and nurturing to prisoners. The key point here is that the dramatherapist is not an integral part of the organisation in the way that prison officers are. Therapists are employed on a sessional basis, as part of a particular initiative of a prison department, rather than being employed as a permanent member of staff. This can lead to more extreme splitting. Another point is that prisons do not only function as places to lock people up. They can also provide treatment programmes for specific issues, like substance abuse or sex offending. Prisons can have a rehabilitation package that will include looking at the prevention of future offending. In these cases the same mechanism will be at work, but perhaps with less impact.

In a hospital setting the balance is towards treatment rather than purely custodial. There is not such a clear split of the carers and the punishers as there appears to be in prison, as here there are nurses and not prison officers. However, staff often split patients into the mad or the bad. The patient is either seen as mentally ill, with this excusing their offending, or malicious and not worthy of care and treatment. The mad patient is often described in asexual, infantile terms, while the bad one is seen as untrustworthy and dangerous. The difficulties and deprivations of early life are not thought about for both kinds of patient. The bad patient is rarely seen as also having been abused and in need of understanding.

It is very difficult to maintain the capacity to think about the patient and staff as a complete person or rounded individual. The nature of the setting and the offending can turn people into caricatures.

The patient

The rationale for providing therapy in secure settings is that the crime is linked to the internal world of the patient (Welldon 1997). Welldon states that it is important to understand the person who committed the crime as this will give us, and the patient themselves, an insight into why they offend in that particular way. This can help prevent further crimes and lead to a better assessment of whether they are likely to commit another crime. She says: 'The point about forensic patients is that internal scenarios are acted out concretely; fantasies, nightmares or dreams become concrete reality' (Welldon 1997: 58). A simple example would be a man who was neglected by his mother as a child. He later kills his girlfriend because she is about to leave him. The man experiences not just that he is being abandoned by his girlfriend, but the event triggers the maternal abandonment, and the murderous feelings he had as a child towards his mother. He could kill his girlfriend for leaving him. Unconsciously he feels he could kill his mother. The loss of his girlfriend leads to him losing the ability to think. Instead of simply feeling murderous towards his girlfriend, he does murder her. But in the killing, he also kills his mother who left him.

It is important to recognise that the patient is going to continue to have difficulty in thinking rather than acting and that this has implications for the dramatherapy session. The offence will be re-enacted in some way in the room. This does not mean that the patient will actually assault or rob people, but that it will feel like that for the dramatherapist. The drama-therapist may feel invaded, killed off or held to ransom. She will find this bewildering unless she is able to understand the dynamics of working with offenders. Welldon outlines key points on transference with these patients:

1   The need to be in control, which is apparent from the moment they are first seen and also during treatment.
2   Early experiences of deprivation and subjection to seductiveness make them vulnerable to anything which in any way is reminiscent of the original experiences.
3   A desire for revenge expressed in sadomasochism as an unconscious need to inflict harm.
4   Erotization or sexualization of the action.
5   Manic defence against depression. (Welldon and Van Velsen 1997)

It is important for the dramatherapist to understand how these points are at work in the treatment. It is crucial that the supervisor is aware of this in order to ensure that the work is safe.

The reason that these patients act rather than think is that, due to problems in infancy, they have not developed the capacity to think. Welldon makes this point, based on an understanding of Bion (1967). The relationship between the mother and the baby forms the basis for the baby to learn to think, through the mechanism of projective identification. The baby is unable to speak but makes his or her needs known by crying. This leads the mother to work out what the baby needs. When this goes well the baby discovers, for example, that the terrifying feeling is hunger. When he or she cries, the mother works out that the baby needs feeding and gives either a bottle or a breast. In this way the baby learns that feeling (hunger) leads to a thought (I am hungry). When things go wrong the baby is left with unbearable feelings, which he or she cannot understand and is desperate to get rid of. When the baby had a relationship with a mother who did not understand and put things into words, he grows up with a difficulty in being able to understand and put things into words. Instead he acts impulsively in order to rid himself of powerful, frightening feelings. This dynamic will be at work in the dramatherapy sessions, but the dramatherapist can offer an opportunity to repair the early damage.

There is another point from Bion (1967) that is important for this setting. At times of great anxiety, or because of difficulty in the relationship between mother and child, the baby cannot tolerate any sense that there is a gap between himself and the mother. The baby is unable to cope with any frustration. He is overwhelmed with extreme feelings which he needs the mother to understand and deal with immediately. If this is not done, the baby feels that he is being annihilated. The baby needs a perfect and complete understanding from the mother to rid itself of strong feelings, nothing else will do. In this state the baby, and later the patient, cannot make do with something being good enough, they need a perfect understanding or they feel they are dying. This process also happens when we are adults and suffering great anxiety. It is more pronounced in people who have not experienced enough containment from their mother in infancy. It is a feature in psychosis, therefore it is likely to occur in treatment. It is also likely to be found running through the staff working in these settings.

The patient Welldon describes above does not necessarily have a diagnosis of mental illness. However, her points are central to understanding the processes at play in therapeutic work in secure settings. Some of the patients a dramatherapist sees will not have a diagnosis, though it could be argued that most prisoners could be seen to fit one of the definitions in the *Diagnostic and Statistical Manual of Mental Disorders* (*DSM-IV*) of personality disorder, in particular, antisocial personality disorder (APA 1995).

The diagnostic criteria for antisocial personality disorder cite three elements from seven types of behaviour, including law breaking, aggression and deceitfulness. Dramatherapists will have a caseload of patients with a range of diagnoses including: psychopath, the range of personality disorders, schizophrenia or some degree of psychosis. *DSM-IV* highlights that as well as the main diagnosis there may be other conditions which also need treatment such as substance abuse. Dual diagnosis (i.e. schizophrenia and substance abuse) complicates treatment. Both elements of the diagnosis need treatment. It is important to bear this in mind, as well as the fact that each element of the diagnosis might need specialist input. Alongside this, the dramatherapist and supervisor need to be aware that working with people who have a personality disorder or who are psychotic needs specialist skills too.

It is important to note that black and ethnic minority individuals will be over-represented in the patients. Individuals who are black or minority ethnic are more often diagnosed as schizophrenic and more likely to receive a custodial sentence if they have committed a crime (Fernando 2003). At the same time the dramatherapist and other therapists are predominantly white. The supervisor and dramatherapist need to consider how the patient can be allowed to feel that their experience is valued, without feeling that they have to fit into a white perspective. For example, if myths and stories are used, do they come from a range of cultures? When we consider our hopes for the patient in recovery from mental ill-health, are we trying to mould the patient to a white, middle-class norm, rather than a model of what is healthy for that individual? This and different cultural attitudes to mental illness are explored by Littlewood and Lipsedge (1989).

Patients are also likely to have problems with literacy and numeracy. This can lead to poor self-esteem and low expectations of work. A substantial number of patients will have been victims of physical, emotional or sexual abuse, and have been brought up in families where domestic violence is common. This is essential in considering offenders. The emphasis can be on patients' dangerousness and abusiveness, while the patient's experience of abuse can be minimised or ignored. In order for the patient to be able to change and develop empathy for others, they will need to explore their experiences of abuse and feel that someone has empathised with them.

Dramatherapy as a treatment

Dramatherapy can be a very useful intervention in forensic settings. Patients have not just thought about stealing, attacking or assaulting, but have acted this out. Dramatherapy is both active and structured, which can be useful in helping these people to express difficult thoughts and think about them. The physical nature of dramatherapy can raise anxieties and the implications of dramatherapy techniques have to be carefully considered in a place where security is important. The dramatherapist needs to be particularly careful in working with people with psychosis where patients' perception of reality can be very fluid. She may be working with a patient who has sexually assaulted a woman because he believed that when the woman flicked her hair this meant she wanted to have sex with him.

King (2000) has written about the value of dramatherapy in prison as a way of increasing self-respect and practising change, rather than focusing on developing insight. McAlister (2000) describes the importance of drama-therapy in a medium secure hospital in developing the patient's capacity for symbolic thinking and working through developmental stages where the patient might be stuck. She has also written about the significance of dramatherapy in the treatment of patients with psychosis (McAlister 2002). I have highlighted the usefulness of dramatherapy as a method to increase the patient's awareness of their emotional state and their capacity for insight (Stamp 1997, 2000). Winn (1996) writes about dramatherapy in a regional (medium) secure unit. The focus is on exploring identity and roles, to enable a move towards a more fluid and healthy role repertoire. He also emphasises dramatherapy as a group activity which promotes the capacity to relate and connect, as opposed to the patient isolating himself.

Issues in supervision: the organisational setting

Splitting and relationships with other professionals

If only there were more dramatherapists working here

Professionals working in forensic settings are subjected to powerful projec-tions from the patient group. These projections manifest themselves in oppositions within staff groups and in extreme responses from the organisa-tion, as described by Hinshelwood (1993) and Stamp (2000). One staff group, for example, nurses or prison officers, can see a patient as difficult, as a deliberate troublemaker or even as evil. Another group, for example, therapists, can see them as vulnerable and in need of support. This splitting can be most extreme at times of changes in the organisation and can be more easily located in a therapist working individually with a patient. The inten-sity of the work, and the fact that no one else is present, lends such a relationship to carry particular projections. In the case of a dramatherapist, the fact that it is a young profession can exaggerate this, with dramatherapy being less established, less familiar to other professions, and so more open to prejudices and fantasies based on ignorance. When such splitting takes place it can be very hard for the dramatherapist to have enough distance to understand what is happening. She may find herself at the butt of jokes about what she does, being seen as over-involved with the patients and without a proper clinical awareness of the patient. She may see the other staff as harsh, clinical and with no real understanding of the patient. The supervisor may feel protective towards the dramatherapist as a fellow dramatherapist and be drawn into the splitting. In extreme cases the fixed viewpoints of the professionals can cause the work to be dangerous. Entrenched attitudes between staff can lead to less discussion of information and erode respect for their professional opinion.

How do you understand and support the dramatherapist in providing treatment for a forensic patient?

What's in this for me?

In order to understand the splitting processes in play, it is essential that the supervisor understands his or her attitude to the organisation and to the patient. I have discussed splitting in terms of the organisation, I now look at splitting in relation to the supervisor and the patient. I have described some of the underlying motivations for working in the field of forensics (Stamp 2000). These may include the desire for control, narcissism, sadism, delinquency, and so on. These dynamics hold true for the supervisor as well, but with added complexity. When the supervisor works in the organisation, they are also part of the projective system around the patient. She or he will be similarly influenced by the organisational dynamics. This can make it harder to see the overall picture and limit the thinking about the material brought to supervision.

If the supervisor is not part of the organisation, she or he can be in a freer position to observe the dynamics at work. However, they may be unaware of key aspects of the work or the organisation at times when the dramatherapist is caught up in particular projections, and thus not able to articulate all that is going on. This may be unconscious and can be very difficult for the supervisor to pick up until much later.

In situations where the supervisor has no experience of working with forensic patients, it is vital that the supervisor questions the reasons for taking on this supervision and familiarises themselves with all of the elements involved in this work. There is always an element of voyeurism in supervision, which is especially strong in forensic work. The supervisor can find themselves unwillingly witnessing deeply disturbing and traumatising offences, at one remove, through the role of supervisor. This can be more traumatic for them than the dramatherapist if they are not familiar with this work and do not have a relationship with the patient to mitigate the picture.

However, another aspect is the danger that the supervisor is mirroring an abused/abuser relationship from the patient's early life. The supervisor is party to information about the patient without the patient's knowledge or consent, for their own interest. They do not have a relationship with the patient, nor do they have experience of their own clinical work, but use the supervisory role to learn about this area rather than experiencing it. In doing so they are able to get right into the patient's life, their history, their clinical notes and so on, without the patient having any say in this. This may be a symbolic repetition of an abuser invading the victim's body for their own use, as the supervisor may be blurring their own need to feed their interest with the need to provide the thinking and containment of being a supervisor.

What is the link between the supervisor and the organisation?

I feel I'm being kept on the outside

It could be argued that dramatherapists are attracted to having a marginal status to be counter-culture and anti-authoritarian. It is still a relatively new profession. It is at the junction of two other disciplines, drama and therapy which means that it straddles two areas of thought, fusing them both, but it is also influenced by other strands of thought. These are coloured by the training, experience and interests of the individual dramatherapist. Forensic psychiatry is also a new field but prisons and special hospitals are well established. Generally forensic settings are, by their nature, authoritarian systems. How does a supervisor respond to the organisation? What fantasies do they have about introducing a more enlightened philosophy? How comfortable would they be in locking people up? These themes will come up for the dramatherapist and supervisor throughout the work and need to be considered before taking on the job. It is important to negotiate in the contract what should happen if the supervisor has concerns about the work. For example, are there situations where they contact the dramatherapist's manager without notifying the dramatherapist? If there is a breach of security involving the dramatherapist, the supervisor will have to think about their accountability. When there is no direct link between the supervisor and the organisation, the dramatherapist becomes the only point of contact and everything is refracted through this lens. This adds to the pressure of the supervisory relationship and also mirrors the lone parent family relationship that many of the patients will have experienced. Because of these issues, I feel it is important that there is a clearly understood relationship between the supervisor and the organisation.

Before the supervisor takes on the work, they should agree with the dramatherapist what contact there is between the supervisor and the dramatherapist's manager. The manager should have some basic information about the supervisor, about their professional suitability for the work and how they can be contacted. It may be useful for the supervisor to agree times when they would discuss the supervision arrangement. This could either be an understanding of when they might need to have contact, or they could fix an annual review. The organisation may have policies or procedures covering supervision, which the supervisor should have copies of. It would be helpful to have information about security issues, like what is not permitted in the clinical areas. Another area is guidance on what happens if the patient admits guilt of a crime while on remand, or discloses other offences, particularly towards children. Finally, the dramatherapist and supervisor need to be clear on the ethical constraints on writing about clinical material.

Issues in supervision: the patient

Information about the patient

Why do I feel terrified of their patient?

I have raised the issue of the impact of hearing details about crimes on the supervisor. Another issue is that the dramatherapist and/or supervisor may not have enough information about the patient. Basic information is the nature of the Index Offence (the crime which led to the patient being imprisoned), details of any previous crimes committed, any history of mental illness, a description of the family and of the patient's early life. This core knowledge gives the dramatherapist and supervisor a framework to understand the session material, especially the transference to the dramatherapist.

As Welldon (1997) highlighted, the offence can be seen as a re-enactment of the patient's unconscious material. Knowledge about the offence is essential as this is going to be repeated in the dramatherapy session until it is understood and the underlying issues resolved. It is also likely to be re-entacted in the supervision session. If the supervisor does not have detailed information about the patient, they are less equipped to understand both the clinical work of the dramatherapist and the dynamics in supervision. This will affect the supervisor's capacity to understand the work and support the dramatherapist, which impacts on the dramatherapist's ability to treat the patient safely. For example, the dramatherapist reports that, while working with an individual patient, the patient consistently makes small actions which cause her to feel invaded and off balance. He may suddenly ask her personal questions or move uncomfortably close. The events may not seem significant in themselves as they appear to be around the edges of the main focus of the work. In supervision, they can, reasonably, be seen as examples of the patient's impulsive personality. They could also be seen as enactments of sexual or violent assault. If the patient has committed such an offence, it is vital that the dramatherapist is able to make this link and work with it in the treatment. In this example, the dramatherapist may feel mild irritation at the incidents; it may be the supervisor who is terrified in the recounting of the session.

There is an argument that the dramatherapist and supervisor work with the material presented without additional information about the patient. This limits the range of views to understand the patient, and there is a danger that organisational splitting is overlooked. For example, the patient may be perceived as doing well in dramatherapy sessions by the dramatherapist and supervisor, while the patient is threatening staff on the wing. The dramatherapist and the supervisor would need to be very experienced in forensic work to be aware of what is being revealed in the material without the information to confirm this.

Transference issues

Oh God, she's in love with him

As well as the dramatherapist and supervisor feeling afraid of the patient, they are also likely to experience feelings of love and intimacy. In some cases they may fall in love with the patient. The phenomenon applies regardless of gender or sexuality in the dramatherapist and patient. The patient falling in love with their therapist can be traced back to the beginnings of psychoanalysis, when Freud became aware of the phenomenon of his patients falling in love with him. He understood this as a manifestation of the intense love that the baby and young child has for his or her mother, transferred to the analyst. This became known as transference. For therapists working with forensic patients, who have been neglected, abused or sexually abused, Welldon (1997) points to the significance of seduction, erotisation and sexualisation in the transference. This is intensified by the fact that the patient is locked up, has contact with fewer people, and that there is an increased dependency on the dramatherapist. Therapy is likely to be the first time the patient has had a regular relationship with a reliable and committed adult.

The dramatherapist will be affected by this transference material and have their own countertransference response. At times this response will merge with the dramatherapist's own personal issues, for example, when they have problems in their own relationships and find it hard to stay within the boundaries of the professional relationship. The supervisor and dramatherapist need to be able to understand what is happening in an open and non-judgemental way to neutralise the powerful, often disturbing, feelings.

The supervisor too will have their own fantasies about the patient. This might include ideas about being in love with the patient, what I call 'the Laura syndrome' after the 1944 film where a detective investigating the murder of the eponymous Laura, falls in love with her, though he never meets her. In the film there is no contact between the detective and Laura to challenge his romantic thoughts about her. She becomes enormously important to him, where in life he might find her boring, irritating, ordinary. This same process can happen to the supervisor who hears about the patient but never meets them. Although Nitsun (2007) suggested that the erotic transference is a sign of health, it has particular implications in forensic work. I think Stoller's (1986) reading of the erotic transference as an attack is essential here. I see it as a perversion of the therapeutic relationship, which mirrors the skewed maternal relationship, where caring becomes sexualised. This needs careful handling so that the underlying needs the patient has to be attached to someone (de Zulueta 1993) are understood and inform the supervision.

Expertise

They don't know anything about this

I have described the likely profile of the patient and the experienced range of difficulties, all of which could benefit from specialist treatment. The primary job of the dramatherapist is to identify what they can offer and develop a therapeutic relationship. It is important to bear in mind the difficulties the patient has and how this affects the dramatherapy treatment. For example, if the patient has drug and alcohol problems, are they receiving treatment for this? If not, how is this going to be addressed in the work? The dramatherapist can have omnipotent thoughts about being able to tackle issues without needing particular expertise or further training. This could be an unconscious communication from the patient about the patient's problems in allowing themselves to be dependent, in this case on the dramatherapist. This can also happen with the supervisor, where they find themselves supervising work on substance abuse without having experience in this field. There may be no need for extra skills or training. The key point is that the dramatherapist and supervisor need to be aware of what might be underlying the avoidance of additional input on specific issues of the patient.

Linked to this issue is the point of the patient's need for perfect understanding. If the dramatherapist, or supervisor, suddenly feel that greater expertise is needed for the work, it could be that this is a manifestation of the patient's anxiety and their resulting need for perfect understanding from the dramatherapist. It may be a symptom of greater investment in the work by the patient. He may feel worried about an approaching break in treatment, or the dependence on the dramatherapist, and find this frightening. Another element of the work is the judgemental feelings that percolate through the organisation. These feelings are partly in response to the crimes that patients have committed, which may not be able to be expressed directly to the perpetrator so become projected elsewhere. Feeling critical and punitive can be an indication of the patient's often punishing superego, which can get pushed into staff. This can manifest in the supervisor being critical of the dramatherapist's ability to manage the range of needs the patient has. There needs to be a balance between feeling you know it all and feeling you know nothing.

I recommend that the dramatherapist and supervisor identify the treatment issues and ensure that they read literature or do specialist training. An understanding of psychosis and personality disorder and the implications for dramatherapy treatment are essential. Other areas of importance are substance misuse and working with forensic populations. Different settings might call for a knowledge of adolescents or women. What is as important as specialist training is the supervisor's and the dramatherapist's capacity for self-reflection; to be able to scrutinise their thoughts and feelings and make use of them in this work.

Issues in supervision: dramatherapy

Dramatherapy techniques

This work isn't safe

In high security settings there will be severe restrictions on what can be taken into the workplace. Do you as supervisor choose to know what is banned or not so that you can advise the dramatherapist? What are the implications of not knowing? Should physical contact be used when patients might be psychotic, or have been abused, or have committed a sexual or violent offence? Whatever you do or do not know about security as a supervisor, it is important that your supervisee discusses the issue with you, especially if they are unfamiliar with the setting. You may feel that the work is not safe. How do you manage this? There are different levels of security operating at one time.

Level one is the physical security where doors have to kept locked. The dramatherapist will need to be aware of the security policies and have to follow them. If they do not they will lose their job. It is important that the supervisor is clear on the importance of physical security. It is useful for the supervisor to be familiar with the policies, so that they can support the dramatherapist, and have a fixed reference point to leave them free to think about the relational and unconscious levels.

Level two is the relational one of how people relate to each other. The relationship between the dramatherapist and the patient gives the patient an opportunity to express and explore difficult feelings, rather than act out on the ward or the prison wing. They develop an attachment to the dramatherapist which enables them to feel safe and contained. However, this attachment can also cause them to feel anxious because they may be unfamiliar with such a relationship, or because they then fear that they will lose the dramatherapist. This can lead the patient to be more volatile.

Level three is the unconscious level where material is acted out. This can be seen in the projections from/to the staff groups, described above.

Working safely involves being able to think about all three levels. It may be useful for the supervisor to have them in mind in supervision and think about the relationship between them. For example, the dramatherapist may be involved in a projective system where the prison or ward staff see her as overinvolved in the patient and unable to see his dangerousness. This may lead to her having an unconscious response by forgetting to lock one of the doors. If the supervisor and dramatherapist are able to think about the unconscious processes this may be prevented.

It is worth mentioning issues arising from working with patients who are psychotic. The dramatherapist needs to be careful about boundaries. The patient needs to be clear about reality and fantasy in the session. It is useful to have rules written down and brought to each session. Concerns about the patient's mental state need to be handed over to the prison or ward staff.

A final point in this section is about the need to explore the negative transference, as well as the positive transference, in the treatment. There can be a focus on drama as a medium where the patient can be engaged and find the sessions enjoyable. The dramatherapist receives projections of being a benign, loving maternal figure, while her negative aspects are projected on to other staff members. It is important that the dramatherapist takes up the unfavourable elements of herself too, and brings them into the sessions. If this is not done, the danger is that a harmful split develops, which cannot be sustained. The split may lead to the patient eventually experiencing the dramatherapist as bad but unable to tolerate this, leaving treatment.

Professional differences

I could do this better

The supervisor may have had a different training to the supervisee. Each dramatherapist has their own way of working. The nature of the setting, with the complexity of the patients means that the supervisory relationship is going to be severely tested at times and unresolved tensions about different approaches is one point where difficulties could erupt. I have mentioned Bion's point about the baby, and later adult, needing perfect understanding. When the dramatherapist is under attack from the patient they will be looking for greater containment from supervision, and may feel a lack of support if the supervisor does not perfectly understand their method of working. Early discussion about perceived differences in approaches and the development of trust are important. Openness about the underlying dynamics is crucial.

It is important that the supervisor knows about the different drama-therapy approaches and can think how she might work with them. If the dramatherapist employs dramatic distance she may work in the metaphor and not state explicitly what is happening in the session. How can the offence be addressed? There needs to be a good enough 'fit' between the supervisor's and the dramatherapist's approaches for the supervision to be effective.

Conclusion

Dramatherapy can be a useful treatment in secure settings. The nature of the patients means that splitting is a significant issue. As well as needing careful thought by the supervisor and dramatherapist, a knowledge of psychosis is also essential.

1   It is important that the supervisor and dramatherapist understand the dynamics at play and constantly scrutinise their response to the patient's material. The dramatherapist and supervisor need to be open and thoughtful about the material at all times. This may call for use of personal therapy.
2   In order to understand the complexity of the issues that the drama-therapist faces, the supervisor has to have had experience in working in forensic settings.
3   They need to know the issues relating to working in the particular setting.
4   A clear contract of accountability needs to be negotiated between the supervisor, the dramatherapist and the dramatherapist's manager.
5   The supervisor has be aware of security – concrete, relational and unconscious.
6   The supervisor needs to be familiar with the theoretical approach of the dramatherapist.

A final point is the issue of frequency and mode of supervision. Because of the complexity of this work and the psychological demands on the drama-therapist, it is important that supervision is regular, even when it is a small part of the dramatherapist's caseload. Group supervision is ideal for forensic work as the group can help monitor the dynamics in the organisation, in the patient/dramatherapist dyad and in the supervisor/dramatherapist dyad. The group also enables the supervisees to learn from a range of case material.

References

American Psychiatric Association (APA, 1995) *Diagnostic and Statistical Manual of Mental Disorders – DSM-IV*, 4th edn, Washington DC: APA.
Bion, W. R. (1967) *Second Thoughts*, London: William Heinemann.

De Zulueta, F. (1993) *From Pain to Violence*, London: Whurr.

Fernando, S. (2003) *Cultural Diversity, Mental Health and Psychiatry*, Hove, UK: Brunner-Routledge.

Hinshelwood, R. (1993) Locked in a role: a psychotherapist within the social defence system of a prison, *Journal of Forensic Psychiatry* 4, 3: 427–40.

Holloway, P. (1995) Dramatherapy in acute intervention, in S. Mitchell (ed.) *Dramatherapy: Clinical Studies*, London: Jessica Kingsley Publishers.

Jennings, S. (ed.) (1987) *Dramatherapy: Theory and Practice for Teachers and Clinicians*, London: Routledge.

Jennings, S. (ed.) (1992) *Dramatherapy: Theory and Practice 2*, London: Routledge.

Jones, P. (1996) *Drama As Therapy: Theatre As Living*, London: Routledge.

King, J. (2000) Community dramatherapy at HMP Magilligan, *Dramatherapy: Journal of the British Association of Dramatherapists*, Spring.

Klein, M. (1975) *Love, Guilt and Reparation and Other Works 1921–1945*, London: Hogarth Press.

Littlewood, R. and Lipsedge, M. (1989) *Aliens and Alienists: Ethnic Minorities and Psychiatry*, London: Unwin Hyman.

McAlister, M. (2000) An evaluation of dramatherapy in a forensic setting, *Dramatherapy: Journal of the British Association of Dramatherapists*, Spring.

McAlister, M. (2002) Dramatherapy and psychosis: symbol formation and dramatic distance, *Free Associations* 9, 3: 353–70.

Menzies Lyth, I. (1981) *The Functioning of Social Systems as a Defence Against Anxiety*, London: Tavistock Institute of Human Relations.

Mitchell, S. (ed.) (1996) *Dramatherapy: Clinical Studies*, London: Jessica Kingsley Publishers.

Nitsun, M. (2007) *The Group as an Object of Desire: Exploring Sexuality in Group Therapy*, Abingdon: Routledge.

Pearson, J. (ed.) (1996) *The Sesame Approach*, London: Jessica Kingsley Publishers.

Stamp, S. (1997) Holding on dramatherapy with offenders, in J. Thompson (ed.) *Prison Theatre*, London: Jessica Kingsley Publishers.

Stamp, S. (2000) A fast moving floorshow – the space between acting and thinking in dramatherapy with offenders, *Dramatherapy: Journal of the British Association of Dramatherapists*, Spring.

Stoller, R.J. (1986) *Perversion the Erotic Form of Hatred*, London: Karnac.

Welldon, E.V. (1997) Forensic psychiatry, in P. Clarkson and M. C. Polarny (eds) *Handbook of Psychotherapy*, London: Routledge.

Welldon, E.V. and Van Velsen, C. (1997) *Practical Guide to Forensic Psychotherapy*, London: Jessica Kingsley Publishers.

Winn, R. (1996) Dramatherapy in forensic psychiatry, in J. Pearson (ed.) *Directing the Self Through Drama and Movement*, London: Jessica Kingsley Publishers.

Key terms

Aims of dramatherapy supervision (Chapter 9, p. 147). Tselikas-Portmann (1999) draws on literature outside dramatherapy with Holloway (1995) for her definition of the tasks of supervision. She sees them as 'promoting the reflection on professional practice, the building up of professional skills, developing or preserving the ability to conceptualize the situation (case), reflecting on the professional role, preserving emotional awareness and enabling self-evaluation (thus promoting autonomy)'. She defines the functions as: 'advising; eventually instructing; modelling; consulting; supporting and sharing; monitoring' (pp. 25–6).

Countertransference (Chapter 8, p. 139). The term, 'countertransference' actually refers to the transferential reaction to a client's or student's transferences, but some people use it to refer to the transference from the therapist to the patient, even if it has nothing to do with the patient's transference. For example, if a therapist has an aversion to tall people, this needs to be addressed so that encounters with such patients are not contaminated with unfair attributions. In other words, therapists can have transferences to patients just as much as vice versa, and teachers can have transferences with students.

Cross-cultural supervision (Chapter 7, p. 112). Refers to different cultural patterns of supervision and to supervision content, process and outcomes.

Definitions of supervision (Chapter 1, p. 9). Grant (1999) has described the core of supervision to be the act of a therapist presenting their work to a supervisor. It is an ongoing process, normally conducted throughout the practising life of a therapist, and concerns and consists of a complex set of relationships.

Developmental model (Chapter 9, p. 156). The developmental approach described by Hawkins and Shohet (2000) and van Ooijen (2000) refers to three stages that the supervisee may be at, dependent on experience, and suggests the corresponding role of the supervisor. For the dramatherapist there is a clear progression from trainee, to newly qualified and more experienced therapist.

Dramatic distancing (Chapter 5, p. 86). The theatre process allows a separation between role and character. Along the continuum of dramatic distancing, the client may work in a fully embodied way, taking account of the feelings, thoughts, motivations, history and dramatic actions of a character. At the opposite extreme, the client may stay with the conception of a person acting a role, in this way more focused on plot rather than deeper psychological processes. Any movement along the continuum of role–character allows for some level of aesthetic distance and enables the possibility of performance.

Field theory (Chapter 3, p. 59). Evans and Gilbert (2005) drawn on the ideas of field theory (Lewin 1952) to look at supervision. They cite field theory's conceptualisation of the individual being interrelated to their environment: the internal world of feelings and thoughts and the external world of their lived context. . . . In this way 'the context or field is a dynamic and interrelated system in which every part influences every other part . . . in psychotherapy and in supervision there is thus a co-created field of mutual reciprocal influence between client and psychotherapist in the former, and between psychotherapist and supervisor in the latter' (Evans and Gilbert 2005: 134). Thus, an interaction is created between 'the current nature of the therapeutic relationship, together with the personal histories of the client, psychotherapist and supervisor will each impact on the field' (p. 134).

Internal supervisor (Chapter 3, p. 55). The idea of the internal supervisor is that the process of supervision is not confined to the sessions between supervisor and supervisee. Over time the knowledge, experience and reflective relationship developed between supervisee and supervisor is internalised by the supervisee. The idea is that the supervisee draws on this within their live practice, as well as in the supervision space.

Intercultural (Chapter 7, p. 113). Intercultural is a term more used in a UK therapy context. The term is chosen to indicate the interactive element in cultural dynamics between the different parties involved in therapy.

Metaphor (Chapter 5, p. 87). The use of metaphor is at the heart of dramatherapy practice. As Mann writes: 'the power of metaphor rests upon its levels of meaning and its ability to be flexible, poetic and intuitive. Its Greek origin literally means "to carry across", implying a transfer of meaning from one frame of reference to another' (1996: 2).

Multicultural supervision (Chapter 7, p. 111). Multicultural alludes to the study and practice of supervision in, and for, different cultures.

Parallel process (Chapter 10, p. 169). Parallel process is a concept that has developed from psychoanalytic theory. It reflects the idea that clients' issues are unconsciously mirrored within the supervisory relationship, or within an institution in which the therapy is taking place. Hawkins and Shohet comment: 'The job of the supervisor is tentatively to name the process and thereby make it available to conscious exploration and learning. If it remains unconscious the supervisor is likely to be submerged in the enactment of the process' (2000: 81).

Process model of supervision (Chapter 4, p. 71). A model frequently used in dramatherapy supervision training is one where the supervisor is taught to operate on a variety of modes within a process model of supervision (Hawkins and Shohet 1989). This approach to supervision has been described as developmental. It emphasises the educational elements of clinical supervision to help the professional develop from novice to independent craftsman (van Ooijen 2000).

Projective identification in supervision (Chapter 12, p. 204). The relationship between the mother and the baby forms the basis for the baby to learn to think, through the mechanism of projective identification. The baby is unable to speak but makes his or her needs known by crying. This leads the mother to work out what the baby needs. When this goes well the baby discovers, for example, that the terrifying feeling is hunger. When he or she cries, the mother works out that the baby needs feeding and gives either a bottle or a breast. In this way the baby learns that feeling (hunger) leads to a thought (I am hungry). When things go wrong the baby is left with unbearable feelings, which he or she cannot understand and is desperate to get rid of. When the baby had a relationship with a mother who did not understand and put things into words, he grows up with a difficulty in being able to understand and put things into words. Instead he acts impulsively in order to rid himself of powerful, frightening feelings. This dynamic will be at work in the dramatherapy sessions but the dramatherapist can offer an opportunity to repair the early damage.

Reflection-in-action (Chapter 4, p. 71). This is a practice-led epistemology in which practical know-how, though informed by theoretical knowing, is grounded in a third, subjective domain of experiential knowledge (Heron 1992).

Reflection-on-action (Chapter 4, p. 71). Through which a practitioner learns skills from recalling past actions and/or preparing for future action, also called experiential learning.

Role approach to supervision (Chapter 5, p. 97). Suggests that the supervisor has a range of different roles. It is important for the supervior to be aware of the role they play and switch supportively between them when required.

Sesame (Chapter 4, p. 69). Creative Arts Therapies Supervision (CAST) training was developed by Sesame trained practitioners, who were consequently trained in the psychodynamic dramatherapy supervision model developed by Marina Jenkyns (1999).

Slow open model of group supervision (Chapter 4, p. 77). A slow open model of group supervision, with a mixture of more or less experienced practitioners, allows for heterogeneity or exchange between supervisees at different stages of anxiety and development.

Splitting (Chapters 11 and 12). In order to cope with the conflict of good vs bad experiences in relation to the same person, a defence mechanism comes into being which Klein called splitting (Jenkyns 1996). Splitting can occur in the relationship between supervisor, supervisee and employing organisation when supervisee and supervisor join in 'blaming' the organisation, rather than recognising underlying forces at play. It can occur between staff within the multidisciplinary team with some staff wanting to 'punish' the patient, while others emphasise care.

Transference (Chapter 8, pp. 138–39). Although psychoanalysts first described transference, the dynamic being referred to is ubiquitous in human relations, being nothing more than the tendency to overgeneralisation of experience (Kellerman 1983). If one has had an unpleasant experience with a teacher with a moustache, there may be a slight tendency to expect a repetition of that experience when one encounters another teacher with a similar moustache years later. The earlier the experience, the deeper and often more unconscious is the reaction. Students and experienced practitioners have transferences as much as patients. It is hoped that they can learn to become more aware of their own dynamics and tendencies, so as to update the reality in the present. Sometimes this activity can be difficult, and part of the task of supervision is to use the evidence of transferences evoked in the course of working with clients as an opportunity to help students to address them more consciously and constructively.

Author index

Subject index